SPORTS

COMMUNICATION

DIMENSIONS, THEORY, APPLICATIONS, AND CULTURE

SECOND EDITION

ALAN JAY ZAREMBA
Northeastern University

Kendall Hunt
publishing company

Also by Alan Jay Zaremba
    Crisis Communication: Theory and Practice
    Madness of March: Bonding and Betting with the Boys in Las Vegas
    Management in a New Key
    Mass Communication and International Politics
    Organizational Communication 4th Edition
    Speaking Professionally 2nd Edition

Cover image © Shutterstock.com

www.kendallhunt.com
Send all inquiries to:
4050 Westmark Drive
Dubuque, IA 52004-1840

Copyright © 2022, 2019 by Kendall Hunt Publishing Company

ISBN 979-8-7657-0666-4

Published in the United States of America

Brief Contents

Contents

Preface

January 1, 2022.

At the end of this New Year's Day, eleven college football bowl games were televised in forty-eight hours. In the previous two weeks, an additional twenty-five were available on radio or television.

Fourteen college basketball games were aired on the networks. If you were a subscriber to ESPN+, fifty-six additional games were streaming.

From 7:30 a.m. Eastern Time until three in the afternoon, there were continuous Premier League soccer matches aired on the USA network.

Professional basketball and hockey games were available on TNT, NBA, and NHL channels.

It continued on January 2. A fan in the Pacific Time Zone would have awakened and watched professional football until it was time to prepare for bed. If one did not need to watch any specific game, subscribers to "the RedZone" could have viewed highlights of all contests without moving a muscle. Alternatively, those who purchased the NFL ticket could have watched nine games concurrently, starting at 10 a.m. with the morning coffee.

On December 28, 2021, NFL icon John Madden passed away. Madden was a very successful coach for the Oakland Raiders in the early years of the NFL/AFL merger. However, for a generation of sports enthusiasts, he is unknown as a coach but remembered because, for thirty years, he was an outstanding television analyst for NFL broadcasts. Another generation of sports fans knows him less because of his work with CBS, FOX, and ABC and more because of his extraordinarily popular video sports game, Madden NFL.

On December 29, 2001, a backup NBA center penned an op-ed article for *The Boston Globe*. The center, who'd recently changed his name from Enes Kanter to Enes Freedom, wrote about how essential it was for athletes to use their visibility to speak out about political and social injustices throughout the world. Freedom, née Kanter, is likely to make less of a mark because of his defense or rebounding and more because of how he intends to communicate about social issues.

On December 31, 2001, an Associated Press article confirmed what had been speculation for days. Becky Hammon had been hired as head coach of the WNBA Las Vegas Aces. This was particularly newsworthy because Hammon's previous job was as an assistant coach in the NBA with the San Antonio Spurs. Almost a year ago to the date, Hammon had become the first woman to coach in an NBA regular season contest when head coach Gregg Popovich was ejected from a game. The news of Hammon's appointment came within hours of an exciting women's basketball game broadcast nationally between the number one ranked University of South Carolina and the University of Missouri. It was not long ago when women's college basketball was hardly ever aired on national networks. One can see the highlights of the last thrilling moments of the South Carolina/Missouri game on YouTube.

At his January 1, 2022, postgame press conference, Houston Rockets' coach Stephen Silas relayed that he'd been disappointed with his team's effort in the first half of the night's game against the Denver Rockets. Silas told the reporters that there had been a "spirited debate" during halftime. Whatever had been communicated then, resulted in guard Kevin Porter Jr. bolting from the arena after the halftime discussion. According to *the Athletic*, Porter had gotten into an argument with an assistant coach who'd confronted players, including Porter, during halftime. Porter apologized subsequently for his overreaction.

Sports and communication intersect--regularly and frequently--in real, substantive, and influential ways. Coaches, leagues, teammates, broadcasters, and fans—all are communicators. And their communications affect not only the games we watch but also our political, economic, and social world. The goal of this book is to describe the dimensions, breadth, and effects of this relatively new academic field: sports communication. The Second Edition, as was the case with the First, is intended to be an engaging and accessible text that will appeal to readers and generate class discussion.

What is new in the Second Edition?

- **Features**
  There are still many features intended to stimulate discussion and interactivity.
  ○ Each chapter begins with prompts that encourage students to take and defend a position on a sports communication issue.
  ○ Each chapter also presents an ethical challenge in a recurring *Fair or Foul* segment.
    ■ Is it *Fair or Foul*, for example, to coax high school athletes to attend your university by omitting or exaggerating information-even if such communication behavior is the norm?
  ○ There is a regular feature called *Test Yourself—Apply the Principles,* which interrupts the text by challenging readers to apply what's appeared previously in the chapters.
  ○ The Second Edition has an added feature called *SportsChats*. These are prompts that encourage readers to respond online to sports communication questions. Other students then can react to classmates' articulated positions.

- **Up-To-Date Content**
  The scholarly literature has continued to evolve, and the Second Edition reflects what is new in the field. In addition, there are references in the Second Edition to many of the new popular books that have been written since the First Edition was published.
  ○ Soccer stars Megan Rapinoe and Carli Lloyd have both recently authored memoirs. Rapinoe makes a strong case for athletes to use their platform to speak out for social change. Lloyd discusses internal communication on teams and her challenges in communicating with trainers and family.
  ○ Sports journalist Joan Ryan's excellent book *Intangibles* identifies communication behavior that can lead to positive and negative team chemistry.
  ○ The prolific John Feinstein has written about athletes' use of their platform and issues of race, protests, and sports.

○ Seth Wickersham triggered a conventional and social media flurry with his comprehensive examination of the twenty-year relationships of owner, star quarterback, and coach on the New England Patriots.

○ Julie DiCaro's 2021 *Sidelined* makes powerful points about the media industry's sidelining of women sportscasters.

○ Larry Olmstead's *Fans* makes the case that fans actually have a higher quality of life because of their affection for sporting events.

Readers will find references to these and many other recently published works in the Second Edition.

- **Sports Crises and Communication**
  The Second Edition, like the First, has a chapter dedicated to sports crises. Inevitably, new crises have surfaced in sports that present communication challenges. Among the many in the recent past, there are the issues of NFL coach Jon Gruden's e-mails; Rachel Nichols's recorded phone conversation; Daryl Morey's tweet; Cole Beasley's contentious social media posts, and of course, communication challenges related to the ongoing COVID crisis.

- **Social Issues and Sports Communication**
  The linkages between social issues, communication, and sports are evident nearly daily. Since the First Edition, the Milwaukee Bucks hired a woman to be the first play-by-play announcer in any sport; broadcaster Kenny Smith removed his microphone and walked off of an NBA TNT telecast in protest of a senseless shooting; athletes have been allowed, if not encouraged, to write social justice messages on their game day attire. The Second Edition reflects what is new as it relates to the interdependent relationship of sports, communication, politics, and society.

The interdependent relationship of sports and communication is apparent when studying teams, sports organizations, fans, crises, ethical challenges, and the multifaceted ways new and conventional media affect sports. I hope readers will find this Second Edition to be a comprehensive introduction to this exciting new field.

Acknowledgments

Sports Communication: Dimensions, Theory, Applications, and Management is my third book with Kendall Hunt. I feel very fortunate to have worked with KH on these projects. I've published with other companies in the past and have had positive experiences with most. However, no publisher has been more supportive and professional than the people at Kendall Hunt. Paul Carty, Kendall Hunt's Director of Publishing, was my initial contact and has been as helpful and encouraging as one could be. I've enjoyed speaking with him about the books and, in general, about the Sine Curve we call life. I can see why the Kendall Hunt list is as extensive and as successful as it has been.

I've had the great good luck to work with several developmental editors over the years. There has been no editor better than Angela Willenbring: knowledgeable, diplomatic, professional, timely—just an excellent colleague. Paul had told me that I would love working with Angela. He was so right. I also was able to meet, over the years, many of the Kendall Hunt staff. We've met in person at conventions in Salt Lake City and Baltimore and Pittsburgh. And, of course, due to the pandemic I've become acquainted with new members of Kendall Hunt via Zoom. To a person, the people at Kendall Hunt have been welcoming, professional, and genuine—in a world where saccharine is often the norm.

Each chapter in this book includes a section with a practitioner; someone in the sports world who understands the importance of communication. These practitioners took time out to be interviewed and I am grateful for their contributions: Olympic hockey player Kendall Coyne; Publisher and Moderator of scoutfriars.com, Rich Coren; President and General Manager of the Charleston RiverDogs, Dave Echols; University Athletic Director Peter Roby; Head University of New Hampshire Hockey Coach Hilary Witt; sports photographer Bob Donnan; former head of A.S. Roma's Digital and Social Media, Paul Rogers; Sports Information Director Matt Houde; former ESPN broadcaster Sarina Morales—thanks to you all.

Finally, as always, thanks to Donna Glick, who has endured the irascibility of an author on more than one occasion. Her support, love, and patience is a necessary foundation for such an all-consuming enterprise. Donna's dad was a very successful high school basketball and track coach. He, Don Glick, left a legacy throughout the Shenandoah Valley of respecting the value of communication when working with young athletes. Thirty-five years after his passing, people from the community speak about how what he communicated affected their athletic performances and, more significantly, their lives after sport competitions were over. Years ago, I attended a ceremony during which Don was inducted into his alma mater's sports hall of fame. His wife—Donna's mother Jean Glick—gave a beautiful speech at the event talking about the value of sports education and her husband's contribution to it.

I dedicated the book I wrote about college basketball fans to my dad, Meyer Zaremba, who, as legend has it, inadvertently tossed me in the air when I was only a few months old while he was watching a particularly exciting college basketball game. Dad was not only a fan, but an excellent athlete in his own right. He played tennis competitively well into his seventies and early eighties, and was a terrific softball hitter. Dad was also a successful educator retiring after years as a school principal. My mother served as the rock-solid foundation for Dad's various activities. In another era she would have been a good athlete herself. Very good hand-eye coordination; poised under pressure. Together, my parents created a strong ethical foundation for their children's growth on athletic fields, and in all arenas.

In the National Football League, analysts often talk about "coaching trees." This refers to the legacies of head coaches who mentored others who subsequently became coaches themselves. The coaches so mentored become part of a coaching tree. Dennis Green and George Seifert, for example—both successful head coaches in the 90s—are said to come from Bill Walsh's coaching tree because Green and Seifert were assistants to Walsh on the great San Francisco 49er teams in the 1980s.

As is the case with coaching trees, we all—coaches and non-coaches—are branches on trees that have been rooted by the elders and mentors who came before us. It's appropriate that I dedicate this book to Meyer and Helen Zaremba and Don and Jean Glick—parents who provided resilient roots, particularly as it relates to sports, communication, and education.

About the Author

Alan Zaremba earned his Ph.D. from the University of Buffalo and his M.S. and B.A. from the University at Albany.He has been teaching at Northeastern University in the Department of Communication Studies since 1981. From 1976 until 1981 he was on the faculty at the State University of New York College at Fredonia. In 2010 Dr. Zaremba was appointed as the founding associate dean for undergraduate programs in Northeastern's then new College of Arts, Media and Design, a position he held for seven years.

Dr. Zaremba has won four awards for excellence in teaching.He is a recipient of the State University of New York Chancellor's Award for Excellence in Teaching—a statewide designation—and has also received Northeastern University's Excellence in Teaching Award on two occasions. in 2001, he was one of two alums to receive his alma mater's excellence in education alumni award.

Dr. Zaremba is the author of six other books including *Organizational Communication* now in its fourth edition, and *Speaking Professionally: Influence, Power, and Responsibility at the Podium*, in its second edition.His 2009 book on sports fandom—The *Madness of March: Bonding and Betting with the Boys in Las Vegas* was described by one reviewer as "an essential read for anyone who wants to get a better window on one of the more interesting gambling and sports subcultures."Another book, *Crisis Communication: Theory and Practice* has been described as "an invaluable text."In August 2008, Dr. Zaremba was the keynote speaker at the Eighth Annual International Conference on Knowledge, Culture, and Change in Organisations held at Cambridge University in the UK. He is the author of the Sport Communication chapter in Professor Mark Nagel's new Sport Management text and has been invited to contribute, and has written, chapters for several other books dealing with Sports, Communication, Crisis, and Education.

Chapter 1

Sports Communication: An Introduction

© Andrey_Popov/Shutterstock.com

Chapter in a Nutshell

Sports communication is an emerging area of study. It is based on the premise that there are interdependent relationships between sport and communication that affect culture, economics, politics, team performance, educational systems, and social interaction. This chapter introduces this field of study and the text.

Specifically, at the end of the chapter, students will be able to:

- Describe the range of issues examined by those who study sports communication.
- Identify incidents that reflect how sports and communication intersect.
- Identify perspectives for examining the field.
- Understand the goals, sequencing, and features of the text.
- Explain social construction theory.
- Describe some specific communication challenges related to the language of sports.
- Explain the distinction between Stimulation and Catharsis theories.

Sports Communication Prompts

- Below you will see statements pertaining to some aspect of communication and sports. For each item
  - Decide whether you agree or disagree with the statement.
  - Explain your rationale for the position.
  - Support your position with examples.
1. A winner is someone who wins. It doesn't matter how she or he plays the game.
2. Whether they like it or not, athletes are role models. So are coaches.
3. Communicative behavior of American athletes and coaches during international competitions is relevant to global perceptions of Americans overall.
4. The media, new or old, can make or break an athlete's career.

I know March Madness is a copyrighted phrase, but through the 1980s our network created college basketball. Yes, you had Magic and Bird the year before, but you can argue that was more of an NBA-maker than a college-maker. NBC, then CBS, had the Final Four, but they were standing on the shoulders of this cultural phenomenon that we kept creating, reinforcing and embellishing night after night through the winter and during the tournament. ESPN was the seminal impetus for creating what that tournament was.

ESPN Sportscaster Bob Ley
(*Those Guys Have All The Fun*, p. 61)

We created college basketball.

Former ESPN president Chet Simmons

The media at an event like the Olympics is like the media on steroids. The media's goal and the team's goal are not the same. They want a story. We want to win a gold medal.

Kendall Coyne, Captain USA Women's Hockey Team

At a press conference in the fall of 2017, Nick Saban, the head football coach of the University of Alabama Crimson Tide, likened sports journalists' articles about his football team to "rat poison." At that time, Alabama was the number one college team in the nation. However, on the Saturday before the press conference, the Crimson Tide had only narrowly prevailed when it played a weaker rival. Coach Saban contended that the problem was that the players were influenced by what had been communicated in the media about them. The team, claimed Saban, had been reading the glowing assessments of its quality. The coach suggested that because of the favorable media reports, players had become complacent and were not working industriously to compete. Saban likened the favorable media content to toxins, specifically rat poison, that had infected and affected team performance. In subsequent seasons, Saban continued to use a rat poison analogy when referring to the media's influence on team performance. After the December 4, 2021, SEC championship game when underdog Alabama defeated Georgia, Saban commented that because sports reporters had favored Georgia during the week leading up to the game, the "rat poison" had had a positive effect. The toxins served to motivate his team and, consequently, were—as he put it—"yummy."

Kentucky men's basketball coach John Calipari has used a similar metaphor. When his team was playing in the NCAA men's basketball tournament, Calipari warned his team, "don't drink that poison," referring to media analysts' and other experts' positive assessments of the team. "If they drink the poison," Calipari said, "we'll be done on Thursday" (Scarborough, 2018).

C. Vivian Stringer, the head coach of the Rutgers University women's basketball team, had 1,055 career coaching victories going into the 2021-22 season. At that time, there were only five women's or men's basketball coaches who had won more games. One of Stringer's defenses is called the "55 Press." It has five foundational principles.

Rutgers players and fans celebrate C. Vivian Stringer's 1000 career wins

© Cal Sport Media/Alamy Stock Photo

- No fouls, body checking, or silly reach-in fouls.
- No stripping of the ball; steals happen off passes only.
- No trapping in the middle.
- Recognize "house on fire," trap is busted, hustle back on D.
- Communication, communication, communication.

Rick Tocchet, the former head hockey coach of the NHL Arizona Coyotes, was interviewed about factors that affect team success. "Obviously," he said, "you have to have the right system. And you need to have good players and goaltending and all that kind of stuff. But to me, the number one thing is communication with players. You've got to talk to these guys. You've got to communicate. In the old days, coaches didn't communicate much with players. It was just, 'Do it my way, or the highway.' That doesn't work anymore."

During a New England Patriots game against the Carolina Panthers, on four separate occasions, the Patriots' defensive backs were apparently befuddled. Prior to these plays, viewers could see defenders hurriedly and almost frantically signaling to teammates in a way that suggested that the players were unclear about who was supposed to do what. On two of these occasions, an offensive player found himself alone and able to score easily when defenders had botched the coverage. Patriot coaches on the sideline could be seen lifting their heads in exasperated disbelief when two defensive backs converged on one opponent, leaving another open in the end zone. After the game, a Patriot safety was asked about the problem. "It's communication. It's assignments, just busted coverage. At the end of the day, it starts with communication. You can zone in on that."

What is Sports Communication?

Sports communication is an emerging area of academic study. It is based on the assumption that there are interdependent relationships between sport and communication. These linkages not only affect team and league success but also influence our culture, economy, language, politics, educational systems, family interaction, and even international relations.

In this text, we will define sports communication as *the study of how communication and sports are linked and why it is important to explore the linkages.* Early research in sports communication suggests that there is a "significant and intimate connection between communication and sport," and there is "potential for continued scholarship that explores the intersection of the two" (Kassing et al., 2004, p. 381). *The International Journal of Sport Communication* publishes a good deal of that scholarship. The journal's goal is to publish research that "provide[s] an all-encompassing view of the field by covering any topic related to communication in sport, through sport, or in a sport setting" (https://journals.humankinetics.com/page/about/ijsc). As we will see shortly, and as is apparent from the journal's mission statement, the field of sports communication is wide-ranging.

"All analyses end in definition" is the way one author began a monograph (Smith, 1973, p. 9). By this, he meant that the residual effect of analyzing and discussing a subject should be a more definitive understanding of what has been analyzed. The overarching goal of this text is to be similarly descriptive. At the conclusion of the book, students who may have had a general interest in sports communication will have a more definitive understanding of the nature and dimensions of the field. Toward that end, we will explain what sports communication includes and why the field is important in the twenty-first century—even for those who are not necessarily sports enthusiasts. In order to accomplish this, we will address the following questions:

- What is the scope of sports communication study?
- What theories and principles can be applied to challenges related to sports communication?
- How can teams and leagues communicate efficiently?
- How is sports communication relevant to society, culture, and politics?
- What is fandom, and how do fans fit into the study of sports communication?
- What ethical questions and challenges surface that pertain to sports communication?
- How does new as well as conventional media affect sports figures and organizations and the public's understanding of sports?

A First Look at Scope

Often the examination of sports communication centers on how the communication media—new and traditional—has affected sport and society.

- March Madness, for example, is an event that has become larger than it was because of how ESPN and then other networks began to cover it. Office members belong to betting pools during March; retailers offer March Madness sales; the President of the United States has filled out his bracket on national television, and fevered alums tweet all through contests.
- Super Bowl Sunday is akin to a national holiday because of pervasive media coverage. Many people—even those who are not fans—attend Super Bowl parties. Revenues generated for a single thirty-second advertisement during the game are startling. Ski resorts and theatres have fewer customers during this time. Some upscale restaurants simply close because regular patrons are more likely to park in front of home televisions or visit dedicated sports bars. Liquor sales soar. Grocery stores are congested with shoppers buying snacks for the game. A "wardrobe malfunction" during halftime of the game can become international news instantaneously.
- The proliferation and success of dedicated sports networks is an indication of the apparently insatiable desire for sports programming. ESPNU, NFL, MLB, and NBA networks are examples. Many local dedicated sports networks not only broadcast events but, on the same day, rebroadcast games in digested forms filling the networks' voracious need for programming with programs for voracious consumers of sport.

- New media has had a dramatic effect on sports. Because of new media, viewers and listeners have become empowered to criticize players and owners and do so anonymously. Often athletes become targets of malicious online comments. With the advent of legalized betting, these communications from disappointed bettors can become frighteningly vitriolic (Sullivan, 2021 p. c1). The speed and reach of new media have had an effect on leagues and international relationships. In October of 2019, Daryl Morey, then the general manager of the Houston Rockets, tweeted support for Hong Kong protestors and, nearly instantly, created havoc for the National Basketball Association and bruised relations between China and the United States.

While examining mediated communication and sport is important, the link between communication and sport is more nuanced and diverse. The nature of this diversity is revealed when one reviews issues and challenges for those who study in this area.

- How do coaches communicate with players? Coaches with trainers? Owners with agents? Recruiters with prospective college athletes? College academic advisers and professors with student-athletes?
- What plans are, or should be in place for sports organizations when they have to communicate during crises? How does a team respond when an athlete or coach has behaved reprehensibly? Urban Meyer, the then coach of the Jacksonville Jaguars, created headaches for ownership in October 2021 for off-field actions after a loss to the Cincinnati Bengals. A video of Meyer surfaced on social media suggesting that the coach was enjoying, or at least not rejecting, a dancer who was moving against him provocatively. Did the Jaguars have to address this issue? If so, with whom should they have communicated? Season ticket holders? Other league owners? Players on the team? Should the messages to all audiences be the same? How should the messages be communicated? Via e-mail? Should there be a public apology posted on a website? Team meetings?

Urban Meyer had problems both on and off the field during his time coaching the Jaguars.

© ZUMA Press, Inc. / Alamy Stock Photo

- Can communication foster team culture? Can, for example, a slogan like "You'll Never Walk Alone" or "Just Win Baby" affect team culture and performance? Can a team or sponsor's logo have an impact on player identification with, or a fan's allegiance to, a team? In September of 2021, the former National Women's Hockey League (NWHL) rebranded itself as the Premier Hockey League. Does a name change like this affect league culture? Does it communicate anything substantive to players or fans? Does the communication behavior of a head coach have an effect on team culture? Does an individual player's communication behaviors affect team cohesion such that it matters if a player is, or is not, "good in the locker room"?

- Did the fifth consecutive United States women's basketball gold medal in 2021 have an effect beyond that particular competition? Did the large television audience for the 2018 U.S. women's Olympic hockey gold medal match and eventual victory signal a change in the popularity of women's sports? How did and does the discourse surrounding Title IX affect society and opportunities for female athletes?

- How does ethnicity factor into sports communication? How did Colin Kaepernick's nonverbal communication during the playing of the national anthem affect attitudes toward race? Was Jackie Robinson's performance during the 1951 pennant chase an accelerant for civil rights legislation in the following decades? Is it true, as John Feinstein suggests in *Raise a Fist, Take a Knee*, that race—even in the third decade of the twenty-first century—is a factor when hiring team general managers and head coaches? (Feinstein, 2021, p. 57; 134–135).

- Why do fans become fans? Who are these people who are the lifeblood of sports organizations? How does a team/league communicate in order to create and nurture a fan base? Is a team website a factor that can generate or dilute enthusiasm? How significant are Twitter and Facebook for fans and/or the cultivation of fandom? How do fans themselves communicate about sports? Did the phenomenon of twenty-four-hour talk radio and online discussion groups provide a healthy outlet for zealous fans, or does it foster sophomoric, if not coarse, communicative behavior?

- The intersection of sports and communication is evident in the availability of books and films about sports. *Major League, Bull Durham, Million Dollar Baby*, and *Field of Dreams* are fictional examples, but there are legions of nonfiction books and films about sports. One can read about the nuances of the North Carolina academic scandal in at least three books that were published within a year of the investigation. Both Carli Lloyd and Megan Rapinhoe have written memoirs about their experiences as Olympic athletes. In a short period of time, at least five books about Bill Belichick and the so-called "Patriot Way" have been published. A bench-warming basketball player wrote a book about his life as an itinerant hoopster (*Can I Keep My Jersey*). Pioneering ESPN anchor Linda Cohn describes her journey to Sports Center in *Cohn-head. Three Nights in August*—in more detail than even some fans may desire—points out the intricacies of managing a professional baseball team and the challenges associated when communicating with professional athletes. John Saunders's memoir *Playing Hurt* debunks any notion that sports media celebrities are above psychological turmoil. Documentaries like ESPN's *30 for 30* series relay stories and contribute to the narrative regarding sports and specific events. How have films and books nourished interest in sport and reflected the enthusiasm large numbers of people have for sport?

- The pregame and postgame press conferences receive more exposure than ever before. Increasingly, sideline reporters ask coaches questions during the contests. Perspiring athletes are interviewed after the games and, sometimes in hockey, between periods.

How important are these communications? Can a coach's sideline communication affect fan perspective of the merit of the coach, team, and league?

- Ethical issues are apparent in all avenues of life, and the intersection of sports and communication is not an exception. Do journalists and teammates have the obligation to out an athlete who is engaging in reprehensible activities? Does an athlete who endorses a beer product have an obligation to consider the influence of endorsements on reckless consumption? When high school athletes are recruited, what ethical constraints do college recruiters have when they communicate with prospective players and their families? Do advertisers and networks have an ethical obligation to ensure that times for sporting events are not altered to manufacture larger audiences when these scheduling revisions could affect the competitive nature of the game?

- Globalization is real, and sports communication has affected globalization. Before satellites, Americans knew little about the most popular sport in the world. Now American children aspire to play "football," and fans are riveted during broadcasted World Cup competition. The popularity of basketball beyond the United States is reflected in international players now having an opportunity to play in the NBA and marginal NBA players being able to play professionally in leagues throughout the world. The 2021 Olympic competition in men's basketball is hardly what it had been in earlier decades. Now teams outside of the U.S. are formidable opponents because the game has spread internationally. The once indomitable U.S. did indeed win Gold in 2021 but lost to Nigeria, Australia, and France during the course of the competition. To what extent has sports and the communication of sporting events affected international relationships? Is the world "flatter" because of sports communication?

- What theories and principles can be applied to challenges related to sport and communication? Theories are often considered abstractions and have been presented by some as the antithesis of what is practical. Yet they can be relevant. Students have perhaps heard the expression, "There is nothing more practical than a good theory." Understanding how, for example, systems theory can be applied to teams and leagues not only can improve team and league performance but can also eliminate crises that can and have surfaced when principles of systems theory are ignored. How do the tenets of Classical Management Theory apply to sports communication? Does Scientific Management make sense in sports contexts? Is the current rage regarding sports "analytics" just an application of Frederick Taylor's "one best way" mantra? What are the applications of Human Resources, Cultural, and Critical Theories? How can Image Repair Theory be employed after crises?

- How is sports communication relevant to interpersonal, family, and fan relationships and communities? Television has been likened to a "cool fire." As opposed to families sitting around the fireplace as they might have in the early part of the twentieth and prior centuries, families might gather around the "cool fire" of the television. Those who study sports communication take this a step further. Television may still be a focus of attention, but for some families, it is sport on various forms of media that is the magnet for gatherings. Beyond the living room and family, sports bars, for example, have become places where fan communities gather to watch games. The Harp, the Buffalo Bills tavern in downtown Boston, is a place to be if you wish to gather with western New Yorkers to support the Bills in New England. Walk in there with Patriot gear, and you are something of a pariah. A Rebecca Watts article "The Florida Gator Nation

Online" describes how new media nourished Florida State University fan subcultures. Communicating using social media has allowed people who do not know each other and are not physically near one another to opine about the wisdom of plays seconds after they have been made so that thousands of people are communicating in the same way as a cluster of friends in a clubroom might have interacted in the past.

The awareness of the breadth of sports communication is an important foundational plank for study in this area. Narrow conceptions of the field lead to parochial explorations and, consequently, limited if not illusory conclusions about the effects of sports on communication and communication on sports. Were one to just focus on media and sports or public relations and sports, the results of the inquiry would be incomplete. Any conclusions about the field based on limited inquiry would be misleading, as they would suggest, implicitly at least, that the study of sports communication excluded significant areas.

© Evgeniy Kalinovskiy/Shutterstock.com

Sports Communication in Everyday Life

Once you begin studying sports communication, you may be startled at its pervasiveness. Almost daily, you can see examples of how communication and sport are linked. One such example is apparent when we consider how we communicate about non-sports-related issues. It becomes clear that sports have permeated our language and culture. A sure thing is a "slam dunk." The leader of your work team may be called your "quarterback." You may hear colleagues complain when they don't receive a bonus contending that the "goalposts" have been moved. People who have no interest in sports might comment that an associate working on a project "dropped the ball." Consider some other common sports metaphors that are part of our discourse.

- That meeting was a game-changer.
- We've got them on the ropes.
- It's no longer a level playing field.
- We're stuck playing defense.

- They struck out with that plan.
- We scored some points at the hearing.
- The special prosecutor is on a fishing expedition.
- They're down for the count.
- This could be a whole new ball game.
- At the interview, she hit it out of the park.
- The negotiation is a bust. We're not even at second base.
- Do you have any sort of game plan?

Robert Palmatier and Harold Ray have produced a book, *Dictionary of Sports Idioms,* that includes nearly 2000 such sports expressions. Dale Herbeck's study "Sports Metaphors and Public Policy" discusses the pervasive football metaphors that were used to describe Operation Desert Storm. Writers have referred to pervasive sports metaphors as "sportuguese" and "sportspeak." However labeled, it refers to the same phenomenon—our discourse is filled with sports terms reflecting the influence of sport on our society.

Not only our discourse but also our sports news reflects how frequently communication and sports issues are intertwined. The following is a "sweet sixteen" sample of such issues.

1. In September 2021, The Milwaukee Bucks made Lisa Byington the first woman full-time T.V. play-by-play announcer in major men's pro sports. Said Byington: "I understand the groundbreaking nature of this hire, and I appreciate the fact that during this process that aspect was addressed but never made a primary focus. In fact, I applaud the Bucks for taking the first steps toward making hires like this more of the norm in the NBA. Because it's time." The *Nine for IX* documentary, *Let Them Wear Towels,* produced years before, describes the long and difficult road women sports journalists faced as they attempted to gain access to do their jobs as sports analysts and reporters.

2. Forty years after their unlikely "Miracle on Ice" victory, Mike Eruzione and members of the 1980 U.S. hockey team congregated in Las Vegas to celebrate the anniversary. The reunion coincided with a campaign rally for President Trump's reelection. The president asked Eruzione and members of the team to wear red "Keep America Great" caps. Eruzione and several teammates complied. Subsequently, the team was heavily criticized for wearing the hats. Eruzione claimed that the team's appearance at the rally was coincidental and apolitical. The team tweeted a response to the criticism.

   To us, this is not about politics or choosing sides. This is about proudly representing the United States of America. Whether your beliefs are Democratic, Republican, Independent, etc., we support that and are proud to represent the USA. It is an honor and privilege!

3. The NFL announced on September 5, 2021, that players would be allowed to display messages of social justice on their helmets. Players could choose from *End Racism, Stop Hate, It Takes All of Us, Black Lives Matter, Inspire Change,* and *Say Their Stories.* The league also announced it would stencil the slogans "It takes all of us" and "End Racism" in end zones.

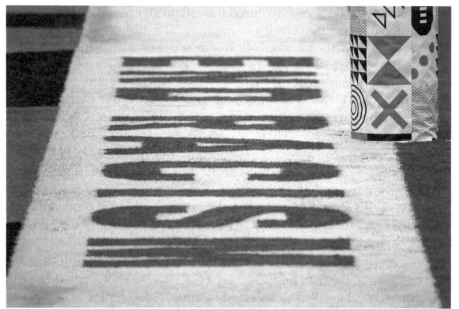

The end zone on October 4, 2020 in Cincinnati

4. An article appeared on the first page of the *Sunday Boston Globe* that continued onto a page in the sports section. It was about hockey coaches who were suspended for allegedly berating adolescent girls who were being coached by them and groomed to be college hockey players. The coaches were portrayed as being excessively critical and demeaning when communicating with the players.

5. Cole Beasley, an unvaccinated wide receiver for the Buffalo Bills, used Twitter to rant against vaccination requirements. He disparaged Dr. Anthony Fauci on the social platform as well. In the summer of 2021, Beasley and a teammate, Jerry Hughes, became combatants in a Twitter debate arguing about the merit of the vaccines and the potential ramifications of not getting vaccinated. Disputes among teammates are not uncommon, but social media escalated the tension and made public a disagreement that might otherwise have been kept private.

6. In September 2021, Celtic great Bill Russell was inducted as a coach into the Basketball Hall of Fame. A newspaper story before the event reported that at a preseason meeting during his second year of coaching, Russell told the team that players and teammates were equals, and he sought their help. Wayne Embry, one of Russell's players then, commented, "I respected that because it indicated his intelligence and also his willingness to listen. Most coaches don't do that, and I think it was a big factor in [our success]." Another former player on that team, Rick Weitzman, said, "If someone had an idea in the huddle, they were free to speak up. And he listened and took in what was being suggested. If he liked it, he'd go with it, and if he didn't, he wouldn't. He made the final decisions, but he listened to everybody." Bill Russell passed away ten months later on July 31, 2022. The next days' newspapers were filled with articles that were as much about how Russell used his platform to communicate and advocate for social change than his athletic prowess.

7. A cover of *ESPN the Body Issue* featured basketball star Sue Bird and her romantic partner, professional soccer player Megan Rapinoe. The athletes stood side-by-side, naked, on the cover. Bird twirls a basketball; Rapinoe poses with a foot standing on top of a soccer ball. It was the tenth anniversary of the Body issue. The words "Body 10" appear across the athletes' midsections. "The way I see it," Bird commented, "it is more how you want to change the conversation or change the narrative of things. I think having a gay couple on the cover; hopefully, it just becomes the norm. 'Oh, another couple is on there.' You know I think for us to be on it is the first step in that direction."

8. Sports reporter Shira Springer commemorated the anniversary of the passing of Title IX by listing nine recommendations related to women, communication, and sport. Among these are to (a) change the name of the World Cup games to the men's World Cup and women's World Cup games; (b) recognize how women athletes have used their microphones for social change; (c) challenge the NFL and the NFL Player's Association for their tepid reactions to domestic violence.

9. On June 7, 2018 the Chicago Cubs defeated the Philadelphia Phillies 4-3. Chicago's fourth run came in the fifth inning when a Cub was initially called out trying to score on a sacrifice fly. The call was reversed when a video replay showed that the Philly catcher, Andrew Knapp, illegally blocked the plate.

10. NFL icon John Madden passed away on December 28, 2021. While Madden was an outstanding football coach, he was remembered as much for his work as an NFL broadcaster and for the football video game Madden NFL. A group of non-sports fans may recall Madden, not because of his coaching, or broadcasting, or the video game, but because of his appearances in beer commercials.

Al Michaels and the late John Madden broadcasting ABC's Monday Night Football.

11. Philadelphia 76ers president of basketball operations Bryan Colangelo resigned when it was discovered that his wife had tweeted information about the team that criticized members of the organization. An investigation concluded that the tweets reflected

"careless and in some cases reckless" sharing of team information. Colangelo himself was unaware of his wife's tweets and denied that he had been reckless, but the investigation "revealed that Mr. Colangelo was the source of sensitive, nonpublic information contained in certain posts."

12. The *Smithsonian* magazine published an article about the great New York and San Francisco Giant Willie Mays. The online version of the article *Even Today, Willie Mays Remains a Giant in Baseball History* allows readers to click on a picture and see the moving image of Mays's famous catch in the 1954 World Series. The article informed that there was an exhibit at the Smithsonian that included Mays's cap, cleats, and baseball glove, all signed by Mays. On the cap, Mays has also written, "Say Hey." The center fielder was called the "Say Hey Kid" by sports reporters during his career.

13. The Boston Public Improvement Commission voted unanimously to change the name of Yawkey Way, the street outside of Fenway Park. The name was officially renamed Jersey Street. The street name was changed because there had been allegations that Tom Yawkey, the long-time owner of the Red Sox for whom the street was named, had been a racist. In response, the Yawkey Foundation issued the following statement:

> We are deeply disappointed with today's decision. The effort to expunge Tom Yawkey's name has been based on a false narrative about his life and his historic forty-three-year ownership of the Red Sox. The drastic step of renaming the street, contradicting the honor the City bestowed upon Tom Yawkey, will give lasting credence to that narrative and unfairly tarnish his name...

14. Two blocks from where the University of West Virginia Mountaineers would play in a March Madness "Sweet 16" game at 7:30, a sports bar called, modestly, *The Greatest Bar,* was packed. In the establishment were scores of West Virginia fans; so many that the tavern had set up a makeshift beer stand away from the large main bar to accommodate the revelling Mountaineer supporters. At a signal from someone, the place rocked with the fanatics belting out the John Denver song, "Almost Heaven West Virginia" 600 miles from the West Virginia border. At 7:30, game time, few left the establishment. The people in the tavern were not going to the arena. These West Virginians had gathered at *The Greatest Bar* to share the experience of watching the contest on the many television screens in the bar.

15. The U.S. Women's Ice Hockey team defeated Team Canada in a Gold medal Olympic game in PyeongChang, South Korea. The game was aired live from 11 p.m. to 2:15 a.m. Eastern Time on NBCSN and despite the late hour still drew 2.9 million viewers. It was the most-watched midnight hour program in NBCSN history. One columnist wrote, "Women's hockey has stolen the show at the Winter Olympics." The game would win an ESPY for the best game of the year. beating out the other two nominees—a thrilling Rose Bowl contest, and a similarly exciting World Series contest.

16. Shortly after basketball superstar LeBron James criticized President Donald Trump, Fox newscaster Laura Ingraham broadcasted an editorial piece in which she told James "to shut up and dribble." James responded "I actually laughed when I first saw the reports. We will definitely not just shut up and dribble." Previously, former Washington Wizard basketball player Etan Thomas published *We Matter: Athletes and*

Activism. The book contends that athletes have accepted their responsibility to speak out for important social causes. In the introductory paragraph, Thomas writes: "Athletes have a unique ability to influence fashion, pop culture, and politics with their actions. It is refreshing to see many acting on their convictions."

Compartmentalizing The Field

Clearly, sports communication issues are pervasive and diverse. In *Casing Sport Communication,* Tucker and Wrench describe the field's breadth. "As long as the study links an aspect of communication with one of sport the sky is the limit" (Tucker and Wrench, 2016, p. 2). The "sky" may or may not be "the limit," but the field is, incontrovertibly, deep and broad.

The question becomes how should one intelligently go about studying such a multifaceted phenomenon. All exploration, academic or otherwise, requires a plan and focus. To survey a plot of land, one doesn't just hire a crew to race about the territory hoping that reports from helter-skelter expeditions will yield a clear understanding of the terrain. One needs to consider how to structure the exploration. "It is imperative to identify a framework that compartmentalizes and presents the diverse field of sport communication as a cohesive whole" (Abeza, 2014, p. 299).

Chapter 2 in this text is called *Sports Communication-Focusing the Lens.* At the conclusion of that chapter, we present a visual model for framing and examining this growing field. In this introductory section, let's begin constructing the framework by considering some ways analysts could compartmentalize issues in this growing field.

SPORTS COMMUNICATION WITHIN CONTEXTS

Organizations

The WNBA, FIFA, the PAC 10, the International Olympic Committee, the NCAA, the NHL, and the athletic department at your university can all be studied as organizations. Researchers argue that regardless of the quality of the product—organizational success is a function of how units within the organization communicate. The WNBA can have the finest athletes in all sports, have outstanding teams in its league, and play competitive, excellent basketball, but inefficient communication within the league and with its external stakeholders will affect the success of the enterprise. Sports communication scholars examine the communication challenges for sports organizations as it relates to these organizations' internal and external interactions.

Teams

The team is a second context for examining sports communication. The axiom, the whole is greater than the sum of its parts, is not always true. More accurately, the whole *can be* greater than the sum of its parts. How teams communicate will determine the chances for a collection of individuals to become more effective as a team. From this vantage point, the study of sports communication involves coaching styles and coach-player interaction, as well as interpersonal communication among teammates and the role communication, has in creating team culture.

We know that communication is important during a game, and we regularly hear comments that a team needs to, for example, communicate better on defense or that a particular player is a good communicator. When researchers look at communication from a team perspective, we examine the multiple ways communication and team success is linked.

Fandom

A third context centers on the fan. In this context, we examine communication as a factor that affects fandom. How do fans communicate with each other? Why do fans become fans? Why do fans spend time communicating about sports, and how can a team use communication as a tool to cultivate fandom? On a sports talk radio program, a caller once issued a blistering rant complaining about a New York Met outfielder. According to the caller, the player did not hustle, had a frivolous approach to at-bats, and was only concerned with personal stats. The host listened to this commentary and then heard a crashing sound in the background. "What is that?" asked the host. "Ah, my wife just fell down the stairs. You know it really burns my butt that Strawberry never hits the cut-off man." The startled host blurted, "Sir, Darryl Strawberry is relatively insignificant. Go attend to your wife."

If we look at sports communication from the perspective of the fans, we consider questions like why sports bars have become a phenomenon. Is it because there one can cheer and chat with strangers who become instantly like family? If you are in the borough of Manhattan in New York City and want to follow the Spartans of Michigan State who hail from Lansing, Michigan, 700 miles away, you can travel to a tavern called the Mercury Bar and converse with people whom you've never met but seem instantly like members of your social club. If you want to know all there is to know about the Columbus Blue Jackets, just go to unionandblue. com, and you can read about the team and interact with enthusiasts. Click on https://www. facebook. com/groups/mmilv/ and you can meet like-minded fans who travel to Las Vegas to watch the first rounds of the NCAA men's basketball tournament.

EFFECTS OF SPORTS COMMUNICATION

In addition to looking at sports communication in various contexts, we can also look at sports communication in terms of its effects. How has sports communication affected our society, racial issues, women's rights, and politics?

The broadcast of the Battle of the Sexes, a tennis match between Billy Jean King and Bobby Riggs in 1973, is said to have had a dramatic effect on women's rights. It is difficult to overestimate King's influence as she used the platform she earned as an athlete to level the playing field. Title IX has had effects on sports that have transcended sports and leveled the playing field in non-sport areas as well. When Joe Louis knocked out Max Schmeling in 1938, it was more than a boxing match. The 1936 and 1968 Olympics, in particular, were not just about the games. The 1963 basketball contest between Mississippi State and Loyola of Chicago has been referred to as the "Game of Change." The game was not only or primarily an NCAA first-round March Madness match-up. When the University of Southern California played the segregated University of Alabama in 1970, an African American running back for USC named Sam Cunningham scored two touchdowns and rushed for 135 yards. The next year Alabama recruited several Black athletes for its program. Subsequently, Alabama assistant coach Jerry Clairborne commented: "Sam Cunningham did more to integrate Alabama in sixty minutes than Martin Luther King did in twenty years" (Feinstein, 2021, p. 66).

ETHICAL ISSUES

We can also look at sports communication in terms of the ethical issues that surface. Coaches, players, media producers, fans, and team owners are all faced with ethical choices. What types of ethical challenges face teams, athletes, and sports organizations? What tools can be employed when wrestling with these tools. Sports organizations often publish codes of ethics and mission statements that incorporate the values of the organization.

When confronted with ethical challenges, do these organizations review these codes of ethics and ostensible corporate values, or do they default to what has been called "instrumental rationality." Instrumental rationality, as will be discussed in detail in Chapter 7, refers to the tendency to make decisions on the basis of how instrumental that decision will be toward the end of organizational goals.

INFLUENCES OF NEW AND CONVENTIONAL MEDIA

The study of sports communication can focus on television networks that are dedicated to sports programming, periodicals devoted to sports, films, documentaries, research publications, books about sports, and the exploding new media focused on sports. In 1979, a father and son had an idea for a 24/7 broadcasting station that would be dedicated to sports. It was difficult to find backers for what would become ESPN. On July 1, 1987, WFAN— arguably the most famous sports talk radio station—began broadcasting. Could a station survive with such a format?

The success of ESPN and WFAN has proven that there is a voracious if not insatiable audience for sports information and debate. The proliferation of blogs, Barstool Sports type sites, and platforms for electronic sports conversation would be startling to those who had been skeptical of the audience interest in sports. On any given Saturday during the autumn, there could be over twenty college football games available for viewing. If one has a smartphone, and approximately 85% of the United States adult population is so equipped, one can watch many contests regardless of location. On a long-distance driving trip and desire to hear how your Chicago Cubs are faring? Simply tune into a Sirius radio station, and you can get the play by play. Are you living in Albuquerque and desire to watch the Orioles? Buy the MLB package, and you might as well be living in Baltimore.

There is a reciprocal relationship between the media and sports. The financial resources for new facilities, winning coaches, free-agent signings in sports often comes from media money. The success of the media, certainly media devoted to sports, requires engaging sporting events. The NFL contracts with the networks are beneficial, if not essential, to both parties. One reason universities invest in basketball and football programs is that five outstanding basketball players can provide a stunning windfall if the team is selected to the NCAA March Madness tournament. Football is a more expensive endeavor, but exposure on television can increase the number of students who apply to your institution. After Doug Flutie won the Heisman trophy in 1984, the number of students that applied to Boston College increased by over 10%. Some have even referred to this phenomenon as the Flutie factor.

A review of the ten most often cited articles in the sport communication literature all focus on mediated communication in one way or another (Abeza, 2014, p. 309). This could be because of how the field had been oriented, but it indicates that scholars believe that the influences of new and conventional media on sports are important to consider.

Fair or Foul   Questions of Ethics

Should the street outside Fenway Park, Yawkey Way, have been renamed?

- Supporters of the change suggest that Yawkey was a racist, and it is an insult to egalitarians to have to walk on a street named after a racist when they go to the ballpark.
- The Yawkey Foundation's position is that "the effort to expunge Tom Yawkey's name has been based on a false narrative."
- Others contend that if people were to change names based on character, dozens of streets, buildings, intersections in a city would have to be renamed.
- Change the name: Fair or Foul?

Social Construction Theory

One of the challenges in examining the discourse about sports relates to what is called social construction theory. Social construction theory refers to the idea that some words do not have inherent meanings but rather have meanings that have been constructed by our society, by us. Outside the world of sports, one could argue that love, romance, family, and friendship are all words that have socially constructed definitions. In the world of sports, words like winner, athlete, champion, even sport could be said to be social constructions.

Were the 2020 Kansas City Chiefs winners? They won sixteen games that year and lost only three, but they lost the Super Bowl played in February 2021. Were they winners? The NHL Washington Capitals won the President's Trophy in 2016, signifying the team with the best record in the NHL during the regular season. They were eliminated in the playoffs. Would you call the 2016 Capitals winners? Are the 2018 Capitals winners because they won the Stanley Cup but the 2016 Capitals losers? The 2014 women's ice hockey team lost in overtime in the finals of the Olympics. Does that mean they were losers, but the 2018 women's Olympic team that was victorious in a shootout were winners? If you never got off the bench for the 2018 women's Olympic hockey team, are you a winner because the team won?

- How do you distinguish between a winner and a champion?
- What makes someone a good coach?
- What makes a team a dynasty?

Muhammad Ali called himself the greatest. Was he? If so, what made him the greatest? What makes anyone great?

Are bowlers athletes? Hot dog eaters? Marble players?

Do you consider this an athletic competition?

Broadcasters, sportswriters, fans on call-in talk shows, and general managers use terms like *great* or *athlete* or *winner* or *elite.* These are all social constructions. Collectively we construct the definitions. Professional communicators in particular, but even fans, should consider what they mean by these terms when they communicate about sports.

Test Yourself: Apply the Principles

- In your opinion, what makes
  - A person, an athlete?
  - An athlete, great?
  - A player, a winner (not the winner, a winner)?
  - A coach, a success?
  - A sportsperson, socially responsible?
  - A player, elite?
- What are the problems, if any, of different people having different definitions of these terms?
- Is it the role of a sports broadcaster, journalist, blogger, or fan to help define these terms for those who use them?
- Was
  - Hulk Hogan an athlete?
  - Andy Murray great?
  - Rene Portland a successful coach?
  - Tom Yawkey socially responsible?
  - The United States 1972 Olympic men's basketball team champions?

Defining Sport

We can debate about what is meant by a "winner" or "loser," or what it means to be "the greatest," but for the purposes of consistency in this book, we need to define what we mean by sports.

What counts as a sport? *Sports Illustrated* once ran a story about the game show *Jeopardy!*. Does that make *Jeopardy!* a sport? Poker competition is often televised on ESPN. Is poker a sport?

Rodriguez, in her text, has defined sport as "a game like activity requiring rules, containing a competitive element, and requiring a level of physical exertion" (Rodriguez, 2016, p 124). In *Research Methods in Sport Studies and Sport Management*, Veal and Darcy define sport as "physical activity which is rule-based and competitive" (Veal and Darcy 4) in *To Play the Game: An Analysis of Sports* has defined sport as a "repeatable, regulated, physical contest producing a clear winner." (Bell, 1987, page 2).

All these have important and recurring elements. Sports do require a physical dimension. They do involve competition. They are rule-based. We'll add to these components to create an applicable definition for our study of sports communication. We will define a sport *as a physical activity; that has rules for competition; and an outcome that is not predetermined.* Below is a discussion of the key components of this definition.

PHYSICAL ACTIVITY

Tennis, golf, archery, road racing, bowling, badminton are all sports. Chess and marbles are not, even though some people could make cogent arguments that another definition would include these activities. There has to be a physical dimension in addition to any mental dimension for a sport to be a sport. Chess and marbles are, by this definition, games, not sports. Some could contend that chess and marbles do require physical stamina and some exertion. Yet, the physical activities involved in playing chess, marbles, dominoes, poker are different. Obviously, what is or is not sufficiently physical can be debated. There is, however, a fundamental difference between poker and marathon running, between checkers and volleyball, that makes one a sport and the other a game. There is contentious debate about whether what are called e-sports are indeed sports. Some who author arguments against categorizing e-sports as sports actually entitle their writings "E-sports are not sports"(Parry, 2020, p. 3; Smith, 2022)[1] E-sports refers to competitive video game playing. There are certainly high-level e-sport competitions. Universities have e-sports teams that are housed in their athletic departments. There are also professional e-sports leagues. However, those who balk at labeling competitive video gaming as a sport contend that sport requires physical and motor skills in a way that e-sports do not and that simply calling something a sport does not make it a sport. Regardless, e-sports—whether they are sports or games—have been researched by those who study sports communication. One could make the case that e-sports can be examined in the context of sports communication if for no other reason that unlike backgammon, chess, and poker, e-sports by design require sophisticated communication technology.

---

[1] Smith's piece with the title, "E-sports are not sports" is found in an e-sports blog https://www.contendercary.com/blog/esports-are-not-sports/

RULES FOR COMPETITION

Frisbee football is a sport but simply tossing a Frisbee with your friend is not a sport. A sport has to have rules for competition and a competitive element. There are rules and even federations for Frisbee football. When you are in the park throwing a Frisbee, it is a recreational exercise, not a sport. Similarly, practicing putting is not a sport. Batting practice is not a sport. Home run derby-type competitions are sports, but batting practice is not. During batting practice, Frisbee tossing, and putting practice, there are no formal rules for competition, and there is, in fact, no formal competition.

AN OUTCOME NOT PREDETERMINED

High school and college wrestling is a sport. Professional wrestling is not a sport. This might raise the ire of professional wrestling enthusiasts, but if the outcome of the competition is predetermined, then despite the physical activity involved, and even though strong women and men ostensibly compete, professional wrestling is not a sport. Racecar driving is a sport; competitive weightlifting is a sport. Driving to work is not a sport (though some motorists appear to believe that there is a competition of some sort). A fixed tennis match is not a sport. In a sport, a winner will be determined and cannot be predetermined.

Book Organization

It can be exciting to consider the multifaceted dimensions of sports communication. A challenge for this text is to organize the content to provide a sturdy foundation for analysis and subsequent study.

Toward this end, the next two chapters discuss communication principles and theoretical underpinnings. While nearly anyone associated with sports organizations recognizes the importance of communication, there can be wildly disparate notions of what communication means. Chapter 2 describes the diverse perspectives and provides a definition that will be used in this text and is valuable for future study. In chapter 2, we also present two complementary approaches to the study of communication: transmission and constitutive perspectives, and explain how these are applied to sports communication. Throughout the text, there are references to factors that affect the transmission of information as well as the constitutive effects of interaction in sports contexts.

In Chapter 3, we present theories that will help readers conceptualize communication in sports contexts. We focus on systems theory and how this conceptualization explains the pervasive and multifaceted nature of communication in sports organizations. Systems and their complementary theories can assist those who desire to assess how effectively their sports organizations communicate while concurrently suggesting steps to take for improving how your sports organizations communicate with various stakeholders.

The fourth chapter discusses a pervasive issue in sports: crisis communication. The college sports world was rocked when it was reported that NCAA coaches accepted bribes to enroll non-athletes into their programs as if these students were indeed scholarship-worthy athletes. How should the institutions these coaches represent, respond? How does the NCAA itself respond? What could have been done to preempt the crisis, and what can be done subsequently to address the damage? When misogynistic comments are made on websites like Barstool Sports, to whom should Barstool communicate? What should the leaders of these groups say to which publics? This chapter identifies proactive and reactive approaches to crisis communication in sports contexts. We explain what is meant by image repair theory and the various approaches used to repair a sports organization's image after a crisis.

In Chapter 5, we look at communication within team contexts. We introduce the term nonsummativity and discuss factors that affect positive nonsummative results. In this chapter, we also look at sports communication in terms of organizational culture. When New York Yankee GM Brian Cashman fired long-time manager Joe Girardi, he referred to the "connectivity and communication issue" with players (King, 2017). Is this important? Or is communication as it relates to culture and success relatively insignificant?

In Chapter 6, we examine the effects of sports communication on society, history, and culture. When Tommie Smith and John Carlos made their loud nonverbal statement in the 1968 Olympics, did that affect history? Hundreds of flashbulbs exploded when the captain of Mississippi State University shook hands with the captain of Loyola University in March of 1963. Did that handshake and event affect the world beyond sports? Title IX has revolutionized access to sports, and because of that revolution, our society has become more equitable. In Chapter 6, we discuss how culture has been affected by sports communication and the ongoing discourse about how active athletes should be in communicating for social change.

In Chapter 7, we examine ethical issues for sports communicators. We identify the types of ethical challenges that surface and provide tools that can be employed when faced with ethical dilemmas; specifically, we discuss what is called "the categorical imperative" and juxtapose that approach with "utilitarianism." In Chapter 7, we also introduce the phrase "the normalization of deviance" and explain how this can be a factor in sports communication contexts.

In Chapter 8, we look at fandom. Why do fans become fans? The subtitle of Larry Olmsted's 2021 book, *Fans* is *How Watching Sports Makes Us Happier, Healthier and More Understanding*. Does it? Does watching sports make us happier even when we follow teams that are regularly unsuccessful. Does watching nine hours of football on a fall weekend make us healthier and more understanding? Fan is short for fanatic, and this is—according to writers like George Dohrmann, author of *Superfans,* and Justine Gubar, author of *Fanaticus*—an apt term to describe fan behavior and communication. Scholar Dan Wann has developed methods for examining the intensity of sports fandom. What are the best methods for communicating with fans? How can one account for someone who decides to attend a game as a "rally banana?"

Chapter 9 is dedicated to looking at communicating with the public. How have sports figures used, and been affected by, media coverage? What are the effects of new media on how and what is communicated? Your university likely has a dedicated sports information staff. What are the challenges for these people when they attempt to get messages to external audiences? In addition, in this chapter, we look at how artists have communicated with the public about sports with their films, books, and documentaries. We also discuss how scholars communicate to the public about sports. We identify journals where academics publish research about sports communication and specific articles that represent the breadth of the field. At the end of this section, students may consider avenues of sports communication research for their own examination.

Text Features

There are several features that appear throughout the text.

- **Sports Communication Prompts**
  - At the beginning of each chapter are statements that require a reaction. A statement might read: *There is nothing wrong with trash talking*. Readers will be asked to (a) Agree or Disagree with the statement, (b) provide a rationale, (c) cite examples that support the position taken on the prompt.
- **Fair or Foul: Questions of Ethics**
  - Within each chapter, one of these ethical challenges will appear. For example, "A recruiter informs a prospective student-athlete that she will be a starter as a freshman when no such guarantees can be given. Assume the high schooler is aware of such misrepresentations. And the recruiter assumes the prospective athlete is so aware. Is the attempt to persuade the student unethical?" Readers are asked to indicate whether the action is "fair" or "foul" and provide a rationale for their opinion.
- **Test Yourself—Apply the Principles**
  - This feature asks students to apply a principle that had recently been presented within the chapter. In this chapter, for example, A Test Yourself feature appeared after the discussion of Social Construction theory.
- **Practitioner Perspective**
  - Interviews with practitioners appear throughout the text, indicating these practitioners' viewpoints on issues relevant to the topics in the chapter.
- **First-Person Narratives—Sports Communication and Society**
  - This feature found at the end of each chapter presents narratives initially written as blog posts that are germane to sports communication.

Chapter Conclusion—Take-Aways

- Sports communication is a diverse field. As such, it requires a framework to understand its dimensions and facilitate the exploration of relevant areas.
- The study of sports communication includes:
  - Sports media
  - Communication in sports organizations
  - Communication on teams
  - Fandom and how communication cultivates fan interest
  - Effects of sports communication on politics, culture, economics, education, and society
  - Ethical issues relevant to sports communication
- Daily interactions use many sports terms and phrases reflecting the ubiquitous nature of sports in society and public discourse.

- Many words used in sports—e.g., winner, champion, elite, athlete can be viewed as social constructions.
- Sports communication issues are pervasive and are likely to be seen as even more pervasive when one is immersed in the study of the field.
- The book has several features that can be used to complement what appears in the text. These features include Sports Communication Prompts, Fair or Foul—Questions of Ethics, Test Yourself— Apply the Principles, Practitioner Perspectives, and First Person Narratives.

QUESTIONS

- Which of the areas of sports communication study are most relevant to your academic interests? Career goals?
- What terms other than sports terms are social constructions? Do any of the conventional constructions for sports terms vary from your own sense of the words?
- What does it mean to say that sports communication issues are pervasive?
- In the last week, identify an issue that surfaced in the world of sports that is applicable to the study of sports communication.

Practitioner Perspective

Kendall Coyne

Team USA-Women's National Team-Captain
Gold Medal Winner 2018
Silver Medal Winner 2014
Six-Time World Champion

Member of the Professional Women's Hockey Players Association (PWHPA)

photo courtesy of Jeff Cable USA Hockey

AZ. Generally, how does communication affect the success of Team USA at international competitions?

K.C. Not only is internal communication imperative to the success of Team USA at major competitions like the Olympic Games, but it is also equally important away from major competitions because we are a team comprised of the best players across the country. We spend more days away from each other than we do with each other. If we do not communicate internally when we are away from each other, we will not be as prepared as we can be going into a competition when we get together. Over the years, our internal communication networks have evolved with technology such as GroupMe, Zoom, and our video analysis software that stores games, shifts, and scouting breakdowns. We have even done virtual team building activities with our mental skills coach, since we spent an exceptional amount of time away from each other during the Covid-19 pandemic. Given the landscape of the Women's National Team, we must be able to adapt and evolve to the new technology that becomes available because it allows us to internally communicate even if it can't be in person. In short, effective communication is imperative. Internal communication is essential for success at elite levels and all levels. The best teams I have been on are the ones that really take the time to get to know each other. Get to know what excites someone, what their passions are outside the rink, and that is done through communicating.

AZ. You were the captain of your college hockey team for two years. And you are now the captain of Team USA. Are there additional responsibilities a captain has in terms of communication?

K.C. Absolutely, and even if you do not have the title of captain, you can be a leader on a team and assume additional responsibilities. As a captain and leader, you have to be someone who will communicate effectively with teammates and always be an ear for them. There may be times when a player is uncomfortable expressing herself to the head coach. You have to be able to listen and respect the player's trust and confidence when such trust is requested. You are also responsible for relaying information from the coaching staff to the players. Something basic like inform the players that they have to be in the video room at a certain time or what the dress code is for the travel day. In addition, as a captain, you must be willing to effectively communicate and address the hard issues teams go through during a season. If you do not address the tough issues in a timely manner, they will linger and often times infect the team culture because the problem lingered for too long.

All these responsibilities are the same whether I am with my college team or Team USA. However, since the Women's National Team rosters are changing at every competition, I must make sure I am communicating effectively right away with the players and staff. We are all coming in from different locations, teams, and coaches daily, so from the time we arrive at a training camp or competition, our communication has to be clear, effective, and efficient with each other if we want our play to be sharp. We cannot afford to have any clogged networks given this landscape. As a captain, I am having many conversations with our staff to ensure all questions and comments are shared from a player's perspective. In addition, during a competition, there are so many things that are unpredictable, and that is why as a leader, you need to thoroughly communicate as many details as you can with your staff and team before a competition starts so that you are prepared to adjust and adapt to whatever is thrown your way.

AZ. Hockey is a very fast sport. In what ways is communication important for hockey players during a game? Given the speed of the competition, is it even possible to communicate effectively while on the ice?

K.C. Yes, it is possible to communicate effectively while on the ice, even though the pace of the game is very fast. You will notice a lot of verbal communication happens during a T.V. timeout and right before faceoffs. This is a critical time to communicate any in-game adjustments you need to make based on how the game is going. When the game is live, quick commands for communicating are used to help improve the awareness of your teammates. Calling for a puck, letting your teammate know they have time, sending direction based on what you see without the puck.

Communication from the bench is also imperative and not just during timeouts or after a shift. As a winger, when I am in the defensive zone on the same side as our bench, I rely on the communication from the bench to let me know what they see so when I get the puck, I can make the best decision possible with it. For example: Are the defensemen pinching? Do I have time? Is the middle open? Should I chip the puck out? Should I go off the glass? You will hear players yell things like: "Glass, Boards, Middle, Time, etc." My awareness is a skill I am constantly working on so I can make the best decision with the puck, but when you have awareness plus communication, it is like having an extra player on the ice. We always say, "Communication is free." Use it.

Lastly, a lot of the communication is nonverbal and instinctual. For example, if you introduce yourself to someone and they stick their hand out, you instinctually stick yours out too and shake their hand. In the game of hockey, it is the same thing. So many habits become instinctual. That is how you nonverbally start communicating. When my teammate puts her stick in a position, I know she is ready to receive the puck, and that is exactly where she wants the puck.

AZ. You created quite a positive stir with your performance in the 2019 NHL All Star Skills Competition. How has that affected media demand for your comments on various topics related to the game? Has it become more difficult for you to communicate with all those who seek you out after that achievement?

K.C. After becoming the first woman to compete in the NHL All-Star Skills Competition, my following increased immensely. There were a lot of people who said they never saw a women's hockey game before, and many who did never believed a woman could skate alongside the NHL All-Stars and even beat one of them. With the increased following and high demand for media after this moment, I knew I had to use my platform to increase the visibility of the sport and awareness around the landscape of the women's game. That moment was beyond special. It would not have happened without all of the players who came before me and those alongside me who have consistently put an incredible product on the ice for the powers that be to believe I could compete alongside the NHL All-Stars. The opportunity surfaced, as you know, when one of the NHL All-Stars could no longer compete. However, the euphoria of that moment does not disguise the reality I returned home to vs. the reality the male All-Stars returned home to after that weekend. The fight for equality in the sport is every day, and it starts with visibility. Having a platform to increase awareness and show people how they can support the game is another avenue that we can utilize to ensure the future generations of young girls and young boys can have the same dream in the sport of hockey.

AZ. How does the media in events like the Olympics and World Championships affect your team's performance?

K.C. The media at an event like the Olympics is like the media on steroids. The media's goal and the team's goal are not the same. They want a story. We want to win a gold medal. A foolish comment by a player can steer the narrative and cause us to lose focus. We are aware of the potential problems and receive coaching about how to interact with the media to ensure that we can retain our focus.

In addition, you have to keep in mind that the media is a major stakeholder in the overall success of women's hockey. As Billie Kean King has said, "You need to see it to be it." It is extremely difficult for people to support, promote and invest in women's hockey if they can't see it. Early on in my career, World Championships wouldn't be on television. Could you imagine the World Cup not being on T.V.? It is unimaginable. When the World Championships are properly covered, people watch. Ratings are high. People become fans. Players become stars. Brands become investors. Dreams become realities. Women's hockey is NOT visible enough. We aren't just an event. We are an everyday product that deserves the platform more than every four years. We will get there.

When Team USA gets to a World Championship, and the World Championship is properly covered, there can be media asks that seem uncommon to some because we aren't on T.V. on a regular basis... yet. We have to adjust as a team to ensure no one is distracted by these asks because we know how important the media coverage is. Some of those examples are the following: a camera crew coming in before warmups, a camera crew shooting you coming off the bus, players being asked to do interviews with the play-by-play person and analyst after practice or the morning of games, being asked to do interviews via phone, zoom, and in-person during the tournament. When the media does their part, we must do ours. It is a two-way street.

AZ. Your Olympic team won an important labor battle with USA Hockey. How did the actions your group took affect group cohesion in the short term? Has it had lasting effects for women's sports beyond ice hockey?

K.C. The exceptional amount of internal communicating we did during the negotiations only made us stronger and more cohesive as a group which I believe played a role in our gold medal victory at the 2017 Women's World Championships. At one point, the leadership group was in a negotiating room with USA Hockey in Philadelphia with our legal team, Ballard Spahr, for twelve hours. Those who weren't in the room listened in on their phones the entire day. Some went on the ice with headphones in and their phone tucked away in their hockey pants. The strength of our communication with each other and the public, no matter what channel, is what made us successful.

Our 2017 boycott has had effects on sport beyond ice hockey. Just like we looked to the pioneers and leaders of women's basketball, soccer, and tennis for advice as they had similar fights, we became a sport that showed we were done getting treated as an afterthought and were demanding equitable support moving forward. We still have a long way to go in women's sports, but our fight set a new standard and expectation across women's hockey, and it instilled motivation in other women across the sports industry to stand up, speak up and show up ready to fight.

AZ. You've played for several coaches. How can a coach's communication affect team success? What are some best practices you've observed?

K.C. The best coaches are open, honest, constructively critical, and complimentary when compliments are deserved. In addition, I believe the best coaches know how to get the most out of each individual player. All players need to be coached differently. A great coach realizes what they need to do and say to get the most out of their players, and that usually begins with communication. I react positively when coaches see me as a person first and a hockey player second. I want someone to care about how I am doing, and I think it is important for the coaches to know how I was doing off the ice in order to be as effective as possible coaching us on the ice.

AZ. You now work for the Chicago Blackhawks. What do you do for them? How important is internal communication on the Blackhawks to your success communicating to external audiences?

K.C. I am a player development coach and youth hockey growth specialist with the Chicago Blackhawks. As a player development coach, the internal communication our department has with our prospects helps us devise a plan that will further improve the player's development which in turn gets them closer to reaching their goal of becoming a Chicago Blackhawk. As a youth hockey growth specialist, our consistent internal collaboration on the needs, areas for growth, and overall improvement in the youth hockey community are imperative in steering what we build and how we externally communicate that with the community.

AZ. Anything else you want to add?

K.C. We covered quite a bit. Let me highlight something I alluded to earlier when speaking about internal communication. It's important on a team that the various groups: Players, coaches, doctors, trainers interact and communicate efficiently. You don't want a player out there with a damaged shoulder doing hit drills because the doctor did not have access to a coach. The coach could think that the player is a slacker when in fact, she is damaging herself by participating in the drill. Lastly, when there is evidence of clear communication in the organization, it eases the players' minds because they're confident an injury or situation will be communicated to the right people in the right time.

First Person | Stimulation vs. Catharsis Theory

In media studies, or what used to be called Mass Communication studies, two dichotomous theories are often used to explain the effects of consuming mediated communication. One theory is called Stimulation Theory; the other is Catharsis Theory.

Used often to examine the effects of watching violence on television and film, Catharsis Theory argues that watching violence does not beget violence. Instead, watching violent acts causes the viewer to purge any latent violent tendencies. So, you watch a film like *Goodfellas*, where people get pummeled and killed, and you do not feel like fighting because the viewing has taken that violent energy and defused it. Stimulation theorists argue the opposite. By watching violent activity, one is likely to go out and be violent as it stimulates viewers to go do what they've seen done. Some readers may be familiar with the famous Bobo doll studies, which supported the fundamental argument of Stimulation Theory.

Which one is it? Are we more inclined to not do what we watch, or does that energize our desire? One could argue that what happens when people watch sports illustrates the merits of both Catharsis and Stimulation Theory. On the one hand, watching sports allows spectators an opportunity, for example, to purge their aggressive tendencies. If you watch a football game or a physical hockey or basketball game, you don't feel stimulated subsequently to tackle your neighbor or cross-check your sibling into a wall. On the other hand, some people, after watching a game, may want to go to the park and kick the ball around like the athletes they observed.

On the T.V. show *The Honeymooners*, a child once asked the rotund Ralph if he might substitute on a stickball team because a teammate had the measles. "What do you say, Mr. Kramden? Can you cover second base?" Before Ralph could spew character-istic boasts about his prowess, his sidekick Ed Norton told the kid, "You are looking at a man who can cover the infield, the outfield, and four sections of the bleachers." There is no shortage of such hefty fans who follow sports teams. It doesn't seem like they have been stimulated to run wind sprints after watching basketball or hockey games.

Chapter 2

Sports Communication: Focusing the Lens

© Chaiyon5021/Shutterstock.com

Chapter in a Nutshell

The goal of this chapter is to provide definition for the study of sports communication. Toward this end, we discuss transmission and constitutive perspectives, factors that affect the communication process, and a model for conceptualizing and studying sports communication.

Specifically, at the end of the chapter, students will be able to:

- Define the term communication in the context of sports communication.
- Describe transmission and constitutive perspectives.
- Identify variables that affect communication quality.
- Describe a model for sports communication study.

Sports Communication Prompts

- Below you will see statements pertaining to some aspect of communication and sports. For each item
  - Decide whether you agree or disagree with the statement.
  - Explain your rationale for the position.
  - Support with examples.
1. What makes coaches winners are their communication skills, not x and o knowledge. You can't be a successful coach without communication skills. You *can* be a successful coach even if you are not an expert in the game—if you can communicate well.
2. Fighting is not good for hockey. It dilutes the inherent value of the game.
3. Spanish or Japanese speaking athletes, or any athletes for whom English is not a primary language, should not have to speak in English when they talk to teammates in the clubhouse.
4. College athletes should not communicate on social media. It can damage the university and the player's brand.

The way I've been brought up is to take critiques and turn them into positives in my game.

Alex Morgan

Coaches who can outline plays on a blackboard are a dime a dozen. The ones who win get inside their players and motivate.

Vince Lombardi

Introduction

In July 2021, when Trajan Langdon, the general manager of the New Orleans Pelicans, introduced Willie Green as the team's new head coach, he spent a number of moments talking about Green's communication capabilities.

What was Langdon referring to? Green's speaking skills? The new head coach's ability to know when to speak and when to be silent? Green's ability to read nonverbal cues? What does it mean when general managers talk about a coach's communication capabilities?

Matt Patricia has had two stints coaching for the New England Patriots. In between these two appointments, he was the head coach of the Detroit Lions. Patricia has been described by his players as "fiery and enthusiastic" and as having a tradition of "connecting with all his players during pre-game stretching, greeting each with a handshake, helmet tap, or bear hug." One of his former players said these gestures are important: "It just lets us know he has our back. He has our back; we've got his back. It's nothing more than just a relationship that he's built with everybody. And when you got that from your coach, knowing that he's going to go down for you, and you're going to go down for him, it makes you want to go there and lay it down for him."

Does it really matter that Patricia taps players on the helmet during stretching exercises? Is what Patricia did during pre-game warm-ups a form of communication?

Matt Patricia connects with a player during warmups.

© Zuma Press, Inc. / Alamy Stock Photo

Defining Communication in Sports Contexts

We can assume that athletes, coaches, broadcasters, sportswriters, bloggers, conference commissioners, athletic directors, fans—all those who are involved with sports—acknowledge, generally, that communication is important and that all benefit when communication is efficient. Nevertheless, despite this general consensus, there is a lack of clarity about what exactly communication means in sports contexts.

The goal of this chapter is to create some focus that will be foundational to the rest of the text and future study. Specifically, this chapter will (1) clarify what is meant by the term communication in sports communication contexts and (2) provide a model for examining issues in sports communication.

COMMUNICATION DURING SPORTING EVENTS

Communication activity is omnipresent in all sports. The third-base coach in baseball signals whether a batter should take a pitch, bunt, or is free to swing away. Catchers signal to indicate what pitch the hurler should throw. When the pitcher does not get or does not like the message, catchers are summoned for a conference that other players may join. A disputed umpire's decision in a game may incite jaw-to-jaw arguments with the official or a teleconference with an arbiter in a distant location who reviews a recording. Managers lumber to the mound to replace a pitcher and signal with their arms if they want the lefty or the righty. The replaced pitcher sometimes registers discontent with the substitution by staring into space or slapping the ball into a manager's hand with greater intensity than is necessary to make the transfer.

Hockey coaches behind the bench rhythmically call out line changes to ensure that players are rested, match-ups are right, and that there are not too many players on the ice. Players who believe they are open for a pass leading to a scoring chance bang their sticks to signal that they want the puck. After a physical scrum, combatants discuss their differences in ways that may be intended to intimidate an opponent or indicate that certain behavior will have consequences.

Coxswains urge rowers to proceed rhythmically to maximize speed. The coxswain does not pull an oar in the entire contest, but her communications are central to the success of the enterprise.

In basketball, a point guard will look to the bench to see if a coach wants to run play one or two, and then after an offensive possession, defenders glance toward the coach to see if the team is to play a zone, man, or press.

Volleyball coaches, before each serve, often using a clipboard as a shield, relay information about where to place the ball and offensive strategy.

On corner kicks, soccer goalies tell teammates how to defend. The goalie will shout out the number of the player each teammate should mark. If an extra attacker comes forward, the goalie may instruct the player guarding the far post to leave that spot and mark that additional opponent.

Soccer goalie dives for a save.

It is obvious to all who have played or watched games that communication is nearly incessant during a contest, whether that communication involves barking at a teammate to switch on a pick, yelling that the pop-up is one that the shortstop will handle, or pointing at a defender indicating whom you intend to block. What may not be as obvious is that off the court and in preparation to compete, communication is similarly pervasive.

Trainers inform coaches about players who are too injured to participate. Sports Information Directors provide information to media representatives and fans who wish to follow their team. Those in charge of facilities report the status of field conditions to coaches and game officials. Compliance officers check with staff to ensure that all adhere to rules. Game day coordinators prepare, up to the minute, written instructions on such minutiae as at what minute the national anthem will be played and at what minute the Jumbotron should begin projecting the recording that extols the virtues of the home team. Prior to contests, coaches gather athletes and issue motivational talks.

New Jersey Devils Jumbotron

After a contest, media representatives interview players asking about performance and strategy. These interviews are more extensive than the snippets viewers at home witness between periods. "Backstage" a room is set up for a postgame conference. Athletes and the head coach are brought in and are asked what must seem like repetitive questions to which the athletes and coaches often give repetitive answers. Sportswriters scribble notes or thrust their recorders into the air so that they can subsequently compose the articles that fans will read later online, in conventional newspapers, and magazines.

ESPN sideline reporter Lisa Salters interviews Lamar Jackson during the 2020 Pro Bowl.

If communication in sports is omnipresent, it follows that communication quality can affect team or league success.

A Jim McBride article about New England Patriot linebacker Kyle Van Noy includes the following excerpt:

…When the defense struggled, players pointed to poor communication. Enter Van Noy. 'I'm just trying to do my job if my job is to communicate to others, so be it…

Being one of the communicators is a role he has grown very comfortable in. *"Yeah, yeah. … We just want to win it doesn't matter who's doing the communicating, cheering, or whatever, we're just trying to win"*   (McBride, 2018).

The article continued with a reference to another player, Devin McCourty, who author McBride characterizes as "also a great communicator." What could Van Noy be good at? Why might McBride refer to both McCourty and Van Noy as "great communicators"?

Transmission and Constitutive Perspectives

Most people think of communication as a transmission phenomenon. That is, the most common conception of communication is that it is the process of relaying a message from point A to point B. We assess whether communications are effective by determining if intended receivers receive messages as they were intended to be received. A third base coach signals to a batter that on the next pitch, the hit and run is on. The batter and base runner read the signal correctly. The runner takes off when the pitch is thrown and the batter swings at the offering. From a transmission perspective, the third base coach's communication was effective.

Similarly, we identify communication as unsuccessful if the intended receivers do not get the intended message. This happens frequently. A notorious example occurred in the NCAA Division I championship basketball game between the University of North Carolina and the University of Michigan. During a timeout near the end of the contest, a University of Michigan assistant coach informed the huddled players that there were no timeouts remaining. The goal was for the players to be aware of this so that they would not ask for a stoppage after play resumed. If they were to do so, the team would suffer a significant penalty. Therefore, the assistant coach told the players there were no timeouts. Nevertheless, a player subsequently did call a timeout, claiming not to have heard the message from the assistant coach. From a transmission perspective, the communication was ineffective. An intended receiver did not get the intended message. As it turned out, this breakdown actually determined the outcome. The University of Michigan was defeated.

The transmission perspective likens communication to the act of filling a bucket with water and transporting it from one place to another. Person A has a message to send to person B, fills her or his bucket with the message, and attempts to transport it so that B can receive it intact. This model recognizes that the bucket can be jostled en route to the destination. Analysts who examine communication from a transmission perspective identify the variables that can affect the receipt of an unadulterated bucket. These variables are commonly referred to as "noises"— impediments that affect the transmission. The transmission perspective recognizes that communication is complex, and the noises that jostle the bucket creating spillage could be relationships, biases, selective perceptions, and several other variables. More about communication noise is presented later in this chapter.

The constitutive perspective provides a different but complementary approach to the analysis of communication. This perspective assumes that while messages must be conveyed to receivers such that there is indeed fidelity between message received and message intended, what is as significant is how communicating shapes relationships. As theorist Robert Craig has written, communication can be seen as a "process that symbolically forms and re-forms our personal identities, our social relations…" (Craig. 2001, p. 125).

If we consider communication from a constitutive perspective, we see that if all we did was examine communication from a transmission perspective, we might be under the illusion that people in sports organizations were good communicators when these same "effective communicators" might be actually ineffective. Consider this example. Assume a coach berates a player in front of her teammates because "she was an idiot for not running the offense correctly." That message might have, in fact, gotten squarely to point B from point A. But if the communication seemed gratuitously caustic as perceived by teammates; if the message seemed to single out a player who regularly appears to take the brunt of the coach's wrath; if the coach used language that players might be familiar with, but consider crude in that particular setting—this successful transmission could affect the shape of that team. It could affect the respect players have for the coach, who wants to play for the coach, who wants to move to this city and work for the organization.

Heather Dinich's story, "The Inside Story of a Toxic Culture," appeared on ESPN.com in mid-August 2018. Dinich reported on a college football coaching staff that communicated in a way that is similar to the hypothetical example above. According to the piece, messages sent to players were often extraordinarily profane and cruel.

Yet someone analyzing these messages purely from a transmission perspective would have to acknowledge that the messages were getting from A to B. It should be obvious, however, that this fact would not make the coaches effective communicators. An analysis of the communications from a constitutive perspective would reveal that the shape of the organization would likely become warped because of the way that the coaches communicated with players.

Prior to the start of the 2017 NBA season, an article entitled "Chemistry is the First Lesson" appeared in the *Boston Globe*. The article described a trip the Boston Celtics would be taking to Rhode Island, only an hour away from where they play their games. The author of the piece, Gary Washburn, wrote, "This trip to Rhode Island is strictly for bonding. The team will have all but one meal together. There is plenty of time for the players to share conversations and swap stories. They will need such a period of togetherness." One of the Celtic players was talking about the value of interacting with his teammates on this retreat. "This [the retreat] gives us a chance to bond together breakfast, lunch, dinner, talking to each other, you're on the bus with each other" (Washburn, 2017).

Consider a sports organization to be some sort of container. Inside the container, there are athletes, coaches, trainers, marketers, compliance officers, security personnel, and a host of others functioning in various capacities. The transmission perspective conceives of communication as events that take place within the container and beyond the container in order for the organization to function effectively. The PR representative asks a player after the game to do an interview for ESPN. Both the request to the player and the subsequent interview can be examined from a transmission perspective.

The constitutive perspective suggests that communication does take place within a container, but as significantly, because of the nature of communication, the size, shape, orientation, even goals of the organization are affected. In short, communication creates an evolving container. The process of communication forms and reforms the entity that is the sports organization.

We will discuss the constitutive perspective in more detail in Chapter 5 when we examine teams and culture. At this point, it is important to be aware that communication should not be viewed solely as a transmission phenomenon. If a team is composed of gregarious, talkative players who regularly kid each other about their abilities and even personal life, then their communications might be more valuably considered from a constitutive perspective than the transmission perspective. Yes, one could assess whether the right-wing understood what the center was saying about his mother, but what is more significant is how that communication is shaping the relationships between the teammates.

When Pelicans general manager, Trajan Langdon, described his new coach's communication capabilities, the G.M. likely meant that the new coach knew the value of transmitting information. In addition, he knew that good communication could form and strengthen the constitution of the enterprise.

Test Yourself: Apply the Principles

- Communication can be examined from a transmission as well as a constitutive perspective.
  - What does each of these terms mean?
- Analyze the quality of each of the following from both a transmission and a constitutive perspective.
  - NFL football players kneel during the playing of the national anthem.
  - Sue Bird and Megan Rapinoe appear essentially naked on the cover of ESPN, the magazine's annual Body Issue.
  - The NHL announces it will suspend play in December 2021 because of the widely spreading Omicron variant.
  - Team tee shirts, "We put the bad in badminton."
  - Lisa Byington is announced as the first-ever female play-by-play announcer in the NBA.

A Manageable Definition

A declaration uttered nearly seventy-five years ago at an MIT conference about communication is as true today as it was in 1950 despite the dramatic changes in communication technology. At this meeting, a speaker named S.S. Stevens remarked, "…no phenomenon is more familiar to us than communication [but] the fact of the matter is that this magical word means many things to many people" (Stevens, 1950, p. 689).

Even in the scholarly literature on communication issues, one can find hundreds of definitions of communication. While the existence of so many definitions reflects that many understand the importance of defining the concept, multiple definitions can actually obscure understanding. Also, in an attempt to be comprehensive, some definitions become cumbersome or esoteric. Consequently, these definitions can be difficult to comprehend or apply.

We will define communication concisely yet comprehensively as *a nonlinear process that occurs when people intentionally and unintentionally send and receive verbal and nonverbal messages.* We'll supplement that definition with the following two principles: Communication does not mean the same thing as understanding. The act of sending a message does not, in and of itself, mean that communication has taken place.

In the next section, we describe key parts of this definition.

COMMUNICATION IS A NONLINEAR PROCESS

Theorist Harold Lasswell developed one model used to examine communication. Lasswell argued that communication could be analyzed by looking at "Who Says What to Whom (In Which Channel) With What Effect" (Lasswell, 1948, p. 37).

Suppose you were a sports reporter writing an article about women's Olympic hockey. The Who would be you, the writer, or by, extension, the publisher of the newspaper, website, or magazine. The What would be the content of your article about the team. The Whom would be the audience you reach or intend to reach. The Effect would be how your audience was influenced by what you communicated.

A problem with this model is that it appears to be linear.

Lasswell may not have intended it to be interpreted this way, but the model as is implies that communication goes one way and ceases when it reaches the receiver. Communication, in fact, is not linear; it is not a one-way phenomenon, especially in the era of social media. Some scholars use the word "process" instead of "act" to describe communication because "act" seems as if communication reflects an isolated occurrence. Any one act of communication is unlikely to be a discrete incident. It is likely to be a function of immediate and past history and should be understood implicitly as a process—the process that occurs when we communicate.

Assume you are a player listening to a coach's pre-game talk. Assume you agree with her message. You nod your head when she speaks about the need to play good man-to-man defense. The coach sees the nodding and goes on to say that she knows the team may desire to double team the ball, but it is important to control the excitement and play tenacious man to man. Your affirmative nodding reaction has had an effect on the coach; she elaborated on her message.

The communication, in this instance, has not been linear. Any one "act" of communication was part of a process. You thought the message was on target, signaled nonverbally that it was, the coach noticed the reaction and then elaborated. Obviously, the persons who are initially the "Who" and the "Whom" can exchange roles and react to one another. Once you've nodded and the coach notices it, you are the Who, and the coach, the Whom.

Let's consider a second example. On March 11, 2018, the NCAA announced, in a novel way, which sixty-eight teams would be invited to participate in its men's Division I basketball tournament.[1] Immediately there was reaction—both to the new format and the teams selected. Fans posted online, callers phoned in on radio talk shows, talking heads talked, the head of the NCAA responded. A police department in Kansas tweeted, "Please do not call 911 to complain about the format for the NCAA tournament selection show. We can't do anything about it no matter how bad it is." Conversations about teams that should have been invited continued days after the selections were made. One conference, the PAC 12, actively challenged the exclusion of the University of Southern California. Bruce Rasmussen, the NCAA chair, responded, "Southern Cal had a nice year [but] When you look at their résumé, they only had two wins against teams in the tournament field."

The communication announcing the invited teams was not linear. It did not stop when it was initially received. And the reactions to the initial messages begat other communications.

COMMUNICATION CAN BE INTENTIONAL OR UNINTENTIONAL

A message does not have to be intentionally sent to be communicated. An athletic director at a major university informed me that some of his coaches habitually came late to meetings. They may not have intended to be communicating anything by their tardiness.

---

[1] Coincidentally, almost exactly two years later on March 12, 2020, the NCAA announced it was cancelling the tournament because of COVID.

However, other members of the group felt that the lateness reflected a lack of professionalism, preoccupation, or disrespect. The fact that the latecomers may not have intended to relay any of these messages does not discount the reality that these messages were communicated.

An athlete may tweet a reaction to a game and, inadvertently, send messages that differ from her intent. A coach speaks to the press and comments, "Samantha Smith is really working out on defense. She is smart and a hard worker." The coach may have communicated positive comments about Smith that were intended, but also unintentionally, that her other defensive players are not as industrious.

When LeBron James announced on July 8, 2010, his decision to play for the Miami Heat, he did not intend to infuriate the entire city of Cleveland. The decision was announced on a dedicated ESPN program that the producers called *The Decision.* On the surface, the message that was communicated was that James had accepted an offer to play in Florida. Other unintentional messages screamed at Cleveland fans and resulted in damage to James that was and may still be difficult for him to shed now many years later—even after James returned to Cleveland to play for the Cavaliers; even after James was central to Cleveland winning a sports championship, a prize that had eluded the city for over fifty years. And even after he left the Cavaliers a second time to play for the L.A. Lakers.

COMMUNICATION CAN BE VERBAL OR NONVERBAL

With the first game of the 2018 NBA finals tied at 107, Cavalier George Hill was on the foul line for his second shot. He had made the first tying the game. There were less than five seconds remaining. Hill's shot hit the front of the rim and bounced directly to his teammate, JR Smith. Smith, instead of going directly up with a shot to win the game, inexplicably dribbled the ball outside. His teammates, especially LeBron James, were incredulous. The look on James's face reflected the power and substantive nature of nonverbal communication.

The Baltimore Ravens scored with seconds left in its December 5, 2021, game against the Pittsburgh Steelers. The touchdown brought the Ravens within one point of their opponent. Ravens coach John Harbaugh put up two fingers, indicating he wanted to go for two points instead of one. The Ravens failed on the two-point attempt. A pass from quarterback Lamar Jackson was a bit too far for receiver Mark Andrews. Had viewers not seen the play but just watched the subsequent reactions of the teams, there would be no doubt that the conversion attempt was unsuccessful. The Steeler defenders jumped up and down in glee. On the Raven sideline, Jackson threw his helmet in disgust.

An example of the power and effects of nonverbal communication cost then Baltimore Bullets coach KC Jones his job. In the third game of the 1975 championship series during a time out, Jones's assistant coach was diagramming a play while Jones kneeled nearby. This not uncommon event—an assistant diagramming a play—was the focus of a television camera. It looked to the unschooled and casual eye that the assistant, Bernie Bickerstaff, was really the coach, and Jones was not leading the team. This tableau was not accurate, but that is what the image suggested. After the season, Jones was dismissed despite an excellent win/loss record for the Bullets. Eight years later, he was hired by the Celtics and proceeded to reach the NBA finals in his first four seasons, winning the championship twice.

A verbal message is one that uses words to convey meaning. The sentences in this book are primarily verbal messages.

The word verbal is sometimes confused with the words *oral* and *vocal*. Any message—whether spoken or read that uses words to relay meaning—contains verbal messages. The NHL Toronto Maple Leafs website https://www.nhl.com/mapleleafs contains verbal messages, as does a postgame press conference when journalists ask athletes questions. Websites and press conferences also are likely to include nonverbal messages. The font and color used for branding on a website and the gestures a coach makes during a postgame press conference are examples of nonverbal factors that can convey messages to receivers. If a website is well-formatted and esthetically engaging, we are likely to get a different impression than we would if the look of the site is primitive or the print so tiny as to make it difficult to read. If a coach uses complementary hand gestures while addressing a group, we are likely to perceive a different message than if the speaker were to stand stiffly in front of the group. Nonverbal messages are often acknowledged when body motion reflects some meaning—commonly called body language. Nonverbal messages are also conveyed by factors unrelated to body motion. Space, time, touch, font are nonverbal factors as well. When the coaches came in late to the meetings referred to by my athletic director colleague, the coaches were, unintentionally, communicating nonverbally.

© Zuma Press, Inc./Alamy Stock Photo

Former Alabama Head coach, Anthony Grant
somberly answers questions after losing to LSU.

Students of communication need to remember that nonverbal messages do not actually mean anything until a receiver decodes them. Even verbal messages do not mean anything until receivers decode them. However, with nonverbal messages, there is considerable room for misinterpretation, as Manusov and Billingsley suggest:

…when we view another's [nonverbal] behavior we may be inclined to judge that it is a direct reflection of some aspect of the other's character, mood, feeling, or belief. We may feel that we really have access to what is really going on in inside the other's mind or heart. But we are also likely to be wrong. (Manusov and Billingsley, 1997, p. 66).

A classic case of problematic nonverbal communication in sport occurred when running back Duane Thomas played for the Dallas Cowboys in 1971. Thomas had been in a contract dispute during the offseason and, after an aborted trade, reluctantly returned to the Cowboys to play in the fall. During the entire season, Thomas refused to speak to teammates, management, coaches, or the media. Thomas was an outstanding running back, but the effects of his nonverbal communication behavior from both a transmission and constitutive perspective were not insignificant. The Cowboys won the Super Bowl that year in no small part because of Thomas's skills, but nevertheless, this productive player was traded in the off-season.

SENDING A MESSAGE IS NOT SYNONYMOUS WITH COMMUNICATING

The act of *sending* messages, in and of itself, does not mean that communication has taken place. This is a foundational but often misunderstood aspect of communication, especially in contemporary times of technological availability. If a trainer sends a text about the injuries on the volleyball team, that does not mean that the trainer has communicated the message despite the fact that a cogent message may have been sent. The recipient may not "do" texts or access a smartphone. A posting on a website does not guarantee communication until the time when the appropriate audience visits the site and reads the message.

Hopper writes clearly, "Communication can be said to have taken place only when messages are received and interpreted" (Hopper, 1976, p. 8). Timm and DeTienne (1995, pp. 15-17) comment that communication occurs whenever someone attaches meaning to a message. Cranmer writes, "Indeed all communication is receiver oriented as meaning is established within the minds of others" (Cranmer, 2019, p. 31).

In short, *message received is message communicated*. And message received may not be consistent with message intended. Or as Red Auerbach, the late coach, general manager, NBA icon, and author, wrote, "When it came to communications, my rule of thumb was simple. It's not what you tell them, [it's] what they hear" (Auerbach, 1985, p. 59).

COMMUNICATION IS DIFFERENT FROM UNDERSTANDING

Some people think of communication as being synonymous with understanding. Occasionally, exasperated colleagues will stop a discussion and say, "We're just not communicating." This seems to imply, "We do not understand one another," or "We can not seem to explain to each other what we'd like to explain." Even when two people who are conversing have trouble understanding each other, they are still communicating. They may not be communicating effectively, but they are communicating.

As significantly, an inability to come to agreement does not necessarily mean that two people are not communicating effectively. A union representative may be trying to reach agreement with league personnel on a new contract. They may be unable to do so but can very clearly understand the other's position. It is not a communication problem. They just disagree.

Understanding the Process

Half the world is composed of people who have something to say and can't, and the other half who have nothing to say and keep on saying it.

Robert Frost

What makes a coach, teammate, athletic director, or general manager an effective communicator? From a transmission perspective, the process may seem to be simple. How difficult can it be to get a message from point A to point B, particularly when A and B are in the same room at the same time and, ostensibly, focused on the communication?

During a timeout in a nationally televised basketball game on January 15, 2018, the then coach of the University of Texas Longhorns, Karen Aston, gathered her team on the sideline. She sat in a chair facing her team with the players congregated in a semi-circle. Aston's Longhorns were playing the University of Connecticut, and the Longhorns were losing. The coach's message was straightforward. She said, "We've got to stop taking bad shots."

This seems clear. The coach is telling the players to be more selective when they decide to shoot. She used common words. She looked right in the eyes of her players. What could be a problem with the transmission of "We've got to stop taking bad shots?"

There could be several. It is possible that there are players on the Longhorns who think all their shots are good shots. It's possible that there has never been a clear discussion of what constitutes a good shot. Perhaps there are players who are convinced that the coach defines a bad shot as one that does not go in the basket, and therefore, the message is that we need to shoot a higher percentage. Perhaps the coach repeats this phrase so often that it has lost its meaning. It's possible that the noise in the arena makes it difficult to hear the coach or the noise in the player's heads—*I'm tired. I hope I can stay in the game. I hope I did well on my exam this afternoon*—is affecting the transmission. It's possible that one player is thinking that the problem is not that *we're* taking bad shots. *The problem is that nobody is passing me the ball, and therefore I, who would take good shots, have not had an opportunity.*

© Cal Sport Media/Alamy Stock Photo

Texas Longhorns Head Coach Karen Aston watches from the sidelines with her team.

None of these factors might have been an issue with Karen Aston's Longhorns. However, the example illustrates why even from a transmission perspective, an apparently unambiguous message may not be successfully communicated.

Throughout the text, we will be discussing ways sports communicators can be effective. In the next chapter, for example, we discuss what is called "permeability" and "requisite variety" as factors that affect how a league, athletic department, sports organization, and broadcasting entity can be more effective. In Chapter 4, we discuss stakeholder theory and image repair discourse when we analyze crisis communication in sports contexts. In Chapter 5, we describe the principle of nonsummativity and how teams, coaches, and players communicate to maximize success. In each chapter throughout the text, we examine challenges and methods for addressing these challenges.

In this early section, however, we present the following general principles that are applicable regardless of whether you are preparing a *30 for 30* documentary, sending a tweet criticizing a goalie, explaining the protocol for COVID testing, writing a book about rugby fans, notifying all teams in your conference about weekend game officials, telling your shortstop that she has to shade to her right, or, as captain, relaying the sentiments of your teammates to the coach. We will discuss the elements of the communication process, common impediments, and general counsel about best practices.

Fair or Foul   Questions of Ethics

- A runner on second base attempts to steal the signal of the catcher. The goal is to identify the upcoming pitch and notify the batter.
  - Proponents of such stealing argue that it is just part of the game. Catchers and pitchers change their signs when a batter is on second, and this is part of the contest—concealing/stealing signs. These proponents contend that as long as a team is not using electronic technology or binoculars to steal and relay signs, any attempt to relay information to the batter is fair.
  - Opponents suggest that stealing signs—whether the sign-stealing is aided by new technology or not—is unethical and gives the batter an unfair advantage in a way that the rules of the game do not allow.
- Is stealing signals fair or foul?

ELEMENTS

The Source

The source refers to that person or persons who, intentionally or unintentionally, send the message. When a message is intentionally sent, the source conceives, encodes, and then transmits the message. During pre-game pep talks, the primary sources are the coaches delivering the motivational message. As indicated in the previous section, communication is a nonlinear process, and therefore, a player who responds—even nonverbally—to the coach becomes the source when that response is observed by the coach. However, the primary sources are those people who have conceived, constructed, and delivered the messages.

The Receiver

The receivers are those persons who decode and perceive meaning. Coach Aston's players, when she spoke to them about "taking good shots," are the receivers in this model. Those who watched the *30 for 30* documentaries are receivers. Quarterbacks who hear the play called in their helmets are the receivers of those communications.

The Message

The message is what the source intentionally or unintentionally, verbally or nonverbally, sends to the receiver. The producers and scriptwriters of the movie *Invictus* created a message about how teams can bring and have brought peoples together even when these peoples have been antagonists in the past. The message in that film is that the success of the Springboks was a unifying factor in South Africa and was a balm that was helpful in addressing the residual effects of apartheid.

Channel

The message the receiver perceives has been sent through some channel. We can decode information using any one of our senses, or by using combinations of our senses. We can derive meaning by sound, sight, smell, touch, and taste. We hear what the commissioner says about game day attire. We see facial expressions that accompany the coaches' pleas for industrious performance. We can smell the sweet field at a major league ballpark and become immediately transported to our first game. If the new ball does not feel right to pitchers, they may ask the umpire for a new one. If a defensive back touches a ball and senses that it is not properly inflated, a two-year science fictionesque saga may ensue.

Feedback

Feedback refers to the responses received from our messages. An umpire calls a pitch a ball, and the hurler glares down at the official to register displeasure. Tweets that endorse a general manager's draft pick are forms of feedback.

© REUTERS/Alamy Stock Photo

New York Yankees' pitcher Orlando Hernandez appeals to the homeplate umpire following a play at first base.

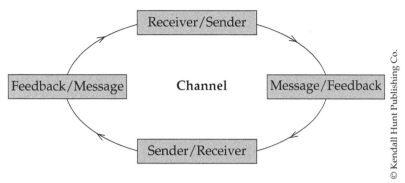

FIGURE 2-1   Communication is a nonlinear phenomenon. The sender becomes a receiver when the audience responds with verbal or nonverbal feedback or nonverbal feedback.

Feedback often does, and should, influence the source of the message. *Feedback-induced response* refers to this phenomenon and illustrates why communication is best conceived of as nonlinear. Feedback-induced response means that feedback from the receiver induces a response from the source. If a captain admonishes you for not hustling and you wave dismissively in response, the captain may grab you by the uniform and, in common parlance, "get in your face" to enforce the initial message.

Efficient communicators are proficient at reading feedback and responding appropriately. Were you to ignore players thumbing through their cell phones while you explain the game plan, you would be encouraging them to miss the messages that you had hoped they would receive.

Since communication is a nonlinear phenomenon, the source-receiver components, as well as the message-feedback components, are essentially interchangeable. A person who is the source of the message also is, almost concurrently, a receiver as well. The feedback from the receiver can be seen as the receiver's message to the source.

The Concept of Noise

Communication noise refers to the impediments that affect the ability to communicate effectively. Noise can literally be external noise such as distracting side conversations or rail traffic outside an opened window. Noise can also refer to psychological interference, such as being preoccupied with another matter while making or attending a presentation.

Message fidelity and message distortion are two phrases used to help conceptualize effective communication from the transmission perspective. When a receiver understands a message the way the source desired the message to be received, we say that there is message fidelity.

Message fidelity can exist despite the presence of noise. Noise is omnipresent. Some writers define noise as that which creates distortion (DeVito, 2001, p. 9). A better way to consider noise is to think of it as a factor that reduces the chances for successful communication but does not guarantee failure. If a stadium makes it difficult to hear the quarterback's call, you might have to increase your volume, or receivers might have to work harder to hear the play, but it is still possible to understand what is being said. Another common example relates to the noise that accompanies distinctive speaking accents. The rosters of sports teams have become increasingly diverse. Accents can be noises. Sometimes, receivers give up when they listen to someone who speaks with what, to them, is a foreign accent. However, if receivers are willing, they may be able to get through the noise that accompanies a speaking pattern that is unfamiliar.

In short, noise should be viewed as an impediment, but like most impediments, noise can be overcome. Speakers and receivers have the responsibility to identify and overcome noise in order to increase the chances for message fidelity.

What are some common impediments?

INADEQUATE COMMUNICATION SKILL SETS

To be effective communicators, people have to have some basic skills. Broadly these skills are the abilities to listen, speak, read, write, and employ new communication technology. In addition, and significantly, people have to exercise the skills they have.

Duane Thomas was a bright man who could speak well. He just decided not to speak. Thomas's behavior on the Cowboys was an extreme example, but many people simply are not industrious and do not use the skills they have. Someone who can read may not thoroughly read the game plan. Someone who is capable of listening effectively may pretend to pay attention as opposed to actually paying attention. Consequently, a communication noise related to skills is partially ability and partially desire to use skills. Revered coaches may be able to get away temporarily with an ignorance of social media. Almost nobody else in the world of sports communication can be so ignorant. If you can't or do not tweet, it may be difficult to get a sense of your fandom and players.

BIASES, CULTURAL IGNORANCE, AND INTERPERSONAL TENSION

Preexisting attitudes toward groups of others can create communication noise. It may be difficult for communicators to "get through" these attitudes in order to accurately transmit or pay attention to messages. The attitudes toward gay athletes described in the documentary *Training Rules* created deafening noise for members of the Penn State women's basketball teams in the late twentieth century up through the 2007 season. Racial tension affecting interpersonal interaction was obvious in major league baseball at the time when Jackie Robinson broke the color line and did not, of course, end because of Robinson's successes. Dave Meggysey's *Out of Their League* is one of many books that discuss racial tension in professional sports (Meggysey, 2005, p. 193). There may not be a more comprehensive work on the topic of how race affects sport than the aforementioned John Feinstein's book *Raise a Fist Take a Knee* subtitled, *"Race and the Illusion of Progress in Modern Sports."* In Chapter 6, we discuss issues of race in sport more extensively.

Ethnocentrism refers to seeing the world through the lens of particular ethnic values. It also implies that ethnocentric individuals feel as if their values are superior. This is anathema to communication either from a transmission or constitutive perspective. Not knowing about another culture, not caring about another culture, or hauling about prejudices—negative prejudgments—will preclude effective transmission of information and corrode the constitution of the relationship between individuals, on teams, and throughout leagues.

Preexisting attitudes toward individuals can create loud noise as well. In Terry Pluto's book chronicling the American Basketball Association, *Loose Balls: The Short, Wild Life of the*

American Basketball Association, two players are singled out as particularly difficult. John Brisker and Warren Jabali created enmity even among teammates. Predating the New Orleans Saints "bountygate" scandal by decades, a coach for the Dallas Chaparrals offered $500.00 to any player who would "deck" Brisker. One player quickly volunteered and punched the opponent during the opening tip (Pluto, 2007, p. 215–220).

Interpersonal noise can be the result of initial interactions. When Bob Costas was hired as a very young man to be the play-by-play announcer for the ABA's Spirit of St. Louis, he was told that he should meet the legendary Jack Buck, who was then the St. Louis Cardinals announcer. Buck was getting a haircut when Costas met up with him. Buck looked at Costas through the mirror while in the barber's chair, and Costas spoke to the back of Buck's head. According to Costas, Buck asked the fledgling announcer how old he was. Costas said he was 22. Buck's response ended this initial exchange, "I have ties older than you, kid" (Pluto, 2007, p. 353).

In sports contexts particularly, noise can also be the result of media representations and the subsequent narrative based on media reports. When Reggie Jackson became a member of the Yankees, he gave an interview in which he talked about himself as "the straw that stirs the drink" (Ward, 2012, p. 220). He referred to himself as the guy who "can put meat in the seats," and that long time Yankee Thurman Munson was someone who "thinks he can be the straw that stirs the drink, but he can only stir it bad" (Ward, 2012, p. 222). Jackson has denied the quotes, but Robert Ward, the author of the *Sport* article based on the interview, insists it is accurate. Regardless, tension surfaced between the two Yankees resulting in what can be labeled communication noise, and that noise affected interactions on the team beyond just Munson and Jackson.

According to a magazine article, when Reggie Jackson joined the Yankees he spoke critically of long time catcher Thurman Munson.

SELECTIVITY AND COGNITIVE DISSONANCE

Researchers have written about four selective stages in the communication process: selective exposure, selective attention, selective perception, and selective retention.

Let's assume that after a game, a player suggests that you all meet at a restaurant. All teammates are invited. If you decided to join the others, you would be *selectively exposing* yourself to whatever messages you might receive at this function. Once there and chatting with teammates, you could listen to what they were saying or become distracted by some other person in the room. You would be *selectively attending* to messages. Once you decided to listen to a teammate, you would *selectively perceive* meaning from what that person was saying. If the person began to list all of his records, you could perceive that he was an outstanding player or an egotistical bore or had an inadequate self-concept—depending on the meanings you perceived from the messages. Following the social function, you would remember some things and forget others. This would be referred to as *selective retention.*

A common noise in the process occurs when people selectively perceive and retain what they want to hear. A coach tells a player that she has a good chance to be a starting pitcher if she works hard during the offseason. If the player selectively hears that as long as she exercises during the summer, she will start, then there is a faulty transmission that could subsequently affect the relationship between player and coach.

Cognitive dissonance occurs when a person holds two conflicting thoughts. These thoughts cannot coexist, and consequently, according to cognitive dissonance theory, a person who experiences this dissonance proceeds to reduce it. A simple example outside of the world of sport occurs when someone, after dinner, is asked if they want a piece of cheesecake. Let's assume conflicting thoughts surface. (1) "If I eat the cheesecake, I will gain weight" and (2) "I would like to eat the cheesecake." According to the theory, these thoughts cannot coexist. The person who has been offered the cheesecake says to himself, "Well, I will take a small piece." Or "It is fine. I almost never have cheesecake." The dissonance is reduced.

In sports communication, this dissonance is applicable as well. A very good case is presented in George Dohrmann's book *Superfans.* A very dedicated fan of the Seattle Seahawks who had been a victim of spousal abuse heard that her team had drafted a college player with a record of domestic abuse. This player was exceptionally skilled. However, there were clear reports that he had physically assaulted his girlfriend. The fan wrestled with the difficulty and reduced the dissonance. She, the fan, commented on social media that every person deserves a second chance. She also opined that some elements of the report suggested that the offense was less than what had been reported (Dohrmann, 2018, pp. 163-164).

CREDIBILITY AND ETHOS

In a baseball clubhouse—perhaps in any competitive group—the impact of information depends as much on a teammate's feeling about the messenger as on the content of the information. Ryan, 2020, p. 61.

Who you are in terms of your reputation may be more important than what you say. Ethos is a term used in communication to refer to how receivers perceive speakers. Your ethos is not something you have; rather, it is something attributed to you. Ethos is a function in large part of credibility. Other factors affecting ethos are power and attractiveness. Ethos is a variable that affects communication from both a transmission and constitutive perspective. A coach who is well respected may have a good deal of success as a recruiter simply because of who she is. A sports radio talk caller who dubbed himself "Butch from the Cape" somehow had listeners riveted to his rants in a way other callers did not. His ethos was high.

SERIAL TRANSMISSION

A common noise in sports communication—particularly when we look at sports from an organizational perspective—is serial distortion. Messages are not always sent directly from sources to receivers. Often there are intermediaries. Even when intermediaries get the messages correctly, they may relay the messages in a way that distorts them. An intermediary can abridge or sensationalize a message and alter its meaning. Some serial distortions are not due to malice but rather lack of industry or an individual's communication style. Someone who is taciturn by nature may shorten a message leaving out key information because they do not feel comfortable either writing or speaking. Another example of serial distortion could occur when a head coach tells an assistant to relay a harsh message, but the assistant dilutes the critical information when speaking to the player.

Recurring Counsel

Below is some general counsel for communicators. In future chapters, additional recommendations are made that are applicable to specific contexts.

KNOW WHEN TO COMMUNICATE

In the course of a game, there are times when it is imperative that coaches and teammates interact and communicate well. On a corner kick, a goalie shouts out match-ups, so the correct defender is marking an appropriate scoring threat. An assistant on a basketball team has to tell the head coach that her center has picked up a fourth foul. The very successful coach of the Duke Blue Devils, Mike Krzyzewski, was asked during one season why he was playing more zone defense than he had in the past. He said that he was playing zone because this year's team did not communicate well. Specifically, they did not know when to communicate when playing a man-to-man. More than in a zone, a man-to-man defense requires players to call out picks, identify switches, recognize offensive plays, and bark out defensive adjustments. In a zone, Krzyzewski said, players defending an area did not have to interact as much.

Outside of the game context, one still must know when it is essential to communicate. A university athletic department representative must communicate with season ticket holders if there is a change to their special parking privileges because of construction to the lot. An academic adviser needs to inform a coach if players have become ineligible. Players need to know where to be when to take the bus that will take them to the airport. There are more subtle examples. A coach must decide when or if to admonish an athlete, establish a policy that she or he knows may have to be broken for certain individuals, or predict a certain degree of success for the season. A league must know when or if to distribute information about referees' performances.

Coach Mike Krzyzewski signals to one of his players.

Knowing and deciding when to communicate is an initial factor that will affect success. People cannot be effective communicators if they are unaware that they need to communicate.

KNOW YOUR AUDIENCE

A key to successful communication is what is commonly called Audience Analysis. ESPN has a target audience for SportsCenter, just as coaches have target audiences for their motivational talks. Commissioners have target audiences for their announcements. Effective communicators study the audience in the same way effective coaches study their opponents. Receivers are not combatants, of course, but learning about them is essential. How do receivers typically access information? Where are they located? What are their needs? What demographic information is relevant? If you want to increase attendance at your home basketball games, you need to learn all you can about potential fans.

Apparently homogeneous audiences can still be diverse. Eighteen- to twenty-two-year-old volleyball players are different from sixty- to eighty-five-year-old potential donors. But even the fifteen volleyball players differ such that communicating to one player from rural Oklahoma may require a different approach than a player who hails from Chicago.

DEVELOP AND CRAFT A MESSAGE

Sometimes messages aren't clearly received because the sources were not clear themselves about what they wanted to say before they initiated the interaction. Even when sources are clear about the message, they need to take, make, or have the time to ensure that what they want to communicate will indeed be part of the message they eventually relay. I may know that I want to encourage athletes to be prompt for team meetings. What I need to say, write, e-mail, or post to effectively relay that message might take some time to consider.

SELECT A METHOD

What is the most appropriate method for communicating a message? A documentary film-maker has decided to relay messages using the documentary, and columnists working for the *Sun-Sentinel*, relay their messages either online or in a traditional print newspaper. But other communicators often have choices.

Does a commissioner meet with league presidents via Zoom to explain changes in vaccination protocol, or would a document attached to an e-mail suffice? Do sports information directors publish a booklet describing the upcoming field hockey season, or can they simply put all information out on the website? Does a fan tweet a reaction to a columnist's opinion or post a Facebook comment?

The capability of a new technology or any method for communicating a message does not make it as good as any other method. A coach could e-mail a player informing her or him that they will be replaced in a starting line-up, but a face-to-face interaction may be better, at least from the constitutive perspective. Seth Wickersham reports that Bill Belichick attempted to defuse a problematic situation that existed between Patriot team trainers and quarterback Tom Brady's personal trainer, Alex Guerrero. The coach revoked Guerrero's access to the Patriot sideline by sending Brady's trainer an e-mail. This method, as well as the content of the message, actually contributed to intensifying the tension. "An e-mail designed to end a problem only created more of them" (Wickersham, 2021, p. 360).

An athletic department's zero-tolerance policy for physical contact for coaches in their interactions with players might be relayed in a day-long retreat or be posted on a bulletin board in a common area—or communicated both in a day-long retreat and be posted on a bulletin board. Later in the text, we will discuss several concepts, including permeability and media richness, that are applicable to the selection of the best method for communicating.

DEVELOP A FEEDBACK CHANNEL

Chances for effective communication are enhanced if there is a feedback channel or channels so that individual audience members can have a way to respond to the messages distributed. There are a number of reasons for creating these networks, but one is simply to ensure that people receive the messages that communicators distribute. These networks have several other functions. Receivers can ask questions, identify concerns the source may not have considered, and reflect reactions to the message. Having a feedback loop does not mean that the source will acquiesce to challenges, only that they are receptive to listening to what others need to say. A professional football coach, having recently moved from the college ranks to a professional job, implemented a system where the defense traveled on one bus and the offense on another. To veteran professional players, this seemed childish, and there was resentment that affected player behaviors. Listening to and creating a channel for reactions to the policy could have affected the dissension and resentment that surfaced subsequently.

IMPROVE COMMUNICATION SKILL SETS

As we have discussed, it is not a given that all can write, listen, speak, read, and use communication technology. Individuals can train to become more efficient in terms of their skill sets. There are ways to improve your backhand in tennis. And there are ways you can train to become a more efficient speaker, user of communication technology, or listener.

ACCURATE IDENTIFICATION OF STAKEHOLDERS

A basic premise of crisis communication (discussed in detail in Chapter 4) is Stakeholder Theory. This theory holds that when communicating during a crisis, organizations need to acknowledge that there are multiple stakeholders, and the individual audience groups may need to receive different messages. If several players on a team are accused of steroid use and will be fined by the league, the commissioner, of course, has to communicate with the offenders, but also the team president, media representatives, teammates who may have been aware of the transgression, fan bases, and perhaps reinforce messages about protocol to an entire league. There likely are other audiences that would need messages as well. The messages that are sent to the varied audiences will be different, if not discrete.

Stakeholder theory can be applied to situations that are not crises as well. If the WNBA changes a policy regarding player base salary, there are different audiences for that message. The key is to identify these audiences and be able to create applicable variations to the separate groups. This is similar to audience analysis described above, but there are some differences. Audience analysis helps communicators know how to send the same message differently. Identifying stakeholders helps communicators assess who has to receive related but different messages. The purpose is not to withhold relevant information from certain groups; the purpose is to make sure that audiences receive relevant information and are not swamped with what is peripheral to them. If a measles epidemic affects who can attend a college basketball game, the players will need to receive a message, so will the fan base. The latter does not need to know the hygienic information that the players require, and the players don't need to know how they can get refunds. Believing that the primary stakeholder for a message is the only stakeholder can be a mistake both from a transmission and a constitutive perspective.

A Sports Communication Model

We have defined sports communication as *the study of how communication and sport are linked and why it is important to explore these linkages.* In addition, we have discussed how sports communication is pervasive, diverse, and powerful. The field is pervasive because there are regular and multiple instances when sports and communication intersect. It is multifaceted because there are many dimensions to the study. The field is powerful because sports communication affects so many aspects of our society and culture. Sports communication affects our economy; influences education at all levels; has and has had political ramifications; addresses racial and gender equality issues; and provides joy and thrills to a large segment of the population.

In the last chapter, we identified a number of perspectives for study in sports communication. We made the point that a coherent examination of sports communication requires a comprehensive plan. We made the comparison between surveying a plot of land and studying a subject. To achieve the former, you would not just send people out without direction because then the study of the land might be incomplete and inaccurate. Similarly, when studying sports communication, we have to consider a method for analysis that will provide results that are comprehensive and complementary. Let's consider a visual representation of what we've discussed thus far about areas and categories of sports communication study.

The Study of Sports Communication

FIGURE 2-2 Areas and Categories of Sports Communication

This model can help visualize the study of sports communication. Each area has an effect on each of the others. Ethical decisions in sports communication contexts can affect Team Communication and Culture. New and conventional media will affect how sports organizations communicate internally and externally. Fan communication concurrently affects and reflects cultural values, business decisions, and economic strength. Note the sample questions that might be explored within each area.

- **Circle 1—Sports Organizations and Crisis Communication**
  - How does the safety committee of the WNBA inform all teams about the protocol to be used when players test positive for COVID?
  - How does the commissioner of the SEC obtain information from conference members that describe recruiting challenges?
  - What are the variables that affect successful league negotiations with media representatives?
  - How does an organization prepare for crises and then communicate in response to the inevitable crises that surface?

- **Circle 2—Communication, Teams, and Team Culture**
  - How do coaches' and players' communications affect the quality of team performance?
  - Can slogans foster team culture?
  - How significant are pep talks for motivation?
  - Does "bulletin board material" affect performance?

- **Circle 3—Effects of Communication and Sports on Politics, Economics, Education, Family, and Culture**
  - How have athletes used their platform to affect society?
  - How have sports events affected politics and the economy?
  - Are athletes responsible for being socially responsible?
  - Have improvements with race and gender relationships been affected by sports and communications regarding sports?

- **Circle 4—Fandom**
  - What is the interdependent relationship between media and fandom?
  - Why do fans become fans, and how does communication foster fandom?
  - How do fans communicate among themselves?
  - How do teams communicate to nourish fandom?

- **Circle 5—Ethical Issues in Sports Communication**
  - During a game, is there a meaningful difference between unethical behavior and gamesmanship?
  - What obstacles in sports contexts prevent ethical decision-making?
  - What is the value of team mission statements and codes of ethics?
  - What tools can be used to help make ethical decisions related to sports communication challenges?

- **Circle 6—Influences of New and Conventional Media**
  - How are sports figures affected by mediated communications?
  - How has new media affected traditional methods of communicating with various publics?
  - What are the hazards associated with using social networks?
  - Have documentaries like the *30 for 30* series changed the narratives surrounding sports?
  - How have books, films, scholarly articles affected the public's conception and understanding of sports?

Chapter Conclusion—Take-Aways

- Communication can be examined from both a transmission and a constitutive perspective.
    - The transmission perspective involves the analysis of whether messages are transmitted accurately from sources to receivers and the variables that affect the transmission.
    - The constitutive perspective examines how communication shapes personal relationships, team culture, and organizational structure.
- Communication is a nonlinear phenomenon that includes both verbal and nonverbal messages that are intentionally and unintentionally sent.
- Among the "noises" in sports communication contexts are interpersonal tension between players, predetermined attitudes about team leaders, serial transmission, language differences, and selective perception.
- Recurring counsel for sports communicators includes: studying your audiences; carefully crafting messages; selecting appropriate media options (including social media); cultivating and nourishing feedback channels; and improving communication skill sets.
- A model for sports communication conceptualizes the field of study in terms of the overlapping contexts of: fandom, ethics, team communication, effects of sports communication on society, organizational/crisis communication, and interdependent effects of media and sport.

QUESTIONS

- Before a basketball game, the starters from both teams were announced. After each player from one of the teams was announced, he ran down a gauntlet of teammates, giving an assortment of handshakes to those assembled. At the end of the run, each player jumped and lurched into a teammate standing at the end of the gauntlet. The player then ran and fist-bumped the three referees who would be officiating the contest. Finally, the player shook hands with an assistant coach from the opposing team who, apparently, was familiar with the drill as he stood near his team's huddle, ready to press flesh with the five opponents.
    - Was the announcement of the starters an act of communication? Running the gauntlet? Fist bumping the officials? Shaking the hand of the assistant coach?
    - What were the goals of the communication?
- During March Madness, a restroom used by student-athletes was papered on the inside wall of every stall with a printed document identifying the prohibition of wagering of any sort on any of the games in the tournament. What would determine if these postings were examples of efficient communication?

- In the 1950s, long before quarterbacks had radios in their helmets, and before sideline coaches used elaborate arm gestures to signal in plays—even before it was common for coaches to make the decisions about which plays to run, Paul Brown, the then coach of the Cleveland Browns, employed a guard shuttle system. Two offensive guards would alternate shuttling in the plays that Paul Brown called. The coach would whisper the play into the ear of a guard on the sideline. That player would run into the huddle, tell the quarterback the play, and another guard would run to the sideline. The process would repeat. In the decades since the 50s, relaying the offensive and defensive plays from the sideline has become more sophisticated. Some college teams get the play, line up to run it, and then, routinely, stop to look at the sideline to see if the play has been altered. When games are televised and coaches radio in the plays, coaches typically cover their mouths with the play sheet so that opponents will not intercept the signal. Regardless of the play called by the coach, the quarterback can shout out code to change the play before it begins.
  - When Paul Brown had his shuttle system, when did communication take place? When Brown told the guard? When the guard told the quarterback? When the quarterback told the team?
  - When quarterbacks use code to change the plays, what are the variables that affect the effectiveness of the communication?
  - Is the process for relaying plays and calling plays an example of something that should be explored by sports communication students and scholars?
- A university held a half-hour ceremony introducing a new athletic director. There was a live audience, and the event was streamed live on Facebook. The university president thanked the retiring athletic director and welcomed the new director. Then, the new director spoke for about fifteen minutes before responding to a few questions. During his comments, he thanked the people at his former university, commended his predecessor, discussed how happy he was to accept the new job and, in broad strokes, mapped out his goals for the athletic department. In his talk, the new director referred to something a mentor from another university had once told him. The mentor had said that the way you spell "fun" was "w-i-n." On Facebook, there was a running commentary from viewers commending both the outgoing and incoming athletic director.
  - What was communicated by whom to whom at this press conference?
  - Does it matter that the conference was available remotely via a Facebook link and that people could make comments live?
  - Is this type of communication an example of something that should be explored by sports communication students and scholars?

Practitioner Perspective

Rich Coren

Courtesy of Rich Coren

Rich Coren is a member of the Basketball Writers of America and author of *Providence College Basketball: The Friar Legacy.* His enthusiasm for, knowledge of, and dedication to Providence College basketball, may be unmatched. I met with Rich to ask about his activities that pertain to this book.

AZ. What do you do for Providence College that relates to Sports Communication?

R.C. As you know, I am the official scorekeeper for home basketball games at Providence. But what is most significant as it relates to your project is that I am the publisher and moderator of an online website dedicated to Providence College basketball.

AZ. What do you do in this capacity?

R.C. I write articles about Providence College basketball that are posted on the site and also monitor the activity of fans who post.

AZ. What is the name of the site?

RC. SCOUTFRIARS.COM https://247sports.com/college/providence/Board/Friar-Talk-102629/

AZ. Do all schools have such sites?

R.C. Large universities from the so-called power conferences all have a website presence hosted by either Scout or Rivals. The hosts earn money from advertising revenue.

AZ. Why do fans visit scoutfriars.com?

R.C. Most people who visit are interested in recruiting information. I learn about who is being considered to play for Providence and share that on the site. I might write about a prospect who has signed, or someone the team has brought in for a workout, or a high schooler that I discover has an interest in playing for P.C. Visitors comment on recruits and other aspects of the team. During the season, fans will post about games, player performance, and coaching decisions.

AZ. Can anyone visit the site?

R.C. There are two tiers of visitors. There is information that is accessible to any visitor for free, and then more detailed information for subscribers.

AZ. What happens when a visitor posts something that is gratuitously offensive about a player, coach, or some aspect of the program?

R.C. I have the authority and will exercise the authority to purge a post or even prohibit a visitor from posting in the future if comments are offensive. Someone can disagree with a thread or coaching decision. But someone who, for example, uses excessive language or discusses personal matters unrelated to basketball will not be able to continue.

AZ. Since you also are the official scorer for P.C., are you ever in a situation when P.C. would prefer that you not comment critically on the site or not allow for critical comments?

R.C. It happens rarely. And most of the time, if someone asks me to take a look at a post, there is some legitimacy to the request. I have established a credible reputation with P.C. and with basketball people, so they trust me to act and write appropriately.

AZ. Ever have a coach angry with you for an article you wrote?

R.C. As I said, most of the time, I find that comments from the team or athletic department are reasonable. There was an instance when a player from Europe, Tuukka Kotti, was being recruited by the then Providence coach, Tim Welsh. I attended a workout session for Kotti and then wrote a piece for the site which identified the attributes of the player. Coach Welsh was more than mildly upset, not because the information was inaccurate but rather because Kotti had been under the radar before I wrote the article. Most coaches are aware of the U.S. players but not familiar with those outside the country. As it turned out, there was no damage because the player ultimately enrolled at P.C.

AZ. You and I have talked before about your work with the media guide.

R.C. Yes, my wife and I design the annual media guide for P.C. Men's basketball. It is a compendium of information about the current team, as well as statistics about career leaders in all basketball categories.

AZ. How do you keep up with all the stats?

R.C. I am the official scorekeeper, so I have access to information about rebounds, scoring, etc. In addition, I have followed the team for decades and have a very good memory for Providence College statistics.

AZ. Ok. You have a good memory? [I flip through the media guide] Which Providence player was the MVP of the 1960 National Invitation Tournament?

First Person   Selective Perception

Communication studies, and other areas of study, for example, psychology and sociology, examine the phenomenon of selectivity in listening and human interaction. There is selective exposure, attention, perception, and retention.

In brief, you expose yourself to messages that you might want to hear, pay attention to what you desire to, perceive meaning by filtering out that which is not palatable, and remember what you want.

The classic example academics like to use occurs when a student asks what she or he needs to pass a course. The professor replies, "Well, you have not attended the class except for one time when you were looking at your cell phone, don't seem to listen, and have not scored well on all the other exams. I guess it is not impossible that you could pass if you somehow reverse direction 180 degrees and study industriously for the final and earn an A+ on it, but it is highly unlikely." If the student leaves and says to her or himself, "No problem, all I have to do is study some for the final, and I will pass." you have an example of selective perception.

It's easy to shake your head when you hear such a story, but the fact is that if you are someone who selectively perceives you may be unaware of the tendency. And if you are unaware of your tendencies, you could go through life assuming that you listen dispassionately and do not filter out what you don't want to hear.

I think what makes people successful in life is their willingness to look themselves in the mirror and ask if they hear just what they want to hear or listen to it all even when "all" can be bruising. Athletes who will not hear that they have a weakness when they bat will always blame something for their low batting average. The ones who listen to coaching may be able to remedy the problems.

Chapter 3

Communication and Sports Organizations

© Joshua Rainey Photography/Shutterstock.com

Chapter in a Nutshell

Systems theory provides a foundation for those who study sports communication. Sports organizations are composed of subsystems that must interact efficiently with internal and external audiences in order to thrive. This chapter describes systems theory, its principles, related elements, and the theory's practical applications for sports communication.

Specifically, at the end of the chapter, students will be able to:

- Define the term "theory."
- Describe systems theory as it relates to sports communication.
- Understand, and apply the following to sports communication.
    o Hierarchical Ordering—Systems, subsystems, and focal systems
    o Permeability
    o Requisite Variety
    o Relevant Environment
    o Entropy
    o Silo Effect
    o Networks and Networking
- Identify and analyze sports communication cases from a systems theory perspective.

Sports Communication Prompts

- Below, you will see statements pertaining to some aspect of communication and sports. For each item
    o Decide whether you agree or disagree with the statement.
    o Explain your rationale for the position.
    o Support your position with examples.
1. It is essential, not just important, that professional coaches and owners listen and respond to fans' opinions.
2. Zoom-type technology proved that leagues will no longer have to convene periodic on-ground meetings with their constituents. The technology saves time and money and is just as effective as face-to-face retreats.
3. If a student-athlete violates an NCAA rule, then the university is to blame for not communicating the rules to the athlete effectively.
4. A great coach must be able to communicate effectively to fans and, in the case of college sports, alumni.
5. Coaches should not consider reporters and other media representatives as the enemy. In fact, sports journalists who follow a team should be treated as part of the family.

We were like the strings of a guitar. Each one was different, but we sounded pretty good together.

Willie Worsley, college basketball player

Introduction

Imagine that you are an athletic director at a university. You oversee twenty sports teams ranging from women's ice hockey to men's and women's crew to football to volleyball to fencing. Each team has a head coach, at least one assistant coach, and many student-athletes. In the case of football, more than 100 student-athletes are on the team's roster.

You are also responsible for supervising the related services for the athletic program. Specifically, you work with trainers, equipment personnel, the facilities staff, the event management team, academic support services, and compliance officers. In your office suite, there is an associate athletic director, three administrative staffers, the community affairs group, and the sports information and promotions staff, which includes two dedicated social media employees. Your job also involves campus recreation. The intramural programs, club sports, and student recreation complex personnel report to you.

Most of your teams play in an NCAA mid-major conference where there are North and South divisions. You meet twice a year with other athletic directors in the conference and then separately with those in the South division. You serve on the media committee for the entire conference. In this role, you participate in negotiations with media outlets for broadcasting rights. Your committee typically meets with the media representatives, prepares a report, distributes the report to all athletic directors, and then administers a vote to determine if a particular package is acceptable.

Some of your teams, ice hockey and crew, for example, do not compete in this same mid-major conference because many schools do not field ice hockey or crew teams. Consequently, these teams play in other leagues, and you have periodic interactions with these leagues as well.

Your school is a member of the NCAA and is compelled to satisfy NCAA protocols. Periodically, the NCAA requests information about student-athlete academic progress and solicits your votes on various issues. An ongoing controversial topic relates to whether athletes should be able to share moneys from sports that are revenue-generating or products that are sold with player names used as enticements. Beginning in the summer of 2021, student-athletes were granted the right to earn money from their "NIL"—Name, Image, and Likeness–without losing athletic eligibility. This created challenges for athletic department leaders and required regular communication in order to be clear about the new protocols. You are on a number of committees for the NCAA, the rules committee for one, and also sit on the women's tournament selection committee for basketball.

In addition to your work with the teams, support operations, conferences, and NCAA, you, of course, belong to the larger university community. You regularly interact with faculty and administration on university policy. You have important connections with the admissions office, registrar, and residential life. For example, at your school, student-athletes are permitted to register early for classes in order to ensure that they can find seats during class times that will minimally interfere with practice and team travel. This is an agreement you were able to reach after meeting with the registrar and then making an oral presentation to the faculty senate.

You are a member of the senior leadership team on your campus, serving with the vice presidents for academic and student affairs, chief financial officer, and the president. Occasionally you meet with the university board of trustees to discuss your programs. The campus radio station covers your football, basketball, baseball, softball, and hockey games.

Occasionally, there will be broadcasts for other sports, and regularly you are asked to speak about your teams by those who have programs on the station. The student newspaper covers all sports and not just with beat writers. Columnists often contribute opinion pieces to the newspaper that can question the wisdom of coaches and administrators. You've occasionally had to write responses to these criticisms.

While you oversee and monitor the athletics' website, which contains information on all teams and all student-athletes on the teams, you also interface with the office of university communications to make sure that there is an appropriate presence for athletics on its and related sites.

You have many audiences external to the university with whom you engage. The alums are a particularly important and, at times, vocal group. It is not rare for alums to send you repeated e-mails suggesting—some subtly, some not so—that you need to make a coaching change in one sport or the other. You want to interact with this group for many reasons, one of which is that they can make monetary contributions to athletics which are fuel for continued excellence. Parents of student-athletes are another external group with whom you must engage. Some can be vocal about promises made during recruitment that may seem to not have been honored.

Another especially key group is the various new and conventional media external to the university who cover—and those you would like to cover—your teams. You have a track star who has broken records that are truly unusual, but for some reason, there is not much space dedicated in the local newspaper, blogs, popular websites, and talk shows that highlight this accomplishment. You are aware that the "media" is a collective term used to describe various types of professional communicators. However, you know that the term—despite the tendency to refer to the media collectively—is comprised of different types that are not all reached in the same way. And the media can be very powerful players in your world.

And then you have fans of your teams—season ticket holders, loyal supporters who travel to away games and are vocal at home—cheering for the student-athletes. Fans are essential for your success, particularly in revenue-generating sports. Engaging with that audience is crucial.

Ohio State Buckeye fans cheer for the team.

The job is multifaceted. *And every single facet requires an understanding of and proficiency in communication.* The success of your enterprise depends on communication quality with these multiple audiences as much as, or more than, the quality of your coaches, facilities, and skills of the athletes.

Systems Theory

Discussions of theory can be off-putting. Even very bright people may sometimes assume that theories are abstractions and, consequently, dismiss theory as the musings of academics who are not grounded in reality. Some theories are, in fact, less than practical, and often theories are described poorly so that whatever value they may have is inaccessible to those who might otherwise like to apply them. It can be thankless work to plow through a complex paper about theory just to reach a conclusion that seems to be irrelevant or self-evident.

Dismissing theory for these reasons, however, is a good example of throwing out the baby with the bathwater. Theories can be extremely valuable and applicable. Systems theory, for example, provides a very practical foundation for the study of sports communication. It is an effective way to conceptualize communication processes and responsibilities. Athletic directors like those described in the introduction to this chapter can employ systems theory to deal with and comprehend their communication challenges. In sports organizations, because of the very many active and vocal external stakeholders as well as the multiple internal stakeholders, systems theory is especially relevant.

WHAT IS A THEORY?

A theory is essentially a speculation, a very educated guess based on study or experience. People conduct research studies that test hypotheses. Hypo is an affix that means "under." Hypotheses are literally under the theory—foundational assumptions that are tested. The results of the test/study can form the bases for a theory.

For example, a hypothesis in a series of studies might be that experience playing a sport and expert knowledge of a sport, are secondary criteria for aspiring general managers when juxtaposed with administrative experience and an understanding of communication principles. Researchers would conduct studies to determine whether the hypothesis can be supported. If the hypotheses could be supported, a theory might be generated that contends that searches for general managers discount playing experience and sport content expertise, and emphasize communication skill and administrative experience. A hypothesis in another series of studies might be that successful college coaches do not fare well when they accept similar positions coaching professional athletes because the communication challenges are not analogous. Researchers would conduct studies to determine whether this hypothesis can be supported. If the hypothesis is supported, then a theory might be developed that asserts that since (a) professional coaches and college coaches have disparate communication challenges and (b) communication is imperative for successful coaching, then (c) success at one level is not the lone or even primary predictor of success at another.

Theories are different from laws. A law, like the law of gravity, is an incontrovertible truth. Theories are conjectures about truth that are based on experimentation and observation. The law of gravity is not a conjecture. It is not a theory. It is a law. Drop a basketball, and it will hit the floor. Every time. Someone cannot dispute a law. Nevertheless, while not incontrovertible truths like the law of gravity, theories can be valuable. And systems theory, particularly so for sports communication.

WHAT IS SYSTEMS THEORY?

The basic tenet of systems theory is that organizations are comprised of subsystems that must work interdependently, not independently. As indicated in the chapter introduction, an athletic director interacts with multiple units. Systems theorists argue that each of these is dependent either directly or indirectly on another. To maximize efficiency—certainly in the long run—no one subsystem can act autonomously. Systems theorists go further and contend that if units act autonomously, then, at some point, there will be a breakdown in the system that can have severe effects—even if an individual unit appears to be functioning efficiently. For example, a systems theorist would contend that despite the great success of its football program, subsystems acting independently and not interdependently were a source of Penn State's embarrassing scandal involving Jerry Sandusky and head coach Joe Paterno. As we will see, systems theorists can argue that the source of the University of North Carolina's student-athlete scandal and subsequent notoriety was a result of poor interaction between subsystems.

The result of poor interdepartmental communication is not always a national embarrassment. However, at the very least, the effect of units acting independently will be a diminution of organizational quality. It is not difficult to imagine, for example, how the athletic department at a university will suffer if event-day staffers do not engage with season ticket holders or trainers on a team do not have access to team coaches.

Systems theory, of course, applies to sport on the professional levels as well—not just at a university. In May 2018, the National Football League owners met in Atlanta. A number of items were on the docket. One with repercussions inside and outside the league was the league's policy regarding player protests during the national anthem. The NFL created a policy that they called a "compromise." The league did not interact with the players or player association when developing the new plan. Once the league made its decision, it had to inform the subsystems in its relevant environment: the players, the players' association, coaches, general managers, media representatives; broadcasting partners; fans; advertisers. And the league had to be ready to respond to the reactions from these audiences.

The reactions were immediate. Fans commented online and on sports talk shows. Newspaper analysts penned opinion pieces in their dailies. Bloggers blogged. Internally, players reacted. Even some owners who allegedly voted unanimously in support of the policy issued statements that indicated a lack of support and confusion. A recurring criticism was that before the policy was formed, the league should have contacted the players' association to obtain its input. Columnist Tara Sullivan wrote that the policy was "a poorly thought out plan, billed as a compromise but established without any player input" (Sullivan 2018).

The NFL Players Association issued the following statement:

The NFL chose to not consult the union. NFL players have shown their patriotism through social activism, community service, in support of military and law enforcement and yes, through protests to raise awareness about the issues they cared about. The vote today contradicts the statements made to our player leadership by [the league] about the principles, values and patriotism of our League.

In Sullivan's article, she comments that neither the NFL nor the players' association wanted to listen to one another: "The NFL has no interest in listening to its players, so afraid of alienating fans and television viewers who pump their bottom lines with cash. Players don't want to hear from those who disagree with their method of protest."

WHAT ARE THE KEY PRINCIPLES OF SYSTEMS THEORY?

Hierarchical Ordering

A premise of systems theory is that an organization is composed of systems and subsystems arranged in a hierarchy. Any system within an organization has subsystems, and each subsystem has its own subsystems, such that any one subsystem can be considered a focal system with its own communication requirements.

In systems theory, the phrase *focal system* refers to the subsystem within an organization that one is studying; in other words, the subsystem that one is looking at and focusing on. In the example that begins this chapter, if you were examining the athletic director's department, the focal system would be that department. If we focus on a subsystem, for example, the football team, we can see how that subsystem can be seen as the focal system with its own subsystems. The football team is likely to have an offensive and separate defensive unit. There may be trainers dedicated to football. It's possible that the team has its own public relations staff or facilities manager. Within any one of these subsystems, there could be further subsystems. For example, the defensive unit might break down and have a group for linebackers and another for cornerbacks. If we select the mid-major conference as the focal system, then the North and South divisions are subsystems. And if we then identify the South division of the conference as the focal system, then its subsystems are the universities within the South division.

Each subsystem is said to be linked horizontally and vertically with other subsystems. That is, each subsystem in an organization is horizontally linked to other subsystems on the same level and vertically linked to systems below it and above it on the organizational hierarchy. On the football team, for example, the trainers, PR staff, offensive unit, defensive unit, facilities staff, and all other subsystems are linked horizontally to each other and also vertically to the leaders of the focal system—in this case, head coaching staff, of the team.

Permeability

All subsystems within an organization need to have permeable boundaries. Information from one subsystem needs to be able to penetrate the walls of other subsystems. If a subsystem has impenetrable boundaries, then the information that needs to be shared cannot reach essential receivers who might, despite their reluctance to make the boundaries permeable, absolutely need the information.

Every subsystem has to be able to get information from the outside and send information to the outside. Systems theorists refer to open and closed systems. A closed system does not have permeable boundaries. It will not function as well as it might and could atrophy or expire in the same way that an organ in a body might atrophy or expire without nourishment from its external environment. If, for example, there are established linkages between trainers and defensive coaches on a team, but if these coaches do not desire to hear what the trainers wish to tell them, systems theorists would say an important subsystem, defensive coaches, have walls that are not permeable. The focal system, the team, may suffer—if not immediately—over time.

Northeastern Athletics & Recreation - Administration

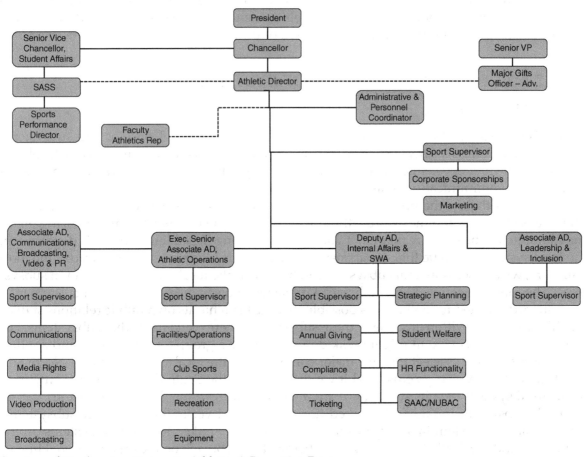

Courtesy of Northeastern University Athletics & Recreation Dept.

Northeastern Athletics & Recreation – Sport Supervision

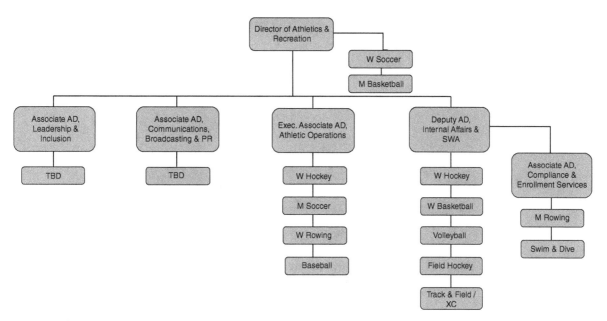

Courtesy of Northeastern University Athletics & Recreation Dept

Organizational penetration is a term used by researcher Phillip Tompkins in his book *Organizational Communication Imperatives* (OCI) and then again in a sequel to OCI (Tompkins, 2005, pp. 88–90). In these books, Tompkins describes the need for organizations to imagine external contractors as units within an organization and penetrate these units in order to be aware of the activities of the contractors. By extension, organizational penetration is used to describe the practice of learning as much as one can about other subsystems internally so that each unit can act with the knowledge of these inherently related entities. It may not seem obvious why the defensive linebackers need to interact with the offensive running backs, but there could be a benefit. Raymond Berry coached the New England Patriots in the mid 80s and would run drills where the offensive ends were asked to play defensive back during some scrimmages. On the surface, this may seem peculiar—and it is an unusual drill—but one can imagine the benefits to receivers when they discover the tribulations and tactics of those who defend them.

If subsystems within a sports organization are not permeable, the result will be a silo effect. Each subsystem will operate autonomously, not knowing or caring about what another related department might be doing. Silos on farms are long tall structures that are used as repositories for grain. Often several of these silos stand adjacent to one another and are not connected in any way. The silo effect is a phrase used to describe organizational units that, like silos in a field, stand adjacent to one another and are not connected. Sometimes silos are created because of competition between units. Other times these silos are created because the organizational culture perpetuates the notion that if every unit does its job, the organization as a whole will operate seamlessly.

Subsystems in an athletic department are inherently interdependent and should not consider themselves discrete entities like silos in a field.

If, in the example with the university athletic director, the South division of the mid-major conference did not interact with or consider the value of interacting with the North division—one can imagine problems that would be seeded. In perhaps a more obvious example, if the SEC, a major NCAA conference, considered itself autonomous and was unconcerned with the tribulations of, for example, the America East, while superficially there might not be much concern, one can predict that roots for trouble would begin to develop. Within a university athletic department, if men's basketball considered itself superior to women's basketball, or fencing or women's and men's soccer—the brittle walls that might form between self-isolating units and the athletes in these units could have negative effects.

Requisite Variety, Relevant Environment, and Chaos Theory

Even if walls are permeable, subsystems may fail to communicate adequately if the subsystem is not equipped to deal with the information that is coming into the subsystem. Requisite variety means that each subsystem has to be as complex and sophisticated in terms of processing information as is the relevant external environment. Information that comes into the subsystem is *input*. The processing of that information within the subsystem is *throughput*, and the information that goes back is *output*.

An athletic director will receive information from fans, media representatives, coaches, conference representatives, the NCAA, referees, vendors, aspiring athletic directors and coaches, and lawyers. The walls of the athletic director's office may be permeable, but if there is not a sophisticated enough system for addressing the influx of information from these various other sources, then communication can and will break down. The hasty remedy for this is to render the walls nonpermeable, that is, to make it difficult for information from certain others to get into the subsystem to avoid being subjected to a deluge. This is shortsighted and will have negative consequences. The long-term solution is to ensure that all meaningful information can be addressed by maintaining a system for communicating internally as complex as the environment external to the subsystem. If the athletic director in the introduction hired a single

According to systems theory, the various units of a team: offense, defense, and special teams, are inherently interdependent, not independent. Within any unit, for example defense, the linebackers, cornerbacks, and linebackers cannot function independently.

staffer to handle all external communications "to ensure" permeability, that "solution" would likely be a catalyst for additional communication problems and—the act itself of hiring only one staffer might seed a culture that devalues communication.

The relevant environment is that part external to the subsystem that is relevant to the system. One might make an argument that there is very little in our universe that is not relevant to any subsystem's environment. Chaos theory, for example, based on the work of the late MIT professor Edward Lorenz posited that what may appear to be irrelevant and unrelated phenomena are, in fact, not irrelevant and unrelated. While we may not be able to quickly understand how or why, chaos theory argues that apparently disparate events are part of some larger composite. In essence, the appearance of irrelevance is illusory. No action is inconsequential, and all actions have some consequence. The theory is sometimes called the Butterfly Effect because it suggests that even the actions of a remote butterfly cannot be disconnected from other phenomena. The nickname for the theory originated when Dr. Lorenz delivered a 1972 paper entitled, "Predictability: Does the flap of a butterfly's wings in Brazil set off a tornado in Texas." The professor's answer was yes. As it applies to sports organizations, chaos theory suggests that the relevant environment may be far greater than what one initially may suppose.

However, there are factors that are more relevant and immediate than others. If any university team is the focal system, the relevant environment includes at least other teams at the school, other teams in a conference, prospective recruits, academic support services, fans, alums, bloggers, broadcasters, conference officials, other coaches, and academic officials.

Subsystems need to have sufficient requisite variety to process incoming communications from the relevant environment, or the result would be, de facto, a closed system. Such a closed system will eventually become disabled because of the disorder that results from not interacting with its relevant environment and its related subsystems. That state of disorder is referred to as entropy. Since systems theorists hold that organizations (as well as organisms) cannot function without permeable boundaries and input, the desired end for a healthy system is the negative entropy that results from interactions with the environment. A systems orientation precludes entropy or at least retards its development. Negative entropy is a desired result.

Communication Networks

If sports organizations are a system of interdependent units, then the organization has to establish communication networks that allow for information to travel from one dependent unit to another. Consider a highway metaphor. In order to drive from one place to another, motorists need roadways. Without Interstate 25 or other alternate routes, it would be difficult to drive from Denver to Cheyenne. It does not matter whether motorists drive vans or minis. They still would have trouble getting to Cheyenne by automobile if there were no viable routes. Similarly, sports organizations require routes to facilitate the transportation of information. Coaches, division heads, athletic directors, conference commissioners must create, cultivate, and nourish these networks in order to permit the flow of information. Networks do not refer to specific messages such as league policies or protocol for game day parking. These examples are analogous to the vehicles that use the highways. The networks refer to the communication channels themselves. Even access to technology does not define or create networks. Technology can facilitate the development of networks but is not synonymous with networks. E-mail, in and of itself, is not a network. Every reader of this sentence has an e-mail address. That does not mean that there are networks that have been established linking all readers.

To some, the distinction between networks and messages may seem to be minor and not particularly meaningful. Indeed, new technologies and social media can blur the distinction. Nevertheless, there is a fundamental difference between messages and communication networks which is not insignificant. To illustrate this, analyze the following examples. They point out that the root of the communication problems is **not** the method of sending information but the absence of any way for important messages to get from one place to another within the organization.

- A trainer is aware of injuries that are affecting the performance of athletes. She prepares an agenda and organizes her thoughts so that she can carefully articulate these problems to the coaching staff. The staff may not have time or the inclination to hear the message. The head coach may tell the trainer to write down what needs to be communicated. However, the coach may never access what is written.

- An academic support services employee is aware of a problem with a class. The class appears to be genuine, but it is actually not a class at all, but a bogus independent study. It is a ruse employed to facilitate maintaining athletes' eligibility. The academic support service staffer desires to relay this, but there is no method of accessing his superior.

- A player is aware that a teammate is using performance-enhancing drugs. Not only is this not in the best interests of the teammate, but it can affect the program if this is revealed. The player informs the captain, who is reluctant to speak with the coach because while it may seem counterintuitive, there is no comfortable network that links the captain to the coach.

- A low-level equipment manager notices something in the men's locker room that is outrageously reprehensible. He sees that a youngster is the subject of sexual abuse by one of the team coaches. Stunned by the sight, the manager attempts to speak to the head coach but cannot gain access and is told to tell his superior. When the staffer tells the superior, the superior tells him that she will take care of the problem—but never herself gets the message to the head coach.

In all four of these cases, there are messages to be sent but no genuine network that allows for the messages to be transmitted.

Types of Communication Networks

There are three basic network systems. One of these, as we will see, has particular applications to focal systems in sports organizations.

Location: External and Internal Networks External networks refer to those channels that carry information from within the focal system to outside its borders or those networks that carry information from outside the organization to inside the organization. In sports organizations, these networks are crucial because so many key stakeholders are external to the system. Fans, media representatives, neighboring citizens, government officials, donors—all these stakeholders need to be reached and need to be able to access the focal system without overwhelming it.

http://aces.wnba.com/contact/

"External networks are channels that link the organization to its outside audiences, as shown on the Las Vegas Aces site."

External networks do not function independently. In order to communicate to external audiences, internal agents must be connected to other internal populations. The NFLPA's criticism of the new anthem policy was that internal networks were not utilized before external units in the league's relevant environment were informed. Some might argue that the league has the right—even the responsibility—to make decisions without exercising internal networks with players. This may be defended, but in this instance, since the players were directly affected by the decision, it was shortsighted not to at least use the network to discuss policy options.

Any channels *within* the organization that carry information are called internal networks. This can refer to *intra*departmental routes and *inter*departmental routes. The focus in sports communication is often on communication with the media and fans—and these are important networks to establish, but internal networks are key as well. A study conducted of eight university athletic departments assessed the major source of communication problems within these departments. The results of focus group discussions and surveys completed by participants indicated that poor internal communication between departments was the greatest source of difficulty (Zaremba and Wiseman, 2015, p. 9).

Often internal channels within organizations exist only nominally and are difficult to navigate. A coach might claim that she has an open-door policy, but it does not seem as if one can comfortably cross the threshold. An outdated website billed as a place where news can be exchanged loses its credibility in the same way a physical bulletin board is not a useful tool if it is crowded with irrelevant information. A weekly zoom meeting designed to share information between assistant coaches ceases to be a valuable network if the head coach uses the forum to speak and not listen to comments from the assistants.

Formality: Formal and Informal Networks Formal networks are those that are prescribed. These are the official, appropriate channels for people to follow when relaying information. Organizational charts indicate who is to report to whom and what the appropriate chain of command is in an organization. The fact that a network is a formal network does not guarantee that communication "traffic" can utilize the particular channel.

Informal networks are those channels that carry information on routes that are not prescribed. Research about informal networks suggests that these routes are faster than the formal network; resilient in that they cannot be destroyed; perceived as credible in the sense that people who receive information on the formal network often check the accuracy with their grapevine sources; natural; and sometimes surprisingly accurate.

Assume the long-time lacrosse coach gathers the team on the first day of practice and explains team rules and policy. As soon as the gathering concludes, some of the first-year players will likely approach the juniors and seniors and ask how much of these policies are enforced. The informal network that naturally surfaced is used to check on the merit of what has been sent along the formal network. Any attempt by the coach to eliminate the informal network will likely serve to stimulate it. The first-year players may put more stock in what the seniors say is the actual policy than what the coach presents as the official policy.

The nature of the grapevine will be affected, for example, by the physical layout of the buildings and offices within the buildings. If Training and Athletic Facilities share a common lounge area and restroom facility, it is likely that an informal network will develop among those people who populate the departments. Common hobbies and activities play a large part in the development of the grapevine. If staffers from different units jog together at lunch, information is likely to be passed along in the course of the run. The friendships that develop because of the common activity will result in social gatherings during which information will be passed along as well. If Smith in Training wants to find out about applicants for the assistant athletic director opening, Smith may not call the Search Committee Chair but contact an Athletic Facilities acquaintance, a committee member whom he knows from morning coffee chats. Even the formal network can affect the growth of the informal network. If you participate on a committee and, in the course of your committee work, become friendly with a person who previously had been a stranger, that developing friendship creates a part of the informal network. The explosion of social media contributes to and expands the informal network. The power and influence of the informal network may be best described to readers by asking this simple question: When you select electives for your schedule, do you rely mostly on what is in the catalog about a course and what appears on the department website about the instructor's credentials, or do you ask fellow students about the course and the teacher? Do you look at what the university publishes about faculty accomplishments, or do you visit a site like RateMyProfessors?

Maybe, In much the same way as students use unofficial networks to find out about an instructor's quality, players may use informal networks to learn the real rules on a sports team.

Direction: Upward, Downward, and Horizontal   In addition to location and formality, networks can be examined in terms of direction. A downward network is one that carries information from upper levels of an organization to those who are below on the organizational chart. The vice president of baseball operations of a team has to relay information to the general manager, and the general manager to the manager, and the manager to the players. Channels established to allow for these interactions are downward networks. The horizontal networks link people on the same level. Upward networks are those that allow individuals on lower levels to communicate with those to whom they report.

Fair or Foul   Questions of Ethics

The National Football League needed to consider its policy regarding players who would not stand for the playing of the national anthem. Many fans and political figures found the behavior disrespectful. Social activists felt that the players were exercising their first amendment rights for a just cause. The NFL announced a compromise policy that required players and league personnel on the sideline to stand but gave them the option to remain in the locker room if they didn't want to stand. The NFL player association responded, indicating they had not been consulted by this policy.

- Was it unethical for the NFL to call this policy a "compromise" policy if the NFLPA was not consulted?
- Was it unethical for the NFL to create this policy without discussing it with the NFLPA?

Feynman's Theory and Upward Networks

The late physicist Richard Feynman was a member of the Roger's Commission that studied the 1986 Space Shuttle Challenger explosion. Feynman is most famous for his work as a Harvard Physics professor. He also wrote some best-selling non-academic books, including, *Surely You're Joking, Mr. Feynman,* and *What do you Care what Other People Think?*

In a *Physics Today* article, Feynman recounted his experience working on the Roger's Commission and discussed some perspectives he had regarding upward communication. Feynman observed that lower-level workers often had valuable information that had not been communicated to managers. In one instance, he attributed this lack of upward communication to the fact that workers had poor written communication skills:

> *They had a lot of information, but no way to communicate it. The workmen knew a lot. They had noticed all kinds of problems and had all kinds of ideas on how to fix them, but no one had paid much attention to them. The reason was: Any observations had to be reported in writing, and a lot of these guys didn't know how to write good memos"* (Feynman, 1988, p. 33).

In another instance, Feynman documented that the engineers at the Marshall Space Flight Center and the managers at the center were not "on the same page." He asked three engineers to write down the chances of flight failure on the basis of *engine* failure. He also asked a manager to approximate the chances of failure. The engineers all predicted a rate of about 1 in 200. The manager predicted 1 in 100,000! (Feynman, 1988, P. 34).

This glaring inconsistency flabbergasted Feynman and the engineers (Tompkins, 2005, p. 120).

Feynman advanced a theory of communication in an attempt to explain how it was possible that the managers could be so out of touch with the engineers.

Feynman conjectured that what happens in organizations is that, at times, heads of units feel compelled to exaggerate the capabilities of the departments they lead. He argued that in order to ensure that resources continue to flow into a department, unit heads feel as if they must highlight accomplishments and downplay the problems. They might, therefore, claim that their units can do various things that they may not be able to do in order to guarantee that the unit will continue to be funded. A coach may speak to an athletic director about an outstanding recruiting class; the academic support head may speak about the percentage of students who are on the dean's list. Perhaps in both cases, there are exaggerations made in order to ensure that the programs are funded and staffed appropriately.

What happens in these instances—according to his theory—is that the upward networks get "clogged." People who are aware of information that would refute the exaggerated claims by the coach and academic support head are discouraged from communicating this information. If coaches were to receive this information, they would be unable to continue to exaggerate the accomplishments to the athletic director. In other words, Feynman contends that leaders sometimes don't want to know certain types of information and actually discourage it from coming up the line. Feynman wrote:

> *I believe that what happened was . . . that although the engineers down in the works knew NASA's claims were impossible, and the guys at the top knew that somehow they had exaggerated, the guys at the top didn't want to **hear** that they had exaggerated . . . It's better if they don't hear it, so they can be much more "honest" when they're trying to get Congress to okay their projects (Feynman, 1988, p. 37).*

Applying Systems Theory Tenets

Let's consider a sports communication case and apply theory we've discussed to the analysis of that case.

UNC ACADEMIC FRAUD CASE

For eighteen years, from 1993 to 2011, student-athletes at the University of North Carolina received credit for classes in the Department of African and Afro-American Studies that were, at best, superficial. These classes required no attendance. At the end of a term, a student submitted a paper. During the course of a semester, students in these classes were not mentored by faculty, nor did faculty at the conclusion of the semester grade the papers. An administrator in the department evaluated the papers—very leniently—and submitted final grades. Students might receive an A or B in a course for a paper that lacked substance. Some paper submissions consisted of an original introduction and conclusion and then pasted content from other sources in between. Some students were aided in their writings by tutors who wrote sections of the papers. Student-athletes took and were encouraged to take these courses to ensure that they maintained their eligibility. Typically, the athletes who took these courses were participants in revenue-generating sports: basketball and football (Wainstein et al., 2014 p. 2).

Initially, students took these classes as Independent Studies. The number of students taking these Independent Studies was staggering—sometimes as many as 300 per academic year. Most departments at nearly all universities offer Independent Studies or something similar. With Independent Studies, a student works with an individual instructor on a mutual area of interest. The student/instructor maps out a study plan and timeline and meets periodically during a semester. The instructor then grades a submission at the end of the term. A very high number of Independent Studies per year in a department might be twenty. Three hundred for an academic year is an alarming number.

In 1999, the department began offering "lecture courses" to complement the Independent Study offerings. Despite calling the courses lecture classes, they were essentially the same as the Independent Studies. The lecture courses were listed as regular classes, students would sign up or be signed up to be in them, but the classes would never meet—students would participate as they had, submitting a paper at the conclusion of the term that would be nominally graded by the student services manager. The advantages of using lecture classes that had no content were that they reduced the very high number of Independent Studies and also finessed the limit on the number of Independent Study courses any one student could take. As significantly, the lecture classes could count toward new university core curriculum requirements, whereas independent study classes could not.

"Bifurcated" classes were a third approach. These were actual classes, but a segment of the registered population did not need to attend. This non-attending segment would, again, write a paper and submit the paper for lenient grading by the student services manager. A similar fourth approach was to add students to a traditional class roster, assign paper topics to these students, and provide grades for the students without the instructor allegedly being aware that these students had been added on.

In sum, student-athletes received credit for classes that were, at best, superficial. They were either Independent Study courses, bogus lecture classes, classes that were composed of students taking the course conventionally and student-athletes who had only to submit a paper, and courses where students who had only written a paper were added on to a conventional roster at the end of the term. Taking these ersatz classes allowed student-athletes to maintain their academic eligibility.

The student services administrator initiated the paper class system. She registered the students, graded the papers, and submitted the grades. She was motivated by her sense of compassion for student-athletes whom she felt needed and deserved assistance, and her passion for University of North Carolina athletic teams. The chair of the department was a hands-off leader. He, tacitly at least, condoned the paper class activity allowing the administrator to act autonomously. Others were aware of the paper classes, particularly academic advisers who encouraged student-athletes to take the courses—and in some cases—discussed with the administrator the grades that were necessary in order for a student-athlete to maintain eligibility.

In 2011, two stunning news items surfaced. Taken together, these suggested academic fraud involving student-athletes and spurred an investigation. The first in July 2011 involved a student-athlete, a football player, who had been suspended from the team for academic violations. The player sought to be reinstated. He acknowledged that he had indeed submitted a plagiarized paper but also claimed that not only were plagiarized papers normal for students enrolled in the class, but astonishingly, there really was no actual class. He had, he claimed, been enrolled in a class that wasn't real and only had to submit a paper to get academic credit. The second revelation came in August of 2011. *The* (Raleigh) *News & Observer* ran a story about another student-athlete. The player's high school record was such that he would not have been eligible to play football in the fall of 2007. One academic deficiency was related to his writing skills, and he, therefore, needed to take a remedial writing course and would do so later in his time at UNC. However, it was made clear in the newspaper story that the player, who needed to take remedial writing, was somehow capable of enrolling in a 400 level course during the summer of 2007 and, remarkably, had earned a B+ in the course. The credit and grade made him eligible to play football (Anderson 2014, p.72-73).

These incidents suggested that there was something problematic going on at UNC. The university began to explore these and related irregularities.

HOW SYSTEMS THEORY APPLIES

An independent agency conducted an exhaustive investigation of what transpired with these paper classes. In October 2014, a committee issued a report of its findings. Two excerpts from the executive summary to that report read as follows:

> *Despite the fact that these classes involved thousands of students and coordination between [the administrator] and numerous University employees, the Chapel Hill administration never scrutinized AFAM's [Department of African and Afro-American Studies] operations or the academic integrity of their course offerings. It was only when media reports raised questions about AFAM classes in 2011 that administration officials took a hard look at the AFAM Department. They were shocked with what they found.*
>
> *We found no evidence that the higher levels of the University tried in any way to obscure the facts or the magnitude of this situation. To the extent there were times of delay or equivocation in their response to this controversy, we largely attribute that to insufficient appreciation of the scale of the problem, an understandable lack of experience with this sort of institutional crisis and some lingering disbelief that such misconduct could have occurred at Chapel Hill. (Wainstein et al., 2014 pages 2; 6.)*

As we have discussed, systems theorists contend that units within an organization are inherently interdependent and must be linked by navigable and horizontal communication networks. In addition, the walls to all subsystems within an organization must be permeable in order for information traveling on these networks to get through to appropriate audiences.

If we are to accept at face value the cited excerpts from the report, there could not have been viable communication networks that linked subsystems at UNC. When the head basketball coach was confronted with the information about the paper classes, his response was that he was "dumbfounded."

If his statement was sincere and the committee's conclusions accurate, the walls of the subsystems at UNC could not have been permeable. The networks were either not there, not used, or illusory. If communication channels had existed as systems theorists contend they need to be, then the head coach would not have been dumbfounded. He would have received information about the fraudulent classes.

The second type of paper class—the lectures—was populated by students who were not student-athletes as well. According to the report, what had occurred was the grapevine carried information about these easy classes, and students began to enroll. One might challenge the assertions that coaches and administrators were unaware of the academic fraud. The scam lasted for nearly two decades. If one acknowledges characteristics of informal networks, that is, the resilience, speed, and credibility, it seems unlikely that the information might not have somehow found its way to audiences on top levels.

APPLYING FEYNMAN'S THEORY

Feynman contended that upward networks become clogged because leaders may implicitly if not actively suppress information that they do not want to hear. One could reasonably make the assumption that this might have been happening at UNC—perhaps without the leaders even being aware they were, in fact, suppressing information.

Even if information had no formal networks on which to travel, the informal networks did carry related information. There was an awareness that bogus easy lecture classes existed. At one point, there were more non-student-athletes enrolled in the so-called lecture courses than those student-athletes who had been encouraged to take the courses.

What could have happened is that coaches who wanted their players to remain eligible had subtly suppressed information that would otherwise have forced the university to suspend or expel an athlete. If the information was available on the grapevine and the academic support service people were aware of the activity either no networks at all existed, or the networks were clogged.

TRANSMISSION VS. CONSTITUTIVE PERSPECTIVES

In the last chapter, we discussed transmission and constitutive perspectives of communication. The transmission perspective of communication analyzes interactions on the basis of whether a message was successfully transmitted from point A to point B. The constitutive perspective analyzes communication on the basis of how communication shapes relationships. A factor that seeded long-term problems in this case was spurious messages transmitted efficiently.

A desire—even a well-intentioned desire—to provide assistance to student-athletes can be used to rationalize behavior that could eventually launch a malignancy. The idea that all student-athletes desire or require bogus courses to succeed is inaccurate, insulting, and invidious. Eighteen years of implicit and explicit messaging that suggested that student-athletes could not succeed without sham courses was the foundation for what became a flawed and warped container. The crisis evolved because the bogus but effectively transmitted messages "athletes cannot succeed without these courses" distorted the organization's constitution.

Test Yourself:　Apply the Principles

Consider a sports organization with which you are familiar either as a player, coach, administrator, sports reporter, or fan.

- Identify at least three subsystems of that sports organization.
- From your perspective:
  - Are the walls of that subsystem permeable?
  - Does it seem as if there is requisite variety within these subsystems to allow for "throughput" and "output"?
  - Assuming that walls are permeable and there is requisite variety, how has the organization benefited?
  - If the walls were not permeable and there is little evidence of requisite variety, what have been the related problems?
- How would you describe the quality of the upward, downward, and horizontal formal networks in that sports organization? The external networks?

Chapter Conclusion—Take-Aways

- In order to communicate efficiently, sports organizations have to conceive of their entity as a collection of interdependent subsystems.
- To communicate interdependently, units within organizations have to be permeable— open to information from other units; and have requisite variety—ability and resources to process that information.
- Systems theory requires establishing formal networks that link the sports organization's subsystems.
  - An absence of horizontal networks may create a silo effect. In a sports context this could mean, for example, that facilities' staffers would not interact with trainers and coaches.
  - An absence of upward networks could undermine coaches' and general managers' abilities to make decisions based on complete information.
  - An absence of navigable external networks can affect relationships with media representatives, fans, community members, and government officials.
- The presence of formal networks does not guarantee that networks will be utilized as designed. Informal networks will exist in every organization, but the absence of credible formal networks will fuel the grapevine.
- Inefficient interdepartmental communication is often cited as a potential source of sports crises.

- System theory principles can be used to identify cases of poor communication in sports organizations.

QUESTIONS

- Assume you are the athletic director of your university.
  - What are the relevant subsystems?
  - What formal networks would you put in place to link-related departments?
  - How would you assure that your unit had requisite variety?
- Consider a league with which you were associated before college. For example, Little League, youth hockey, high school soccer league.
  - What communication challenges affected the league?
  - How would you characterize the quality of communication between subsystems?
  - What recommendations might you make to league administrators for improved internal communication?
- Assume you coordinate the NFL draft. How would you see your communication responsibilities in terms of systems theory?

Practitioner Perspective

Dave Echols

President and General Manager
Charleston RiverDogs.

Courtesy Dave Echols

The **Charleston RiverDogs** are a Single A Minor League Baseball team located in Charleston, South Carolina. They are an affiliate of the Tampa Bay Rays, play their games in a field that is colloquially called, *The Joe* and officially the Joseph A Riley Jr. Park. On a steamy Father's Day, I attended The Joe and saw, despite the heat, an exciting brand of baseball. The atmosphere was festive; many activities for kids at the park, multiple concessions, and friendly attendants. At one point, I was approached by an usher who asked if she could do anything for us, and when we asked for some water, she obliged and returned an inning or so later with cold refreshment. I noticed that she also interacted with other fans, similarly asking how they were doing and if she could be of help. There was a good crowd on this Sunday afternoon with some very knowledgeable spectators cheering the team.

Dave Echols is the President and General Manager of the RiverDogs. He was named General Manager in 2004 and was honored as South Atlantic General Manager of the year in 2013. In 2016, he became President as well as General Manager. Prior to the RiverDogs, Echols was GM of the Brockton Rox in the Northeast League and was named executive of the year in 2003. He has also worked for teams in Kingston, North Carolina, and Columbus, Ohio. I asked Dave about the role of communication as a factor that affects his team's success.

AZ. I imagine your work with the RiverDogs is multifaceted. Generally, how important is it for you to communicate effectively with your various audiences: Fans, Coaches, Players, Parent Club, Advertisers, Grounds Crew, other teams in the league? Is there another audience I have left out?

DE. Ownership is not local, so you could add them into the mix. What about the front office staff? It's extremely important for the RiverDogs to effectively communicate with all you listed, as a whole and each individually. While I am responsible for the overall message, it is important to have everyone relaying that same message…

AZ. Of these audiences, which group has the greatest communication challenges? That is, are there groups that are tougher to reach than others?

DE. All are important, and all have their challenges. When you analyze the question to the utmost, I guess I'd say the fans have the greatest challenges due to the diversity of their interests and our desire to reach everyone.

AZ. What do you think are the keys to successful communication for a person in your role?

DE. Honesty, transparency, and authenticity—all following our game plan for execution.

AZ. Has new media affected your ability to communicate with your various audiences?

DE. It has obviously enhanced it and allowed us to effectively reach our audiences, but it also, in this day and age, demands immediate communication, which at times is a significant challenge.

AZ. Is there an incident that reflects how your effective communication prevented some calamity or addressed a crisis to defuse the potential fallout?

DE. Pretty much every day in the summer and the weather patterns of the southeast dictate an impact on all the audiences who each require one on one communication.

AZ. In your opinion, is organizational culture a function of quality communication?

DE. It does seem to all come back to communication…

First Person   Avatar

A while back, our college had a function welcoming parents of students to the campus. There was a reception, an introduction to an art exhibit, and informal communications between parents, faculty, and the students who had enrolled.

For quite a while, I was conversing with a student who is studying Game Design in our college. The extent of his knowledge was remarkable, at least to me—a newbie if even that—to the world of video games and such gaming.

The student explained what he was studying and also his involvement in games. One of the games was particularly interesting to me. In it, an alternate universe had been created that had rules which governed the activities and capabilities of participants. He was, essentially, someone else in this game represented by an avatar. He/the avatar was a member of a virtual corporation. He had an assignment, much like I or anyone else has an assignment as a member of our organizations. He also had associates from around the world, members of this corporation who wanted to know how he was doing on his projects. There was this complete alternate universe with friends, superiors, staffers—with a goal to do whatever it was that was the objective of the game.

I asked dozens of questions, and he supplied answers patiently and, more often than not, eagerly. Eventually, I asked the question that was hanging around in my head the whole time. Did he ever confuse sight of his real world as he participated in this other one? Could people become so immersed in the game that they confused the avatar with their real selves?

I wonder about this now and again, and not just as it relates to electronic games. Can we become so adjusted to an alternate being we've conceived that we cease to be in touch with who we are? Actors run into this now and again. I was in a play once during my avocational acting days, when the lead playing a maniacal delinquent started behaving maniacally when the curtain came down as well. How long can you play a physician before you think you can write prescriptions? And in a more general sense, how many times can you put on your game face to be someone you are not before you become the person you are not? And then, how long can you be the person you are not before your body rejects or becomes infected by the impostor?

This relates to sports as well as theatre. As a sports executive, as a teammate, with fans, with the media, are sports figures who they are, or have they adopted the persona the game has attributed to them.

A while back, the Giants had a pitcher named John Montefusco, who was nicknamed "The Count." At one point, he took a step back and said something along the lines of, I am John Montefusco, but then I see this stranger on tape that everybody is calling the "The Count."

I think it is wise to take that step back now and again and make sure who you are, in sports or other organizational and interpersonal contexts, is really you as opposed to some avatar that you've created in the course of some game.

Chapter 4

Crises, Sports, and Communication

Aaron Rodgers

© Brian Cassella/TNS/Newscom

Chapter in a Nutshell

Athletes, teams, and sports organizations are often faced with crises. These crises require effective communication to repair the damage caused by the event. This chapter examines crisis communication in sports contexts.

Specifically, at the end of the chapter, students will be able to:

- Define a sports crisis.
- Cite examples of crises that have affected athletes, teams, and sports organizations.
- Identify and describe key terms related to crisis communication.
- Explain how an organization can plan for communication during crises.
- Identify common image repair strategies.

Sports Communication Prompts

- Below you will see statements pertaining to some aspect of communication and sports. For each item
  - Decide whether you agree or disagree with the statement.
  - Explain your rationale for the position.
  - If possible, support your position with examples.

1. Crises in sports are inevitable. Communicating after a crisis cannot restore the image after the damage is done. *The Decision*, not the decision, will forever stain LeBron James.

2. Deflategate was a fabricated issue made worse because of talking heads on the NFL and other dedicated sports channels. If it had not been for the media coverage, there would not have been a crisis.

3. The NFL must communicate transparently about the potential problems with its sport and concussions. They cannot worry about lawsuits.

4. The reason Morey's tweet caused a crisis was because of how the NBA reacted to it, not because of the content of his message.

We do not experience and thus we have no measure of the disasters we prevent.

J.K. Galbraith

When you make a mistake, there are only three things you should ever do about it: 1) admit it; 2) learn from it; 3) don't repeat it.

Paul "Bear" Bryant

Ten Sports Crises

- Major League baseball was rocked when an article in *The Athletic* suggested that the 2018 World Champion Houston Astros included a sophisticated method for stealing signs. The Astros manager and general manager were suspended by the commissioner and then fired by the team CEO. Subsequently, two other major league managers who had been on the Astros at the time of the World Series--Alex Cora and Carlos Beltran--"parted ways" with their respective employers for their involvement. This crisis affected not only the individuals and the Astros but major league baseball itself.

- In the Fall of 2021, Aaron Rodgers, the quarterback for the Green Bay Packers, tested positive for COVID-19. Rodgers had not been vaccinated prior to the diagnosis. However, months earlier, in response to a question about his vaccination status, Rodgers had stated that he'd been "immunized." Media commentators and many fans claimed that the immunization claim was nothing but a lie and that Rodgers had deliberately deceived the League and fans. Rodgers attempted to defend his comments and exonerate himself in an interview program. Some media commentators ridiculed the interview, suggesting that it too was duplicitous and exacerbated the crisis Rodgers, the Packers, and perhaps even the League faced.

- On November 12, 2021, a *Boston Globe* article reported that a high school coach had subjected high school athletes for years to "fat checks." Allegedly these were tests to assess the extent of body fat on an athlete. However, the athletes were told to become naked for these tests. Some body regions that were tested are not routinely examined when testing for body fat. There were claims that some people in the school administration, as well as other coaches, were aware of the "fat check" testing.

- E-mails surfaced during the first weeks of the 2021 football season that revealed that the head coach of the Las Vegas Raiders had made disparaging comments about African-Americans, women, and gays. The Raiders were off to a good start to their season when this story became news. The head coach who allegedly made the comments had won a Super Bowl when he coached the Tampa Bay Buccaneers and also spent time as a prime-time NFL broadcaster. Some of the e-mails had been sent to other members of the NFL, and therefore there were others who knew about the comments and may have, tacitly at least, agreed with them.

- In January 2018, ESPN broadcast a program entitled, "Is Anyone Listening: Crisis at Michigan State." The program was subtitled "Spartan Secrets" and highlighted allegations of sexually-abusive behavior at Michigan State University. The report suggested that student-athletes had been so abused and, moreover, that there was awareness at MSU that the accusations were legitimate. For Michigan State, there would be no suitable time for such a charge to be made, but the damage to the institution was compounded since it arrived on the heels of public charges that the institution was aware that Larry Nassar— a long-time employee—had taken advantage of his role as an athletics' trainer to sexually abuse young women gymnasts.

US Senator Dianne Feinstein talks with Aly Raisman, Simone Biles and Maggie Nichols. The gymnasts are all survivors of Larry Nasser's abuse.

© Rod Lamkey - CNP/picture alliance/ Consolidated News Photos/Newscom

- On January 20, 2019, during the NFC championship game, an official or officials clearly missed a pass interference penalty which would have likely made the New Orleans Saints victorious. The no-call did not give the game to the opponents. The Saints, despite the call, took the lead but relinquished it when the Rams tied the contest at the end of regulation. During overtime, the Saints again had an opportunity to win but lost possession and then lost the game. The Saints fandom, ownership, and local press were furious about the non-call.

- Chronic Traumatic Encephalopathy are three words that the National Football League would prefer never to have heard. They refer to a neurodegenerative disease that occurs when people have had multiple head injuries. A movie about CTE, *Concussion*, described not only the nature of the disease but also how the NFL attempted to discredit and bully Bennet Omalu, the doctor who first became aware of the problem. In a study released in July of 2017, it was found that nearly all of the brains of now-deceased football players reflect that these athletes had CTE (Mez et al, 2017, p. 360). This report caused understandable concern for NFL current and former players.

- On May 2, 2018, an article appeared in *the New York Times* reporting that five years prior, the cheerleaders for what is now the Washington Football Team had been required to travel to Costa Rica for a meeting with season ticket holders. At the meeting, the cheerleaders were obliged to pose topless for photographs, and attendees were invited to observe the photography session. Afterward, some of the women were told to accompany men as escorts to a nightclub event. A few days later, a video posted by *SportsPulse* caustically admonished the organization and owner Dan Snyder.

- TMZ published a report stating that then LA Clippers' owner Donald Sterling was heard on tape criticizing his then girlfriend for associating with African-Americans. The recording would have been damaging to any organization, but this clear racial bias was particularly problematic for the NBA, where an overwhelming number of players and staff members are African-American. Among Sterling's remarks were:
  - "It bothers me a lot that you want to broadcast that you're associating with Black people. Do you have to?"
  - "You can sleep with [Black people]. You can bring them in, you can do whatever you want. The little I ask you is not to promote it . . . and not to bring them to my games."
  - "I'm just saying, in your lousy . . . Instagrams, you don't have to have yourself with, walking with black people."

- In February 2014, NFL star running back Ray Rice was seen dragging his then fiancée out of an elevator after the two apparently had a physical battle. The NFL explored the situation and, in the summer of 2014, suspended Rice for two games. This seemed to many to be a light sentence for physically violent behavior. The situation was exacerbated in September of 2014 when a video surfaced showing Rice punching his fiancee in an elevator such that she was knocked into a handrail and became apparently unconscious. When this video surfaced, the Ravens dismissed Rice from the team, and Rice was suspended by the NFL. The matter became more complicated when it was revealed that the NFL had seen a copy of the punches in the elevator five months previously and still, despite having seen it, suspended Rice for only two games at that time. It was contended that only when the public saw the recording did the NFL suspend Rice indefinitely (Bien, 2014). Issues regarding light sentencing for NFL players surfaced again In August 2022, when a judge handed Cleveland Brown quarterback Deshaun Watson a six-game suspension for alleged sexual misconduct that many—including the NFL—felt deserved a more severe penalty. https://www.cnn.com/2022/08/03/sport/deshaun-watson-tony-buzbee-suspension-spt-intl/index.html

What Is a Sports Communication Crisis?

Sports crises abound. Many other incidents could supplement the ones cited above. You may have already thought about additional crisis events that you've observed or experienced.

We will define a sports crisis as *an anomalous event; that affects stakeholder perceptions of an athlete, team, or sports organization; which requires efficient communication to reduce the damage related to the event.* In other words, a sports crisis has to meet three criteria to be so labeled. It has (a) to be an atypical event, (b) to affect stakeholder perceptions of a sports entity, and (c) to require communication in order to repair the damage the crisis has caused.

If your university's basketball team loses the big game, you have no crisis in the context of crisis communication study, even though fans may consider the loss devastating. If the team's star player is injured, you do not have a crisis in the context of crisis communication, although some people may worry about how the injury will affect the revenues and fortunes of the team.

However, if it becomes known that members of the team were selling their complimentary tickets to scalpers, or the team members were conspiring with gamblers to alter the natural course of the games, then your team, athletic department, and university have a crisis. These situations would be anomalous events. They would likely have a damaging effect on the basketball program, the university's students, and the university's image, if not its financial health. The illicit activities would compel university officials to communicate to various audiences in order to reduce the effects of the crisis.

It may seem clear that a star athlete, coach, or general manager can do something that causes a crisis. However, a sports organization can have a crisis when others peripheral to daily operations behave reprehensibly. During a basketball game, the University of Southern Mississippi's pep squad band created a crisis for the school when band members shouted, "Where's Your Green Card" at an opponent taking a foul shot. Two days after the horrific Newtown murders, President Obama spoke at a prayer vigil for the victims. This address interrupted the broadcast of a Sunday Night Football game. A third-string long snapper for the Division II University of North Alabama football team— whose season had already ended—tweeted during the broadcast. He wrote: "Get that n . . . off the air I want to watch football."

The pep squad band may not report to the Southern Mississippi athletic director. Regardless, the athletic director had to address the crisis caused by the band's chant. The University of North Alabama is hardly a high-profile football powerhouse, but the power of social media and an irresponsible marginal player created a crisis for the institution.

What Do Crisis Communicators Do?

Crisis communication involves identifying internal and external receivers who must receive information during times of crisis. Crisis communicators conceive, create, and disseminate messages to these internal and external receivers and prepare to receive and respond to feedback from these audiences.

More specifically, crisis communicators:

Prepare for crises. While crises are not normal events, one can prepare for them by developing relationships with internal and external audiences, anticipating potential crises, and considering, ahead of time, how to address types of crises that can be anticipated. One cannot know that a third-string backup long snapper will tweet irresponsibly, but one can inform all student-athletes of the hazards of social media. An athletic department can conduct simulations regarding how they would proceed in the event of some social media posting that embarrasses the institution.

Identify audiences. An effective crisis communicator considers who needs to receive information during times of crisis. These audiences will be external to the organization as well as internal. We know or hope that sexual abuse is an anomalous occurrence and that most student-athletes engage intimately only when there is consent. However, an organization could identify the internal and external stakeholders who would have to be notified if such an event occurred.

Conceive and construct messages. Crisis communicators identify units of information that they wish to relay to the identified audiences. Communicators then create messages that are composites of these units of information. One could not predict that a global pandemic would derail our activities and all but put a stop to sports contests. However, one could prepare information about local health care facilities, contact information, and counseling centers that would likely be essential when dealing with any health crisis.

Select the media or medium to be used to relay information. A crisis communicator evaluates methods for communicating and selects the best method for relaying information. What is the best way to convey a message? Should a commissioner tweet; deliver a speech; hold a press conference; use Facebook; post a notice on the web, place an announcement in a well-read publication? Should an e-mail be blasted to all relevant audiences? Should the league request time on an interview program to present its perspectives? The best method will depend on a number of factors, among which are: the nature of the audience, the crisis itself, the league or team's history of responsibility during crisis, relationships the organization has formed with the audience prior to the crisis, and the nature of the message content.

Respond to feedback. Crisis communicators acknowledge, or should acknowledge, that audiences will have questions and reactions that pertain to the information generated by the organization. The event regarding Donald Sterling may have been first communicated on TMZ, but TMZ is not the lone stakeholder that should receive messages. Responses will be sent to multiple audiences. And crisis communicators need to anticipate reactions they will hear/read from various audiences.

Evaluate the success of crisis communication efforts. After the immediate problems related to the crisis have passed, crisis communicators must assess the effort, discuss how they could have been more effective, and record plans for activity if faced with similar crises in the future.

Myths about Crisis Communication

Eric Dezenhall and John Weber's book *Damage Control* is subtitled *Why Everything You Know About Crisis Management Is Wrong*. It is an interesting subtitle. One assumes the antecedent to the pronoun in the subtitle is the reader. It is arrogant to think that all readers are ignorant or have been misguided and less than humble to imply that the lone bearers of wisdom are the authors. Research and case studies, actually, do not support all of the authors' claims. However, Dezenhall and Weber are correct when they suggest that there are misconceptions about how organizations should communicate during crises.

A review of how some behave during crises makes this point well. Leagues have addressed crises by pretending that they will go away; by stonewalling; by denying that which could not be plausibly denied, and even by attempting to intimidate those casting legitimate doubts about the culpability. One could argue that Penn State University did many of these when confronted with charges that the university and football team knew that a coach was an inveterate pedophile. Pete Rose adamantly denied that he had bet on baseball even when confronted with clear evidence. He only eventually admitted culpability when he thought that was his ticket to reinstatement. The NFL's initial reaction to the CTE study published by Dr. Omalu and others included denial and intimidation.

Players have said, "no comment" when confronted with challenges. They have assumed that these two words would avoid complications when in fact, these two words have dug them in deeper. One could make the case that players accused of consuming illegal drugs have done just that. When Alex Rodriguez was initially confronted with the *Sports Illustrated* report that he had tested positive for illegal substances, he said, "You'll have to talk to the union." Asked if there was an explanation for positive test results, Rodriguez told *SI*, "I'm not saying anything."

New York Yankees third baseman Alex Rodriguez chose not to comment on illegal drug accusations.

Owners have attempted to displace responsibility on some third party, assuming that this will remove guilt, when in fact, such communications have reduced the respect and credibility publics attribute to these shortsighted organizations. Donald Sterling's initial response to the recordings of his racist statements was that his girlfriend had provoked the comments.

Misconceptions about crisis communication are problematic not only because they are logically flawed but also because the inaccurate notions become floorboards for communication plans that could not possibly be supported by the warped foundation for construction. Inept communications become part of the crisis itself. Many scandals are recalled more for how the leagues communicated during them than for the activities that created the crises.

Since ineffective crisis communication can exacerbate crises, and since these ineffective communication efforts may be based on misconceptions, it is important to understand fully not only what crisis communication is but what it is not. Consider the following five common myths about crisis communication.

MYTH 1—CRISIS COMMUNICATION IS SOLELY A REACTIVE ACTIVITY.

Crisis communication does, of course, involve responding to crises. However, the successful crisis communicator can prepare for and, in some instances, preempt crises because of proactive activities.

You hope that your football coaches do not accept money from shoe companies. You hope that an assistant coach does not recruit illegally. You hope that student-athletes attend classes and do not inappropriately use social media. However, you do not have to wait until such events transpire to attempt to prevent them, and you can prepare for not entirely unpredictable events. The notion that crisis communication is solely a reactive enterprise might seem benign, but it is not. A reactive conceptualization precludes taking preparatory steps that enable an organization to communicate effectively during crises.

For example, relationships with stakeholders are a key factor in determining the success of crisis communication efforts. Neighbors whose homes are in the vicinity of your football stadium are such stakeholders. Assuming that crisis communication is a reactive enterprise may result in not establishing positive relationships that could have been developed and nourished. If rowdy spectators damage property after a game, the neighbors may be more inclined to believe placating team messages if positive relationships have been established.

MYTH 2—CRISIS COMMUNICATION IS SYNONYMOUS WITH MEDIA RELATIONS. THE PRIMARY ACTIVITY OF CRISIS COMMUNICATORS INVOLVES DEALING WITH THE MEDIA.

The media are important players in sports crisis communication. Media representatives may, in fact, expose the crisis. Fans and sports observers first found out about the Washington cheerleaders because of a *New York Times* article or the reposting of that information on the Internet at various sites. The website TMZ reported Sterling's incendiary comments. Also, after a crisis, the media are important stakeholders for a number of obvious reasons.

However, the media are not the only important audience or player. The media may not even be the primary audience in a crisis situation. There are at least two reasons not to consider crisis communication to be synonymous with media relations. The first is that considering the two to be synonymous means, inevitably, that an organization will be ignoring other key audiences when considering their communication efforts. When Michigan State University faced its crisis with Larry Nassar, it did indeed have to communicate with the media. However, it had other very important audiences. Students, current coaches, parents of students, victims, families of the victims, faculty on campus, dormitory directors, the counseling center at the school—all these audiences were crucial, and care had to be taken to ensure that sensitive messages were relayed to them. Considering the primary audience to be the media would inevitably relegate these other important stakeholders to a relatively insignificant status.

A second reason to see media relations and crisis communication as distinct is that if an organization defines crisis communication and media relations synonymously, it might assume that it does not have a crisis unless the media becomes involved. The results of such a parochial conception can be catastrophic and are ironic. Incidents that became media events might never have become such if the organization assumed it had a crisis on its hands regardless of whether the media was yet involved. Michigan State University had a crisis before the ESPN broadcast. Students had brought the incidents to the attention of university representatives. Journalists had done investigative reporting and, according to subsequent reports, had confronted coaches with the information. Athletes who were not involved in the offenses had, nevertheless, heard about them. Damage to Michigan State, at least from the perspective of internal stakeholders, had occurred. Thinking that the crisis does not become a crisis until it is exposed is shortsighted.

MYTH 3—CRISIS COMMUNICATION IS ABOUT SPIN CONTROL. THE JOB OF THE CRISIS COMMUNICATORS IS TO SPIN A NEGATIVE SITUATION SO IT SEEMS LIKE A POSITIVE ONE.

Should the NFL have attempted to spin the CTE-related crisis? Should the NBA have tried to spin the Sterling crisis? Would it be wise to minimize the effects of concussion-related crises or the frequency of officials allowing biases to affect game scores?

The job of the crisis communicator is not to spin, and it is counterproductive to think of crisis communication in this way. Spinning is a term that has come to be used as a metaphor for taking reality and changing it—spinning it so that it will be seen from a different vantage point. By spinning, the event may seem to be something other than what it is. Take a negative event and spin it a different way, and it may become a positive one. A good spin may make a crisis no longer what it was, transforming it into a more palatable and attractive variation.

This is a prevalent assumption about crisis communication and an especially insidious one because of how it has become normalized. A careful reading of books and articles written by practitioners and academics suggests that spinning is harmful and, at best, will have short-term positive effects. The almost universal conclusion by all—practitioners and academics alike—who have studied cases in crisis communication is that spinning disorients the organization, makes it difficult for the organization to see the crisis clearly, and erodes the legitimacy of the organization.

There are at least two reasons why spinning is inappropriate. The first is that spinning is inherently unethical. It is an attempt to confuse an audience by distorting reality. The second reason is that, from a pragmatic perspective, spinning actually makes crisis communication efforts more difficult. Truth typically does surface, and when truth is juxtaposed with spun reality, the communicators who attempt to present the distorted view lose credibility. As we will see, an important criterion for crisis communication success is organizational reputation. Reputation is typically enhanced by candor and damaged by duplicity.

MYTH 4—CRISIS COMMUNICATION INVOLVES COMMUNICATING ONLY TO EXTERNAL AUDIENCES.

The Washington Football Team, in the wake of the Sports Pulse video, had to communicate with external audiences. However, they also had to communicate with their current cheerleaders, players, and staff members.

Even those who acknowledge that media members are not the primary audience for communication sometimes assume that crisis communication is about public relations. While some people who deal with public relations are aware that internal publics are important, and while external publics are crucial to effective crisis communication, it is essential to remember that crisis communication addresses internal as well as external audiences.

MYTH 5—CRISIS COMMUNICATION IS A LINEAR ACTIVITY.

A common misconception in all matters related to communication is that communication is a linear activity. That is, there is an assumption that communication goes one way—from sender to receiver. Communication is a non-linear activity. Receivers of information respond or can respond to messages that are sent to them. The process of communicating does not end once a message has been generated.

For example, practitioners and researchers counsel spokespersons not to say "no comment" when confronted with questions about a crisis. It is beyond shortsighted and borders on the stupidly foolish to assume that because you say, "No comment," a receiver will simply absorb this message. People do not take in messages like a bullet to the chest. Receivers will not hear, "We have no comment on this matter" as "They have no comment on this matter." Receivers will respond with a host of speculations, such as "Perhaps they have something to hide" or "They do not have their act together." There will likely be follow-up questions if not of a particular spokesperson but of others who, receivers may perceive, are in the know.

The NFL could not declare or intimate that the CTE crisis is meaningless, and it stops there. Communication is not linear.

Key Crisis Communication Terms

Several terms are important to remember when we consider crisis communication.

STAKEHOLDERS

R. Edward Freeman is one of the first authors to use the term stakeholder as it relates to organizational communication. He did so in his book *Strategic Management: A Stakeholder Approach*. Freeman defines a stakeholder as "any group or individual who can affect, or is affected by, the achievement of a corporation's purpose" (Freeman 2018, p. vi). In crisis communication, we use the term stakeholder in the same way. Stakeholders either have a stake in the issues germane to the crisis, or the organization wants these receivers to have a stake in the organization and the crisis. Internal stakeholders are those people who are within the focal system. External stakeholders are people outside of the focal system.

STAKEHOLDER THEORY

Stakeholder theory refers to the assumption that during crises, there are multiple stakeholders, and each discrete group is likely to need to receive different messages. When identifying stakeholders, all internal and external audiences need to be considered, and the appropriate messages for these audiences need to be created and disseminated.

LEGITIMACY

Legitimacy is an oft-used term in crisis communication literature. It refers to stakeholder perception of an organization's behavior. In essence, when an organization is perceived as acting appropriately, it is seen as legitimate; when it is perceived as behaving inappropriately, the organization loses legitimacy.

If, for example, a team is honest when it deals with fans; complies with the law; drafts intelligently; prices fairly, seems to desire to win and treats its players well, the team is likely to maintain a perception among stakeholders of legitimacy. If a team "tanks" at the end of the season; raises ticket prices capriciously; seems to function solely to generate revenue as opposed to acting to meet the needs of supporting fans; and/or appears to attract societal misfits on the roster; the team will lose legitimacy. An organization does not have legitimacy as much as legitimacy is attributed to it (Allen and Caillouet, 1994, p. 45-46). Since legitimacy is an attribution and is a function of perceived behavior "having a noble purpose . . . is no guarantee that an organization will be perceived as legitimate" (Seeger et al., 1998, p. 254). In other words, how stakeholders assess actions will determine legitimacy, not whether the organization's intent was inherently or actually honorable.

During crises, for reasons related to the crisis itself or to communications about the crisis, an organization either gains or loses legitimacy. When it was reported and confirmed that the New Orleans Saints paid players to physically hurt opponents so that they would be unable to play—the so-called Bountygate crisis—the Saints lost legitimacy, as did the entire League.

The Bountygate crisis hurt not only the Saints, but the entire League.

The objective of crisis communication is to repair legitimacy when that is necessary and to ensure that a team does not lose legitimacy in those instances when stakeholders are temporarily holding judgment.

IMAGE REPAIR THEORY

After the report surfaced that cheerleaders had been asked to pose topless, the legitimacy of the Washington franchise was affected. Image repair theory suggests that organizations can repair and attempt to restore legitimacy by communicating efficiently. The theory identifies several different types of messages that can be employed. These approaches include denial, apology, attack, transcendence, bolstering, intimidation, corrective action, compensation, minimization, displacement, mortification, compassion, suffering, and differentiation. Each of these image repair strategies is discussed and explained later in this chapter.

FOUR RS

Relationships, Reputation, Responsibility, and Response are four variables examined in crisis communication research. The fact that relationships and reputation are considered significant supports the perspective that crisis communication is not solely a reactive activity.

Relationships refers to the connection between the focal system--for example, a team or a league–and its various stakeholders. These relationships are established or exist prior to any crisis yet are variables that affect crisis communication efforts.

Reputation refers to the extent to which the focal system is seen as legitimate. Reputation is established or exists prior to any sports crisis and is strengthened or tarnished on the basis of the crisis and crisis communication activity.

Responsibility refers to the extent to which the stakeholders consider the focal system responsible for the crisis. If an athlete commits a violent offense, assuming that the perpetrator had no previous history, the team may not be seen as responsible. The team might not have known that the player was violent, or the violent behavior may be a clear aberration. However, if a second or third or fourth athlete on the same team commits a similar violent offense, stakeholders may begin to believe that the team does not consider the character of its players when they hire or sign them. In this situation, a team could be considered Responsible for a crisis that involves a player.

Response, predictably, refers to how a team or league or player has responded to the crisis in terms of its behavior and communication efforts.

As is likely apparent, each of these can affect the others. The reputation a league enjoys may affect the relationships that the league has with its stakeholders. The relationships may affect the extent to which stakeholders will accept a response. The extent of responsibility for a crisis will affect the nature of the response. The response during a crisis will affect the reputation after the fact.

STABILITY

Stability is a term that has a counterintuitive meaning in the language of crisis communication. Stability refers to how frequently an organization has crises. Therefore, an athletic department, for example, that has regularly violated recruiting protocol is considered to have high stability. There is an obvious correlation between reputation and stability: the greater the stability, the higher the likelihood of a weak reputation. As we saw in the last section, there is also a correlation between stability and perception of responsibility. Finally, there is a correlation between stability and the requirements for responses during crises: the higher the stability, the more challenging the requirements for crisis communicators.

INSTRUCTING INFORMATION

When a crisis involves a health risk, organizations need to communicate how to address the associated risks. In 2020 and 2021, the entire world learned of the importance of such instructing information when we faced the COVID-19 pandemic. Explaining how to preempt the spread of the virus and what to do if you require medical aid is called instructing information. Nightly, during the first several months of the pandemic, on any of the major network news reports, a doctor or doctors informed viewers of ways to reduce the chances of infection. Leagues developed official COVID protocols that were put in place to preempt the spread of the disease. During the last months of 2021 and into 2022, these protocols required canceling games and were having an impact on the quality of the sports product when games were played. Athletes could be prohibited from participating if they had tested positive, and the rules varied depending on whether a player had been vaccinated. Some athletes, like unvaccinated Buffalo Bills wide receiver Cole Beasley, complained bitterly about the rules when he was not permitted to play in an important late-season game. "Just to be clear," he posted on his Instagram account, "COVID is not keeping me out of this game. The rules are." Despite such criticism, leagues are required to communicate instructing information during health crises.

Buffalo Bills receiver Cole Beasley challenged the NFL COVID 19 protocols

© UPI / Alamy Stock Photo

NUGGETS/MESSAGES

The word nuggets is used to identify specific messages that crisis communicators want to convey to audiences. In simple terms, a nugget is a vital piece of a message. Crisis communicators are encouraged to identify nuggets that will be relayed to each group of stakeholders and to stay on message when communicating to the audiences. After the nuggets are determined, crisis communicators create messages that are comprised of these nuggets.

HALO AND VELCRO EFFECTS

The Halo Effect is the tendency for some positive attribution of a unit to remain with the unit subsequently. A program that is known as "squeaky clean" in terms of recruiting behavior, for example, may experience the Halo Effect when accused of some duplicity. The Velcro Effect is the tendency for negative attributions to stick to a company because of negative performance history. As Coombs and Holladay (2001) write, "A performance history is like Velcro; it attracts and snags additional reputational damage" (p. 335). When Jerry Tarkanian moved from Long Beach State to UNLV and then to Fresno State, he had established a reputation, deservedly or not, as someone who recruited players who may not have been academically oriented. An infamous photo of basketball players from UNLV seated in a hot tub with a renowned gambler did nothing to reduce the perception. Because of his past, " Tark the Shark," as he was known, was under constant scrutiny by the NCAA. The Velcro Effect applied to him. He continually pushed back, claiming that other bigger schools were violators, but for some reason, they were getting a pass. He was not because the Velcro effect applied.

SUPPORTING BEHAVIOR AND HONORING THE ACCOUNT

Two clear illustrations of these phenomena occurred in Cincinnati and New England. When Pete Rose was banished from baseball and accused of betting on games, his reputation and relationships among fans of the Cincinnati Reds were such that regardless of the overwhelming evidence, the fans honored the account and promulgated the arguments that he spewed in defense of the alleged transgressions. Except in Boston and thereabouts, there was widespread suspicion that quarterback Tom Brady had indeed deflated footballs. All through New England, however, Coach Bill Belichick's professorial explanation of the Ideal Gas Law seemed to be accepted and spread by many of those with allegiance to the team.

Because of a positive relationship with a team or league or athletic department, stakeholders are more likely to honor the account than had there been a negative relationship. Honoring the account means believing and accepting the account. Sometimes the relationship between stakeholder and focal system is so good that the stakeholder will act as an agent and spread the nuggets in informal and formal conversations with other stakeholders. When this happens, the stakeholders are said to be exhibiting supporting behavior.

Test Yourself:	Apply the Principles

You are the athletic director of a large university. It is brought to your attention that students on the men's and women's hockey teams have cheated on a take-home final examination. A professor has sent you copies of student exams from three students on the men's team and three students on the women's team. On the exams, the professor has highlighted sections that are nearly the same on each test. To date, as far as you know, the professor has not notified anyone else about these transgressions.

- Who are the key stakeholders that need to receive information about this potential, if not current, crisis?
- What different messages do these stakeholders need to receive?
- What methods would you employ to transmit these messages to these stakeholders?
- What vehicles would you put in place to receive feedback from the messages?

Image Repair Approaches

ATTACK

When Roger Clemens was accused of using steroids, an approach he took was to attack his primary accuser. Clemens's lawyer Rusty Hardin attacked Brian McNamee, asking the Clemens accuser if McNamee just "made things up." Hardin told the jury, "We're not going to talk bad about anybody except Brian McNamee." And during the entire trial and during all the pretrial talk, that is precisely what Clemens and his legal team did: attack McNamee's credibility (Frommer, 2012).

Attorneys for Roger Clemens went on the attack as a defense
strategy for their client.

BOLSTERING

Bolstering occurs when spokespersons identify the achievements of a focal system that may be peripheral to any specific crisis. The bolstering is an attempt to offer a positive perspective when the crisis is
shedding a negative light.

After the story about the cheerleaders surfaced, the team posted a statement on its website after the
May 2, 2018, *New York Times* article. In it, the team acknowledged its "appreciation and respect for our
cheerleaders" and went on to refer to the various work the cheerleaders did for the community and with
the military. In general, the team stated how proud it was of the cheerleaders and how the team "will
continue" to "take all necessary measures" to make the environment for the cheerleaders safe.

After the July 2017 study on the prevalence of CTE, the NFL issued a statement indicating that the
League is "committed to supporting scientific research." The NFL stated that the League had "pledged
100 million dollars" for independent medical research, which was a supplement to the 100 million the
League "and its partners are already spending on medical and neuroscience research."

Both the Washington Football Team and the NFL statements are examples of bolstering. The team
spoke about how proud they are of the cheerleaders' community efforts and how the team "supports
them" and will "*continue* to take measures to create a safe and respectful work environment." The NFL
spoke of its financial commitment to scientific research.

COMPASSION

After the head coach and assistant basketball coach of the Oklahoma State women's basketball team
died in a plane crash, the university issued the following statement:

> The Oklahoma State family is devastated by this tragedy. Kurt was an exemplary leader and a
> man of character who had a profound impact on his student-athletes. He was an outstanding
> coach and a wonderful person. Coach Budke elevated our women's basketball program to new
> levels of success. He and his staff raised our profile in the nation's toughest conference.

In March 2019, the Boeing Company faced a crisis for the second time in six months when one of its planes crashed, resulting in fatalities. The company's CEO stated: "On behalf of the entire Boeing team, we extend our deepest sympathies to the families and loved ones of those who have lost their lives in these two tragic accidents."

Compassion is an approach that attempts to avoid the loss of legitimacy by expressing concern, consideration, and sympathy for those affected by the crisis.

COMPENSATION

A way to attempt to restore legitimacy is to compensate those who have been affected by the crisis. Michigan State University announced that it had agreed to compensate the more than three hundred women who had been victimized by MSU employee Larry Nassar. The sum total of the settlement was five hundred million dollars. On that day, the interim president of Michigan State, John Engler, issued a statement. In it, he wrote that MSU had worked hard to make changes that would preclude a "monster" like Nassar from ever surfacing again. The president said that the compensation was a result of "a successful mediation" that had been a priority for then-interim president Engler from the beginning so that an outcome would be "fair and equitable."

Compensation that has come about because of legal action is understandably not as likely to restore legitimacy to the same extent as compensation that comes about before pressure was placed on the organization. Despite the compensation, the university and President Engler were criticized. On June 20, 2018, 130 sexual abuse victims of Nassar signed a letter sent to Michigan State's governing board requesting that the board remove Engler, saying he has reinforced what they called a "culture of abuse" at the university. In addition to criticizing the interim president, the letter singled out individual trustees and strongly admonished them. Individual trustees' behavior was called "appalling" and "horrifying." Eventually, in January 2019, President Engler was forced to resign.

Clearly, compensation is not always successful at repairing legitimacy. But it can be. In a non-sports-related case, for example, a food company, Schwan's, compensated not only those who became ill after consuming a product but those who thought they might be ill and wanted to seek medical attention. To be sure, the situations are not analogous in that in the Schwan case, the company compensated promptly before any legal action was taken. Also, in the Schwan case—while they did not know it at the time they offered the compensation—the problem was not a direct result of bad foodstuffs but rather related to the company that had been contracted to transport the foods.

CORRECTIVE ACTION

In January 2021, Michigan State University posted a letter to the university community entitled "Eradicating RVSM remains key priority for MSU." In the letter, university administrators identified nine separate steps they had taken to preempt and/or address RVSM (Relationship Violence and Sexual Misconduct).

In 2009, the NBA faced a crisis when one of its referees, Tom Donaghy, was accused of—and then admitted to–betting on games that he officiated. Subsequently, NBA commissioner David Stern issued the following statement:

> We would like to assure our fans that no amount of effort, time or personnel is being spared to assist in this investigation, to bring justice to an individual who has betrayed the most sacred trust in professional sports, and to take the necessary steps to protect against this ever happening again.

Organizations take corrective action or speak of taking corrective action when they inform stakeholders about what they are doing to ensure that such a crisis never occurs again. This is a very common and, when genuine, effective form of image restoration.

A famous crisis case in major league baseball involved corrective action. Members of the Chicago White Sox were accused of taking money to intentionally lose to the Cincinnati Reds in the 1919 World Series. Eight White Sox players were indicted on October 22, 1920, and major league baseball lost a measure of legitimacy.

While other organizations during the early part of the twentieth century had been criticized by muckrakers for inappropriate corporate behaviors and consequently had lost legitimacy, baseball had "positioned itself as a public virtue" and had enjoyed strong perceptions of legitimacy. What became known as the Black Sox scandal, however, highlighted that legitimacy could be an ephemeral phenomenon.

In order to restore its image, baseball owners took measures that had been unprecedented. They hired a disciplinarian, Justice Kennesaw Mountain Landis, to be the commissioner of baseball. Prior to hiring Landis, baseball was overseen by a group of three persons. The hiring of the impartial and reputably tough Landis was an attempt to ensure that the game would be seen as impregnable, not a sport that would tolerate questionable behavior. Enforcing that perception, Landis banished the eight White Sox players from baseball despite the fact that the eight had been exonerated in court. While the players had not been found innocent of taking bribes and throwing the games, a jury had found them to be not guilty of defrauding baseball. Nevertheless, Landis banished the players stating that "Regardless of the verdict of juries, no player who throws a ballgame . . . will ever play professional baseball."

DEFEASIBILITY

Sometimes organizations argue that blame should not be attributed to them because it is not feasible that they should be held responsible for the actions that created a crisis.

In the University of North Carolina academic fraud crisis, the university contended that it was not feasible to blame the athletic department for the scandal. They claimed that what occurred at UNC is what happens at many schools. There are easy classes that all students know about. At UNC, the school argued, athletes were only one population among others that enrolled. While the existence of the classes is indefensible, the school suggested that this was not an athletics' issue and, therefore, the NCAA should not punish the athletic department. This defense helped the university in its legal battle with the NCAA.

However, the argument is flawed. The so-called "paper classes" at UNC were initially Independent Studies and were designed specifically for athletes. Athletes did not discover classes and enroll in them. The classes were created for athletes, and athletes were encouraged to take them. Significantly as it relates to crisis communication in sports, the defeasibility approach did not have the effect of restoring UNC's legitimacy, at least among media representatives. Mark Titus, a former college basketball player at Ohio State, now writes about sports and is a contributor to The Ringer, a sports and popular culture website. In October 2017, Titus captured concisely what many sportspeople were wondering. "How in the hell did North Carolina get away with this?" (Titus, 2017).

Similar media reactions were described in an article published in the Raleigh *News&Observer* that used the Titus question in its headline. "'How the Hell Did North Carolina Get Away With This?' Media react to NCAA ruling on UNC" (Bennett, 2017).

DENIAL

One sentence in the Washington Football Team statement regarding the alleged cheerleader incident reads, "Based on the dialogue we've had with a number of current and former cheerleaders over the past 48 hours, we've heard very different first-hand accounts that directly contradict many of the details of the May 2 article" (L. Lewis, 2018).

Roger Clemens, in addition to attacking his accuser, vehemently denied the charges that he had used performance-enhancing drugs. In December 2007, Clemens issued what had become a recurring position: "I want to state clearly and without qualification: I did not take steroids, human growth hormone or any other banned substances at any time in my baseball career or, in fact, my entire life" (Curry and Wilson, 2007).

DIFFERENTIATION

Differentiation is a technique used to explain why what has occurred in your organization is different from an offense that has been committed by another organization.

When baseball pitcher Andy Pettitte was accused of having used illegal drugs, the athlete used differentiation as a complementary strategy to improve his image. Pettitte acknowledged his error, apologized to fans, and clearly expressed his embarrassment. However, in addition, he explained that he had taken the steroids because he hoped the drug would expedite the healing process necessitated by injury. By identifying the purpose for taking the drug, Pettitte intimated that what he was doing was different from the offenses of other baseball players who had used steroids to enhance performance.

DISPLACEMENT

Displacement is a very common image restoration technique. The approach here is to displace blame onto another party.

When the city of Boston could not contain the destructive exuberance of revelers after the New England Patriots defeated the Carolina Panthers in a Super Bowl game played in February of 2004, the mayor of Boston quickly blamed local universities for not policing the students more efficiently. The objective was to displace responsibility from the city for poor preparation onto the universities in the vicinity.

It is a child's game to displace responsibility on someone else; a child's game utilized by many adults when their backs are to the wall. The success of the approach is based on the integrity of the argument, the relationships established by the organization with its stakeholders, the reputation of the organization, and the regularity of crises besetting the organization.

In the UNC case, Deborah Crowder and Julius Nyang'oro were identified as the persons on whom the crisis should be blamed. Neither Crowder nor Nyang'oro should be condoned for their roles in the scandal, however, had it not been for academic advisors and some people who preferred not to see what was obvious for nearly twenty years, the activity that fueled the crisis would likely have lasted far less than twenty years.

INTIMIDATION

Intimidation is often used in conjunction with attacks. When Dr. Bennet Omalu revealed what his research discovered as it relates to football and concussions, his reputation was attacked. The Union of Concerned Scientists posted, "The NFL Tried to Intimidate Scientists Studying the Link Between Pro Football and Traumatic Brain Injury" (Union of Concerned Scientists). The book *League of Denial* makes similar claims (Fainaru-Wada and Fainaru, 2013, pp. 189–191; 197). Regardless of the legitimacy of the claims in the Concerned Scientists article or *League of Denial*, intimidation is a very shortsighted approach to image restoration. It would only be successful if the intimidation mutes a whistle-blower completely such that information that could damage legitimacy does not surface. It is an unethical approach, and given access to information in the twenty-first century, it is an approach that is unlikely to be successful.

MINIMIZATION

Minimization is a technique that is used to downplay the significance of a crisis. McGuire and McKinnon contend that baseball slugger Mark McGwire used minimization when he confessed to his use of steroids. McGwire attempted to minimize the damage by contending that while he took steroids, the drugs did not help him connect with a baseball (McGuire and McKinnon, 2012, p 36).

Some contend that Serena Williams was more heavily criticized for challenging tennis umpires than male players like John McEnroe

When Serena Williams excoriated an umpire during the 2018 US Open, she employed minimization in the same way she did in a prior US Open when she had challenged a linesperson. "People yell at linespeople all the time," she said (Brazeal, 2012, p 244). An interesting sidebar with the Williams incident is that during the years when John McEnroe and Jimmy Connors were tennis superstars, they regularly challenged linespeople when calls did not go their way. These challenges were not mild. McEnroe entitled a memoir *You Cannot Be Serious* which was a regular barbed comment when he disagreed with a call, and not one of his more volatile outbursts. While there were sportswriters and fans who questioned the merit of these challenges, the criticism that Williams received after her incident seems out of proportion when juxtaposed with the attention that counterparts McEnroe and Connors received. This point is underscored in the book, *Sidelined* by Julie DiCaro (2021, pp. 162-166).

MORTIFICATION

When athletes humbly describe their embarrassment at what has occurred, they are, wittingly or otherwise, using the technique called mortification. Often mortification is accompanied by an apology and, all too often, only when the person has been caught. NFL quarterback Michael Vick faced a crisis when news surfaced that he had encouraged and sponsored bloody dogfighting competitions. In his article about Vick, Smith describes the various image repair approaches the now ex-quarterback employed. One approach was mortification. When incontrovertible evidence surfaced, Vick made the following statement:

> I want to personally apologize to Commissioner Goodell, Arthur Blank [owner of Atlanta Falcons] coach Bobby Petrino, my Atlanta Falcons teammates; you know for our-for our previous discussions we had. And I was not honest and forthright in our discussions, and, you know, I was ashamed and totally disappointed in myself to say the least (J. Scott Smith, 2012, p. 159).

PENITENTIAL AND CAUSAL APOLOGIES

Two types of apologies are described in the crisis communication literature. The first, a *penitential* apology, is recommended over the other, a *causal* apology. In a penitential apology, the organization expresses remorse and does not offer any explanation that describes why they are in a position to have to apologize. In a causal apology, the contrition is attenuated by a reason that accounts for why events evolved as they did.

A case that illustrates the distinction between the types of apologies took place in Lubbock, Texas, and involved the Hampton University Women's basketball team. The case involved the wrongful arrest of three African-Americans.

In a Walmart parking lot, a white woman was duped in a scam that is called a pigeon scam. In a pigeon scam, the perpetrators approach a victim and say that they have found some money. The outlaws attempt to con the target by claiming that without a lawyer, they—those who found the money—will not be able to retain the funds. The scammer then offers the target an opportunity to partner and receive some of the found money. If the target would be willing to front the money necessary for a lawyer, then the scammer would hire the lawyer. Then, according to the con, the scammer and the target would share the found money.

It is a bizarre con and might lead readers to wonder who would be sufficiently foolish to be victimized by it. Nevertheless, this scenario played out in the Walmart parking lot. The woman in the car gave the scammers—who were black—money to obtain a lawyer. The target then went home and relayed the incident to her husband. The husband recognized the scam and contacted the police.

The police returned to the parking lot with the target. The police spotted two African-Americans in a car. The police asked them if they had recently found some money. They said they had not. Eventually, a third African-American came out of Walmart, and the three began driving. The police followed the car.

The people in the car were the head coach of Hampton University's basketball team, the assistant coach, and the spouse of the head coach. Hampton University was in town to play Texas Tech the following evening. The lone characteristic that the scammers had in common with the coaches was that both the scammers and the coaches are black. Nevertheless, the police followed the coach's car back to the team's motel. The target rode with the police as they followed. When the police car arrived at the motel, the target was asked if she could identify the scammers. The target did identify the coaches as the scammers. The coach, the assistant, and the spouse were arrested.

This arrest proved to be a national nightmare for not only the city of Lubbock but for Texas Tech University. The city especially was excoriated in the national media. The city police had arrested people who had been shopping at Walmart because of a positive identification that seemed to be based solely on skin color. Angry accusations were made that the city was racist. Subsequently, the target recanted her identification, and the coaches were released. The image of the city, however, had taken a severe blow.

The mayor of the city traveled to Hampton, Virginia to apologize for the incident. However, the mayor's apology was couched with an explanation. She suggested that the police had an excuse. The mayor claimed that since it was not until after the arrest that the target had recanted the incorrect identification, what the officers had done had some legitimacy. She expressed regret, but her apology was causal—there was a reason. There are many more issues related to this crisis. For the purposes of this section, however, consider the value of a penitential apology versus a causal one.

A penitential apology includes no causal explanation. It is simply a statement of remorse.

An apology in the vernacular of crisis communication means what it means in common usage. One party expresses remorse for what has occurred. Sen and Egelhoff (1991) claim that it is always important to show concern for the victim of a crisis (p. 81). And often, that concern is expressed as an apology. Benoit's comment on this matter is often cited in the crisis communication literature. "When a wrong is committed, one should admit it, apologize, and take corrective action" (Benoit, 1995, p. 102).

The default tendency by many, however, is to consider apologies to be problematic because they leave an organization liable for lawsuits and financial liabilities. People simply do not like to apologize because they feel that an apology is, de facto, an admission of guilt. Because an admission of guilt might render the person issuing the apology vulnerable to a financial loss, "often offenders are explicitly instructed by their lawyers, or their insurance companies, *not* to apologize" (Emphasis in original) (Cohen, 1999, p. 1012).

In an exhaustive sixty-page article in the *Southern California Law Review*, law professor Jonathon Cohen challenges the advice that it is unwise to apologize. He argues that from an ethical, cathartic as well as pragmatic perspective, apologies can be beneficial to organizations or individual clients. Cohen cites Massachusetts law specifically as prohibiting equating apologies with admissions of guilt. In addition, the author contends that apologies have the advantages of repairing damaged relationships, facilitating negotiation between parties who might otherwise assume intransigent contentious postures, and therefore actually reduce the chances that an injured party might sue.

> For a legal dispute to occur, injury alone is not sufficient. The injured party must also decide to bring a legal claim. Taking the step to make a legal claim is often triggered by the injured party's anger. An early apology can help defuse that anger and thereby prevent a legal dispute. The lesson here is an important one. While there are risks to making an apology there are also risks to not making an apology. (Cohen, 1999, p. 1022)

SUFFERING

Suffering refers to communications suggesting that, in addition to the victims, the organization is also suffering.

At a news conference after a tragic airplane crash that took the lives of both the women's head and assistant basketball coach, Oklahoma State University president, Burns Hargis, said, "This is our worst nightmare. The entire OSU family is very close, very close indeed. To lose anyone, especially these two individuals who are incredible life forces in our family, it is worse beyond words."

It is likely that this was not a deliberate image repair strategy but rather a genuine expression of sadness. Ten years prior, there had been another horrific crash that took the lives of members of the Oklahoma State men's basketball team. After that accident, the university had written a safety policy that applied whenever players were being transported. That policy, however, did not apply to coaches who were recruiting. In addition to the coaches, the crash took the lives of the pilot and his wife, both Oklahoma State boosters. As a second event in a ten-year span, the university could have lost some legitimacy if stakeholders perceived them to be careless and not sensitive to the tragedy.

TRANSCENDENCE

When the focal system or person at the center of the crisis attempts to put the crisis in the perspective of something more significant, the communication strategy is referred to as transcendence. Essentially, other issues transcend the one that is current.

At one point, when baseball player Barry Bonds was accused of steroid use, he said,

> "This is just-this is old stuff. I mean it's like watching *Sanford and Son* you know, you just, rerun after rerun after rerun. You guys [reporters] it's like, what I mean, you can't—it's almost comical, basically. I mean, we've got alcohol that's the number one killer in America and we legalize that to buy in the store. You've got, you know, you've got tobacco number two, three killer in America, we legalize that" (J. Scott Smith, 2012, p. 50).

| **Fair or Foul** | **Questions of Ethics** |

You are the head coach of a team with several coaches. One of your coaches occasionally makes homophobic remarks during meetings of all coaches. You know this. Years after the coach was hired, several players on the team voiced their concerns about what they claimed were homophobic slurs made during practice. Local media representatives hear about these concerns. Bloggers, newspapers, television broadcasts begin to report on the complaints. You are asked to comment about the accusations.

Setting aside the issue of whether, in the long run, you would be "caught" and just considering this from an ethical standpoint, would there be anything unethical about:

- Denying that you were aware of the coach's attitudes?
- Bolstering—pointing out all that the team has done previously in the name of LGBTQ rights?
- Differentiating the offense by claiming that this offense is not as egregious as those who are sexual predators?
- Minimizing the damage done by the slurs, claiming that the coach did not really mean to be offensive, and most players knew this?

Best Practices

The recurring counsel from both practitioners and researchers includes the following recommendations.

USE ACCOMMODATION VS. AVOIDANCE APPROACHES

In instances when organizations clearly have some level of responsibility, Compensation, Corrective Action, Penitential Apologies, Mortification, and Compassion are likely to repair legitimacy, whereas Attack, Intimidation, Denial, and Displacement are, at best short-term solutions.

ADDRESS THE CRISIS

Rarely do crises go away. In some instances, press coverage of events will not linger as it might otherwise because other more important stories will coincidentally surface. Yet even in these cases, the crises linger, stakeholders remember behaviors or the absence of action. The notion that a crisis will go away is wishfully myopic. The NFL could have hoped that the study published by Dr. Omalu would go away or that the Ray Rice episode would fade, but particularly in a time of social media, crises do not evaporate.

AVOID STONEWALLING

Researchers and practitioners are nearly unanimous on this counsel. "Remember the rule never to say, "no comment." That phrase triggers two negative events. First, 65% of the stakeholders who hear or see "no comment" equate it with an admission of guilt . . . Second, "no comment" is a form of silence which is a very passive response . . . . In a crisis being passive means that other actors in the crisis event get to speak and to interpret the crisis for your stakeholders" (Coombs, 2015, p. 84). "Some of the major reasons incidents turn into crises include stonewalling—not being responsive to the media and the people who need to be informed, or responding with 'no comment'" (Henry, 2000, p. 4). In Seth Wickersham's book about the New England Patriots, *It's Better to Be Feared: The New England Patriots Dynasty and the Pursuit of Greatness*, he reports that Tom Brady's adamant refusal to acknowledge any culpability in the Deflategate scandal (an event the author calls "the most farcical scandal in sports history") concerned the NFL because League executives were worried about long term damage to the League (Wickersham, 2021, p. 325).

STAY ON MESSAGE AND RESPOND QUICKLY

Whatever you have decided are the key "nuggets" of your message, you want to make sure to stay focused on these nuggets and not digress. A crisis management consultant once told me that when she coaches executives, she tells them to stay in the shark cage. If you emerge, you are susceptible to voracious consumers. It is also important to respond quickly, particularly given contemporary social media. "In crisis management, in an online world, timeliness is critical. If you wait, the world is going to define your image for you" (David Henderson quoted in Schworm, 2009, page B4).

REMEMBER YOUR INTERNAL STAKEHOLDERS

It is easy to think of the media and external stakeholders as primary. In fact, internal stakeholders need to know what has transpired and can also act as agents of the organization in the communication effort if they are informed. The documentary, *Fantastic Lies*, deals with a crisis that Duke University faced when some of its lacrosse athletes were accused of sexually accosting an erotic dancer at a party. The school was inundated with tremendous pressure from external sources contending that the school needed to take action against the athletes and the program. It was difficult to ignore the external noise. Internal stakeholders also needed information, as well as a receptive audience for their messages that could have, legitimately, undermined the narrative that the athletes were guilty (*Fantastic Lies*, 2016).

ANTICIPATE POTENTIAL RESPONSES AND BE PREPARED TO RESPOND

It is a standard recommendation for those making presentations to consider questions that will be asked at the conclusion of a talk. Similarly, crisis communicators would be wise to anticipate responses and react to them.

SEE THE MEDIA AS A POTENTIAL ALLY

Organizations and individuals who believe they have been maligned by the media often lash out at the press as conveyors of innuendo and false accusations. The press can be seen as an ally and an agent that will help carry your message in times of crisis. If your team or league has established credibility with sportswriters, bloggers, and the broadcast media, and is offering candid reactions, then media representatives may be inclined to honor the account and exhibit supporting behavior.

BE PROACTIVE AND PLAN INTELLIGENTLY

A university cannot know ahead of time the nuances of a particular recruiting violation or cheating scandal. And a university should take steps to create a culture that reduces the likelihood of such crises. However, these events do happen and can be broadly, considered. Who would be the internal stakeholders in a cheating scandal? What is the contact information for these audiences? What types of messages would we need to be prepared to distribute? What is the best method for distribution? All these questions can be addressed for predictable crises.

In order for a crisis communication plan to work, there has to be a plan in place and a willingness to simulate responding to predictable events.

Chapter Conclusion—Take-Aways

- All organizations need to prepare for crises. That preparation requires considering how to communicate before, during, and in the aftermath of crises.
- In sports organizations, because of media exposure and fan interest, damaging crises occur with frequency.
- Sports organizations need to consider communication during crises as more than just communicating with the sports media but also communicating with their internal and other external stakeholders.
- Crisis communication is not synonymous with spin control.
- Effective communication during crises can repair an athlete or sports organization's legitimacy. Ineffective communication during a crisis can exacerbate the crisis.
- There are several communication approaches when confronted with a crisis. Most scholars and practitioners suggest employing Accommodation strategies like corrective action and compensation as opposed to Avoidance strategies like denial, displacement, or attack.

QUESTIONS

- How can a professional sports league proactively prepare for crises?
- A former NFL player was arrested for physically attacking a police officer. Does the NFL need to communicate to restore lost legitimacy? Does the team for whom the player played need to communicate? Does the player's agent? Who would be two key stakeholders in this crisis? Assume the player was still active. Would your answers to the preceding questions change?
- If Accommodation strategies are typically more successful than Avoidance strategies why do so many initially employ denial when facing a crisis?
- Assume you are a sports communication consultant. What advice would you give to an athletic director at a university who has been told that several of the members of the volleyball team have cheated on final exams?

Practitioner Perspective

Peter Roby

Member of Knight Commission on
Intercollegiate Athletics
Interim Director of Athletics and Recreation-Dartmouth University
Former member of NCAA Men's Basketball Selection
Committee; Athletic Director: Northeastern University;
and Head Basketball coach at Harvard University

Courtesy of Peter Roby

AZ. You worked for ten years as the head of an athletic department. What were the major communication challenges associated with that job?

PR. An athletic director has to appreciate and identify the different stakeholder groups; be clear about the messages that need to be conveyed to these groups; recognize that not all audiences need to or should receive messages the same way, and ensure that the messages communicated to stakeholders are consistent with the department's core values. I had to interact with senior staff, middle managers, coaches, parents, students, alums, donors, colleagues on campus—and many other groups. Then there are external groups, for example, the media and community organizations.

We conveyed a clear message in Athletics, and that was that the educational needs and development of student-athletes was our priority. The realities of the years dealing with Covid-19, you would certainly have to add the health and safety of our students, coaches, and staff to that list of priorities. All who worked in Athletics had to respect that, and their communications had to reflect that. As you know, I am now a member of the Knight Commission on Intercollegiate Athletics. One of our clear guiding principles is that the educational experience and outcomes of college athletes must be paramount. A communication challenge for athletic department leaders is to make sure that message is credibly communicated.

AZ. In crisis communication, we speak about doing things proactively to avoid crisis. In your ten years as AD, there were no major crises in Athletics that required image repair. Sometimes crises are inevitable, but what did you put in place to avoid crises?

PR. It gets back to what I said in response to your first question. I wanted to establish lines of communication with the various stakeholders so that they knew and believed in our values and could comfortably contact me about concerns. We had a situation, for example, where a coach was doing something that could have jeopardized the health of some of our athletes. A trainer felt comfortable speaking with me about that. I had a conversation with the coach and reminded the coach that our values were such that this was not in the best interests of the student-athletes. The coach was not real happy about it, but he accepted my decision. Because I became aware of the problem, I was able to take steps to avoid what could have become a crisis. Because I took steps, our priorities were reinforced. If our culture didn't reinforce student-athlete welfare, the athletic trainer might not have felt comfortable bringing it to my attention. Elsewhere as you know, there have been crises because either lines of communication were not open or values were presented as window dressing.

AZ. How important is it for people in sports to use their platforms to speak out on social issues?

PR. Sport is a significant factor in our society and affects the lives of fans. Consequently, fans can be influenced by the athletes they admire. I view the platform athletes have as very important if athletes use this platform correctly and responsibly.

Athletes need to research the issues and educate themselves. They need to be prepared to articulate why they feel the way they do. Also, athletes should recognize and weigh the risks of speaking out.

My message to our student-athletes was simply to be sure that they were informed on the subjects they were protesting about. And also to ask what they were going to do, subsequently, related to the protest. That is, if a student was not going to do anything subsequently, then perhaps they were not as informed or vested in the cause.

I was on the board of an organization called Athletes for Hope. In the group's early years, I served as an adviser. Alonzo Mourning, Mia Hamm, Julie Foudy, Andre Agassi, and Mohammed Ali were some of the founding athletes. Athletes for Hope has as its mission "to facilitate athletes using their voice and position to make a positive difference in our communities." Sports figures do have a chance to make a positive difference.

AZ. You worked for years on the NCAA men's basketball selection committee. What communication procedures did your group put in place to ensure that there were valuable discussions about the teams that should be selected?

PR. That committee is all about making sure we communicate well to select the most deserving teams. There are ten people on the committee, and one of those persons is the chair. In addition, there are ten to twelve staff members who assist us with our deliberations and communications with the media and public.

In March, during conference championship week, we meet from Tuesday night all the way through selection Sunday. In addition, well prior to that week in March, we convene periodically during the season to discuss the performance of teams. So, by the time we convene in March, we have already been examining and discussing eligible teams' "body of work."

In February, we simulate the communication processes that we will use in March so that when we meet the following month, all will be familiar with the procedure. This is particularly valuable to newcomers on the committee. There is also a "mock selection process" that media representatives go through. This is conducted so that those reporting about the selection can experience the complex and comprehensive nature of how we go about making choices.

When we vote, no member can vote on any team with which they have an affiliation. For example, if you are an athletic director for Purdue, you cannot vote in support of Purdue. If your son is on the coaching staff of Oklahoma, you cannot vote in support of Oklahoma.

We are very careful to do the best we can to communicate effectively in order to identify the deserving sixty-eight teams.

AZ. Any advice to students exploring the intersection of sports and communication?

PR. Well, my first bit of advice is for students to ask themselves why they want to get in the field and what aspect of the field they would like to explore. Learn about the field and do some introspecting. Students need to recognize that sports communication is multifaceted and appreciate the diverse landscape. Then they can identify what they might want to study and pursue.

First Person   Somehow a Crisis

The other day I had the experience that any reader who has regularly driven to the same place repeatedly has had. I pulled into the lot, parked the car, and realized that I could not recall how I got there.

I knew, of course, that I'd left the house, but after leaving Auburndale, a spot on my route, I had only a fuzzy recollection of making the left on Moody, then right on whatever the name of that road is that I have made a right on for umpteen months, made the next right, made the right at the ribs place that I have to go back to, made a left onto the ramp to the Pike, got on the Pike, got off the Pike, swung around Copley passing the Cheesecake Factory, made the left on Mass Ave, waited at the sometimes interminable light, dodged the bicyclists who are forever thinking that there is an actual lane when there is not, made the right on Columbus, and pulled into the garage where the attendant squinted her eyes to make sure I had a parking decal. Couldn't remember much of anything after Auburndale.

I sat there for a moment and wondered how I could have gotten to this spot without remembering anything about the drive. It was as if I had an out-of-body experience with another individual. I was at once:

- The conscious person who was thinking about my classes, whether it is worth it to keep paying for satellite radio, the lure of a warm-weather climate, the snow that was predicted and did not come, the parents of school-aged kids who must be livid that they canceled school on the basis of a forecast of snow when there was not a flake on the ground.
- The autopilot who made all the correct turns without registering them.

There I was in the parking garage and could not remember much of anything about how I got there.

For readers with siblings and particularly large families, this sensation may be even more pronounced. What with going to soccer games, planning for overnights, getting ready for holidays, deciding who is going to pick up the laundry and who is responsible for remembering whose turn it is to mow the lawn—a day can be packed with so many chores that years of such days later you find yourself somewhere and ask how the heck that happened.

And then the metaphor surfaced.

How did we get here? How did we get wherever we are? How conscious have we been of the turns in the road when we've taken them such that we wind up where we may be?

When sports teams, players, sports organizations, fans, sports media entities face a crisis, it could be because they stopped thinking about where they were going and wound up where they are, and they are not where they want to be. Then what?

How athletes drive, plan their routes, make decisions about whether to take I-90 or Route 20 can affect the traffic they run into. Being mindful of activity can preclude finding yourself in a garage and not knowing how you got there.

Chapter 5

Teams, Communication, and Culture

© Dziurek/Shutterstock.com

Chapter in a Nutshell

Communication is a central factor that affects team performance. The success of a team is not simply a function of the cumulative skill levels of the players on the team. This chapter discusses the effects communication can have on teams and team performance.

Specifically, at the end of the chapter, students will be able to:

- Define nonsummativity and how it relates to sports teams.
- List and describe variables that affect nonsummative results.
- Identify characteristics of supportive and defensive team cultures.
- Explain and contrast principles of Theory X and Theory Y coaching styles.
- Explain Critical Theory and Manufactured Consent.

Sports Communication Prompts

- Below you will see statements pertaining to some aspect of communication and sports. For each item
  - Decide whether you agree or disagree with the statement.
  - Explain your rationale for the position.
  - Support your position with examples.

1. A coach's pep talk before a game can affect team performance.
2. Player-only meetings are valuable methods for creating team cohesion.
3. Slogans like "There is no I in Team" have no effect on team performance or wins and losses.
4. Team captains will, inevitably, help assistant and head coaches because the captains will relay information from players to coaches that help the coaches coach.
5. Sometimes coaches have to scream at players to get their points across. Good coaching communication occasionally requires in-your-face conversations. Coaches who, on day one, communicate that they want to be a friend to the players will be unsuccessful.
6. A team's culture is a function of wins and losses, not of how the coaches and players communicate.
7. In the past, captains on teams needed to be able to listen to players' issues and communicate to the coaches. Now, this is unnecessary because players go directly to coaches or simply tweet what is on their minds.
8. Owners of professional sports teams should pay the bills but stay out of the way. When Jerry Jones and Mark Cuban, for example, take their messages to the public, they dilute the authority of the coaches.

A team is as skittish as a herd of animals—like gazelles—and a wrong word or decision can rile them up so they never can really be set straight again.

George Plimpton

The trouble with these guys is that after you've been with them for a couple of weeks you start to play like them.

Baseball player Sid Gordon after having been traded to the hapless 1951 Pittsburgh Pirates

Good Teamwork Skills

NBA analyst Doris Burke after Joel Embiid pointed to himself taking responsibility for an errant pass.

Introduction

There is no doubt that athletic skill is an essential factor that will affect team success. Hockey clubs need players who can skate, defend, and shoot the puck into a narrow opening. Without skilled players, a team is not going to win many games. That is a given, but to what extent is communication and interpersonal relationships an additional and perhaps overriding variable affecting success?

Sports scribes will often write about a player being "good in the clubhouse." Does that matter? Does clubhouse behavior affect team performance such that a player who is "good in the clubhouse" is actually an asset? Long-time baseball announcer Joe Castiglione was once attempting to diplomatically describe a player who had an abrasive personality. "Well," said Castiglione, "he never took the Dale Carnegie course." The announcer was referring to the best-selling book by Dale Carnegie and workshops run by his associates. The Carnegie book was entitled *How To Win Friends And Influence People.* Can a surly teammate affect team performance?

In his book *The Captain Class*, sports reporter Sam Walker writes of the importance of team cohesion and, specifically, leadership. He contends that "the most crucial ingredient in a team that achieves and sustains historic greatness is the character of the player who leads it" (2017, p. xvii) Is this so? Can the captain of a team, because of her character, be a determining factor even if she is not the most talented player?

Often players speak about how they value the camaraderie that develops on a team. Jalen Rose, a former professional basketball player, has been a regular co-host on ESPN's morning sports talk show, *Get Up.* Rose has commented that athletes who leave the game often miss, more than the game, the interactions they had with teammates (April 27, 2018). This comment sounded like a chorus refrain after COVID forced sports to cease in March 2020. When athletes resumed practicing, they said that what they missed was interacting with their teammates.

We have discussed the distinction between constitutive and transmission approaches to studying communication. It is an especially important distinction when examining team communication. The transmission perspective examines communication in terms of whether a person can transmit a message from point A to point B. The constitutive perspective examines communication in terms of how communication shapes relationships. Can the way players interact in the locker room affect relationships such that team performance will be affected? Can the way coaches interact with players affect relationships such that team performance will be affected?

Glory Road is a film about the 1966 Texas Western team that defeated the heavily favored University of Kentucky Wildcats in the NCAA championship. In the face of external pressure and harassment that could debilitate a team, the players gelled under the leadership of Coach Don Haskins. Texas Western won a game that, for a number of reasons, is called the most significant basketball contest in NCAA history.

Miracle is another movie about a stunning upset. It describes how the 1980 U.S. Olympic team coached by Herb Brooks—a team composed of amateur hockey players—somehow evolved so that they were able to defeat a Soviet Union team that some claim was the best hockey team in the world at the time. After the defeat, that Soviet team went on to win 94 of its next 107 games, losing only four of them. *Miracle* includes one of the more riveting pre-game pep talks one is likely to hear. [Players on that 1980 team feel that the speech in the film was very similar to the actual speech Herb Brooks made in Lake Placid] (Littlefield, 2005).

Team USA celebrates its "miraculous" victory against the Soviet Union in the 1980 Olympics.

Can a coach's pep talk actually affect performance in a way that fuels a miraculous victory? Green Bay Packer all-star Willie Davis said that Vince Lombardi "could say something and it would just grab you and do something to you. It was like he could make you rise to play at a level you didn't even know about." (Walker, 2017, p. 74) Davis refers to a halftime speech Lombardi made during the first Super Bowl game. (Then called the AFL-NFL World Championship Game. It was not until the third Super Bowl that the Super Bowl was called the Super Bowl. That third game was indeed called Super Bowl III—even though it was the first time the game officially had that name.) The Packers, huge favorites, were ahead by a slim 14-10 margin at the half. Said Davis, "There was something about that speech that made me play better. . . if you look at our performance in the second half, we raised the bar. We raised the bar because of the conversation he had with us" (Walker, 2017, p. 73).

The University of Tennessee Lady Vols was an annual powerhouse in the Southeast Conference. Year after year, Pat Summitt was able to shape individuals into a collective that was difficult to defeat. Her oft-quoted philosophy was that "Teamwork is what makes common people capable of uncommon results." Her players, judging by the many testimonials in the *Nine for IX* documentary *Pat XO* bought into the team philosophy. They considered the messages from Summitt a key to their uncommon successes.

A Vince Lombardi maxim.

How much of each of these teams' successes were based on player skill level, and how much was based on Coach Haskins's, Brooks's, Summitt's, and Lombardi's ability to communicate and foster cultures that powered the teams?

Consider the question another way. If different coaches had led these teams, might achievement have been less likely, not because of different game strategies or relative levels of coach expertise, but because of the team's internal communications? *You Win in the Locker Room First* is co-authored by Mike Smith, a former head coach in the NFL. In the book, the authors contend that communication is the most important thing a coach can do (Gordon and Smith 2015, pp. 49-50). Vince Lombardi said that "Coaches who can outline plays on a blackboard are a dime a dozen. The ones who win get inside their players and motivate" (Walker, 2017, p. 75).

Yet, the very successful NFL head coach Bill Belichick once remarked, ". . . in the end we can all sit around and kumbaya all day. If you don't block anybody or you can't tackle or you can't kick then I don't really know what you have." (McKenna 2017). He is correct, of course. But given that teams need to perform and have skilled athletes to so perform, it is important to study an additional variable: the constitutive effects of player, coach, and team staff communication.

Nonsummativity

"The whole is greater than the sum of its parts" is an adage we have heard in nearly every arena outside of a math class. As it relates to sports, the saying suggests that a team entity is stronger than the sum of the individual skill levels of the players on the team.

Unfortunately, "The whole is greater than the sum of its parts" is not completely accurate. It is true that in team situations, the whole *can* be greater than the sum of its parts and optimally will be greater than the sum of its parts. However, it is also true that the whole could be less than the sum of its parts.

The principle of nonsummativity applies to teams and all group performance. It means that the whole is not necessarily greater than the sum of its parts but is unequal to the sum of its parts. As Dainton and Zelley have put it, "The point of nonsummativity is that the whole is qualitatively and quantitatively different from the sum of the individual components" (Dainton and Zelley, 2019, p. 162).

A mosaic is a composite of pieces of stone or glass that, when placed together, forms a whole. A sports team, a composite of people, is different. People are not inanimate shards that can be shaped within a frame and solidified with the aid of a grout. The combined effects of communication, management, and industrious preparation can make the team product far better than just a composite of parts. Similarly, for various reasons, a team—despite outstanding skill—can be weaker than the sum of its parts.

Even the casual sports fan can cite examples of a team that performs below the cumulative skill level of the players. Prior to the start of the 2017–2018 NBA season, the Oklahoma City Thunder acquired perennial all-stars Paul George and Carmelo Anthony to complement Russell Westbrook. Westbrook, the prior year, had averaged a "triple-double." This means he had averaged at least ten rebounds, ten points, and ten assists over the course of playing eighty-one of his team's eighty-two regular-season games. This is an achievement of significant magnitude. The only player to have ever done that previously was the great Oscar Robertson, and Robertson did it fifty-five years prior. Adding the stars Carmelo Anthony and Paul George to a team that also had a talent like Westbrook seemed to make the Thunder, inevitably, championship contenders. They weren't. Despite the addition of the superstars in '17–'18, the team was eliminated in the first round of the playoffs just as they had been eliminated in the first round the previous year. During the regular season, the Thunder won only one more game than they had in '16–'17. In fact, with the three superstars in '17–'18, the Thunder nearly missed the playoffs entirely. More talent. Less success. The result of the collection of individuals that comprised the Oklahoma City Thunder was negatively nonsummative. The 2021 Los Angeles Rams added stars Von Miller and Odell Beckham Jr. during the season. The Rams went on to win the Super Bowl, but immediately after the acquisitions there had been turbulence. The Rams were 7-1 when they acquired the players, and three games later they were 7-4. Initially, the addition of outstanding players did not make the team better despite the added talent.

There are many examples of positive nonsummativity as well. The Green Bay Packers under Lombardi had arguably less talent than its annual rivals, the Dallas Cowboys. Yet in championship games both in 1966 and 1967, the Packers prevailed, making the game-winning play in the final moments of both contests. The 1973 Mets had no right being on the same field with the Big Red Machine of the Cincinnati Reds. The Reds had Pete Rose, Johnny Bench, Tony Perez, and Joe Morgan. Yet somehow, the Mets defeated the Reds in the NL playoff series. It was not so much that the Mets beat the Reds but that they had achieved at all with the relatively unskilled athletes that had been on the team. Perhaps the most glaring examples of the whole being greater than the sum of its parts are the 2010 and 2011 Butler Bulldogs. For two consecutive years, Butler advanced to the championship game of the NCAA tournament, winning several games against much more talented opponents. Except for Gordon Hayward, who played in only that 2010 season, Butler had little exceptional individual talent. Nevertheless, Butler almost won in 2010 against mighty Duke and was ahead at halftime in 2011 against three-time NCAA champion, the University of Connecticut. And then there are the startling 2018 Las Vegas Golden Knights, an expansion team in the NHL that somehow advanced to the Stanley Cup finals in its inaugural season.

What Affects Nonsummativity?

CONFLICT

Whether you are examining a committee that meets regularly, a group tasked to solve a problem collectively, or a team that is attempting to win games against similarly-willed opponents, conflict is a factor that can affect team communication and performance. Typically four types of conflict are identified.

Perceptions of Equity

Equity conflict on a team occurs when players, staff members, or assistant coaches believe that there is inequality. Players may feel as if they are not getting enough playing time or their contributions to the team are not valued. Some may believe that they are being criticized more often than counterparts who are off-limits to criticism. Individuals may sense that others are slackers—they don't work hard in practice or at preparation time—yet seem to be getting away with it. The literature on team interaction actually refers to slackers as "social loafers" who undermine team cohesion.

Assistant coaches may experience equity conflict if their voices are dismissed, for example, when discussing game plan options or when they're tasked with relatively menial jobs. An assistant may believe personal friendships have allowed some coaches a seat at the table while they sit, metaphorically at least, on the periphery. A woman trainer on a team may feel marginalized when compared to her male counterparts. When she speaks about player injuries to the coaching staff, it seems as if there are more side conversations and texting. This may cause the trainer to grumble to colleagues and even affect her willingness to contribute as much as she might otherwise.

Equity conflicts exist in two flavors. In the first, players or staff believe they are doing too much and bear a disproportionate burden. In the second, individuals sense that they are not able to contribute as they'd like. When either type of equity conflict occurs, individuals, either formally or as likely informally, articulate their displeasure. While equity conflicts and the concomitant grumbling tend to yield negative nonsummative results, the absence of equity tension will have a positive effect. When players feel as if they are evaluated appropriately and coaches and staff are allowed to contribute equitably, this can have a positive effect on a team.

Process

Procedural conflict stems from feelings that the *process* is unproductive. Players may experience procedural tension when they believe that practice time is not maximized or when drills are implemented randomly, seemingly less to yield better performance and more to subjugate and establish control. An assistant coach who is compelled to attend unproductive game-planning meetings may resent the time sap. She or he may believe the routine is just that, a routine, and not conducive to qualitative team growth. Individuals who experience this type of conflict feel that if processes were different, there would be greater productivity.

When the process makes sense, when teammates believe that drills are designed to help players get better, then that will have a positive effect. You may have experienced this in your classes as well as on athletic teams. When you attend a class, and it seems to be well planned with exercises and readings explained and designed reasonably, that tends to improve your desire to work industriously. You are likely to hear less grousing among classmates inquiring about why the class is being asked to complete a task. Consequently, there may be more participation in the class and greater motivation to work. The atmosphere in your class might be such that students wish to contribute to discussions, thus increasing its value. Similarly, on teams, believing that the process makes sense will improve team performance.

Affective Tensions

Affective conflict surfaces when people on a team begin to dislike one another. Perhaps this could be the result of equity tensions or irrational jealousy, or some prior insult that has festered. In 2015, John Papelbon, a relief pitcher for the Phillies, had a dugout fight with teammate Bryce Harper for all to see. Former Yankee manager Billy Martin and outfielder Reggie Jackson verbally brawled in the dugout when Martin replaced Jackson in the middle of an inning for not hustling. Jeff Kent and Barry Bonds clashed when the two were, nominally, teammates on the San Francisco Giants. Neither Kent nor Bonds had much to do with the other players on the team. Sports broadcasters Brent Musburger and Jimmy the Greek Snyder famously had a barroom brawl after one of their *NFL Today* broadcasts. Teammate bickering on the 2021-22 Boston Celtics fueled a "players only" meeting in the first weeks of that season.

Affective conflict does not necessarily guarantee a negative nonsummative team effort. Teams like the old (and successful) Oakland Raiders were depicted as not the most cordial, yet they were often in the playoff picture. Typically, however, affective tension is not healthy. An assistant coach may not agree with anything another assistant suggests—even when the ideas have merit—because of personal tension. The result may be a less effective strategy. A point guard may avoid passing to a teammate with whom she has a dispute. Players on teams that fuel negative energy are called "cancers." The metaphor is apt because their negative influences tend to metastasize. "Like secondhand smoke, the leakage of emotions can make a bystander an innocent casualty of someone else's toxic state" (Goleman, 2006, p. 14).

Again, the opposite can have a positive effect. Ryan writes about "super-carriers" like ex-baseball player Jonny Gomes, who fuel positive chemistry on a team (Ryan, 2020, pp. 49-75). Players and coaches may claim to have, and actually have, love for each other. Some coaches earn such respect that players want to excel for the coach, and others seek out opportunities to play in that environment.

Substantive Conflict

A positive type of tension is called substantive conflict. This means that there is disagreement among team members about the best way to prepare and compete. This is a good thing because it can generate creative approaches and dismiss stale ones that are not working. Substantive conflict also reflects respect for all participants. Earlier in the text, there is a reference to NBA player Wayne Embry's comments about the positive effects of substantive conflict on the Bill Russell-coached Boston Celtics.

The absence of substantive conflict can have a deleterious effect. Good teams generate such conflict. Coaches, for example, might ask each other to identify reasons why a certain plan will not work. In group interaction generating substantive conflict this way is called Risk Technique. It means simply that when one identifies a solution to a problem, all team members are compelled to list a reason, aka risk, to the proposed solution. By compelling team members to identify risks, even if they actually believe the plan has merit, a team can generate a stronger plan by minimizing risks they may not have otherwise identified.

EMOTIONAL INTELLIGENCE

Announcers and coaches often speak of a player's basketball or soccer or football IQ. What this means is that the player plays intelligently and makes intelligent decisions during a game.

Being smart, of course, is an asset, but in addition to assessing a game IQ, it is wise to consider a player's EIQ or emotional intelligence quotient. Salovey and Mayer have defined emotional intelligence as "the ability to monitor one's own and others' feelings and emotions, to discriminate among them and to use this information to guide one's thinking and actions" (Salovey and Mayer, 1990, p. 189). Goleman identifies five criteria reflecting emotional intelligence. He argues that people with high emotional intelligence know their emotions, can manage their emotions, are capable of motivating themselves, can recognize emotions in others, and can effectively handle relationships. In short, high EIQ teammates are self-aware, have empathy for others, can regulate themselves, and have social skills that allow them to interact with others (Goleman, 2005, pp. 43-44).

It may be difficult to ascertain if someone is emotionally intelligent, but it is not difficult to realize how important emotional intelligence can be to a team's success. When Scott Pioli was hired by the Kansas City Chiefs to be its player personnel director, he commented that his task was not to find players who were extraordinarily skilled. His task was to find players who would make the team better.

The distinction is not insignificant. Any fan of sport knows how a personality who has trouble establishing relationships with teammates can cause stress. Terrell Owens was an outstanding talent, but he created tension wherever he played. Owens appears on at least two lists of the worst teammates in sports history (Kelly, 2018; Herrold, 2010). His statistics are outstanding; the teams' performances not as much. It is meaningful to point out that when the Philadelphia Eagles made their Super Bowl run in 2003–2004, Owens was injured for the first two play-off Eagle victories. He returned for the Super Bowl and had terrific numbers in that game, but the team lost. Subsequently, Owens criticized quarterback Donovan McNabb intimating that had McNabb been emotionally stronger, the Eagles would have been victorious. Such self-centered behavior is typically not conducive to team success.

Terrell Owens has the dubious distinction of being considered one of the worst teammates in sports history. Many players considered Jeff Kent an abrasive personality as well.

What is ironic about the Pioli example is that he was dismissed from the Chiefs in early 2013, and at the time, the criticisms of his work as general manager suggested that he himself was challenged as it relates to emotional intelligence. This, of course, could be a narrative fueled by a few disgruntled people. Pioli, after working with the Chiefs, was hired by the Atlanta Falcons as assistant general manager and has been highly praised by colleagues. Regardless of Pioli's emotional intelligence, the point is that EI can be a factor in creating positive nonsummative results. Theo Epstein was the general manager of the Boston Red Sox when they won their first World Series in decades, and then the Chicago Cubs a few years later when the Cubs won their first World Series in decades. Epstein has commented about a player's influence on a team beyond that player's athletic skill set. "The truth…is that a player's character matters.…The player's impact on others matters…The willingness to connect matters…Who you are, how you live among others, that all matters (Epstein quoted in Ryan, 2021 p. 223).

CLIMATES, CULTURES, AND COMMUNICATION

Cultural theory is based on the premise that there is a phenomenon that can be labeled "organizational culture" and that culture affects the performance of collective entities, for example, teams. Researchers like Edgar Schein--as prominent and prolific a writer as there is in this area--claim that there is "abundant evidence" that culture affects performance (Schein, 1999 p. xiv). Culture reflects "a pattern of shared tacit assumptions that [are] learned by a group…What really drives daily behavior [are these] learned, shared, tacit assumptions…" (Schein, 2019, pp. 51-52). A supportive culture is said to have a positive effect on performance, and a defensive culture has the opposite effect. Culture is an important concept in communication studies because communication is a factor in the creation of culture. Duke basketball coach Mike Krzyzewski has said, "You cannot merely expect culture to be a natural occurrence; it has to be made a part of your everyday routine." Daily communication will affect team culture, and team culture will affect daily communication.

A phenomenon related to culture is organizational climate. Taguiri defines climate as the "relatively enduring quality of the internal environment . . . that (a) is experienced by its members (b) influences their [the members'] behavior, and (c) can be described in terms of the values of a particular set of characteristics (or attributes) of the environment" (Taguiri, 1968, p. 27). The climate "is the internal emotional tone . . . based on how comfortable organizational members feel with one another and with the organization" (Kreps, 1990, p. 193).

Researcher Daniel Denison (1996) wrote an exhaustive article attempting to make the distinction between climate and culture and discussed the possibility that the two words were essentially interchangeable and dissimilarities were based on one's vantage point. A good way to think of the distinction is to consider team culture as the root of what becomes the team climate.

Many authors use, appropriately, a weather metaphor when describing the climate. They argue that "nasty" "cold" conditions retard the development of positive relationships, and "warm," "sunny" conditions are conducive to interaction. In essence, the climate is the atmosphere on a team that either encourages or discourages communication. A supportive climate is likely to encourage interaction and the flow of information. A defensive climate is likely to retard the flow of information. Using the weather metaphor, one might think of culture as the weather factors, when taken collectively, generate the weather conditions—the climate.

Stefan Bondy wrote a piece for the *New York Daily News* about New York Knickerbocker Coach David Fizdale. It is titled "David Fizdale Stresses Culture and Accountability as Knicks Introduce him as Head Coach." An excerpt from the coach's remarks indicates the importance he placed on culture and climate:

> I will roll up my sleeves and work really hard—tirelessly—to build this culture, to rebuild this culture back, to give these guys a great opportunity to build basketball success and eventually where we can all hold the trophy together. Culture and accountability. I'll be putting those words on walls in a lot of places. (Bondy, 2018)

Ultimately Fitzdale was not successful as coach of the Knicks, but his comments about the importance of culture are meaningful, nevertheless. In Joan Ryan's book *Intangibles*, the author cites former baseball manager Chuck Tanner who said, "If you have good chemistry, it's like you traded for a superstar." Later in her book, Ryan writes about the 2010 World champion San Francisco Giants, a team she followed as a reporter. "…this complex interplay of relationships, was coalescing into something all its own—a culture. …this culture became like a gravitational force, bending everyone toward each other and a common goal (Ryan, 2020, pp. 15, 23).

SUPPORTIVE CULTURES

Charles Redding is a pioneer in the area of organizational communication. Redding contended that the climate was a very powerful factor affecting overall communication quality. He argued that the climate was even more significant than individual communication skill sets. In other words, teammates with marginal skill sets in a supportive climate would exercise the skills they had such that their ability to communicate might be greater than someone with better skill sets in a defensive environment. A simple example: A player has an idea about a way to defend a star opponent. In a supportive climate, a player with weak communication skills might nevertheless find a way to express how to defend the opponent; in a defensive climate, someone who is quite capable of speaking eloquently might not contribute to the discussion.

Redding identified a number of characteristics of what he called the Ideal Supportive Climate.

- **Pursuit of Excellence**
  - The first criterion is an emphasis on high-performance goals. If a cultural norm is that a team strives to win championships or some other realistic high-performance goal, the climate will reflect that cultural norm, and players and coaches will industriously pursue excellence.

- **Organizational Credibility**
  - A second criterion is communication credibility. Do coaches and players trust what they hear? Players and coaches who earn a reputation for being credible, even when the messages players may hear are not palatable, plant the seeds for a supportive culture.

- **Supportiveness**
  - A third criterion is supportive communication. Supportiveness in this context does not mean indiscriminate stroking. It means communicating support when it is deserved and communicating constructive criticism when it is not. Blanket "attaboys" can actually undermine team culture. Two researchers, Frank Smoll and Ronald Smith, have done extensive research regarding how athletes react to coaching feedback. In their article, "Enhancing Coach-Athlete Relationships," the authors discuss findings based on surveying more than 1000 athletes and observing 85,000 behaviors of some eighty coaches. The research supports two related principles: (a) athletes react favorably when excellence is acknowledged and react negatively when excellence is ignored, (b) athletes are receptive to criticism when errors have been made when that criticism is accompanied by recommendations regarding how to improve (Smoll and Smith, 2006, pp. 23-29). (Interested readers might review the interview with Olympian Kendall Coyne that appears at the end of Chapter 1. In the interview, she makes very similar remarks about the importance of genuine and constructive criticism).

According to a study published by Frank Smoll and Ronald Smith athletes are receptive to criticism if suggestions for improvement accompany the criticism.

DEFENSIVE CULTURES

As opposed to the ideal supportive climate that Redding described, a professor named Jack Gibb identified characteristics of defensive cultures and climates.

- **Excessive and gratuitous criticism**.
  - ○ Players on a team have to be able to listen to constructive criticism that is intended to make players get better. The sixteenth-century French writer Michel de Montaigne's comment on this point is as true now as it was five hundred years ago. "We need very strong ears to hear ourselves judged frankly . . . those who venture to criticize us perform a remarkable act of friendship." However, if teammates and coaches have only one note, and that note is constant and often gratuitous criticism, the result will be a defensive culture.

- **Manipulation**
  - ○ If players regularly hear messages like, "this is your role," when it is apparent that the role is designed not for team benefit but to satisfy some other agenda, the result will be a defensive culture.

- **Indifference to Individuals' Personal Needs**
  - ○ There is no merit in coddling players. It can undermine an emphasis on team excellence. However, a genuine concern for a player's legitimate needs is conducive to a supportive environment. If players and coaches get a sense from others on the team that people are indifferent to their personal needs, it can have a negative effect.

- **Condescension**
    - ○ A respect for authority is likely to be a healthy factor in determining team performance. If players do not respect coaches, practices may become valueless, with some teammates working hard and others not practicing as diligently. However, an attitude of superiority on the part of coaches and players can have deleterious effects. We've heard of players having an "attitude" or that some athletes who may or may not be superior behaving as if others are not as valuable.

- **Intransigence**
    - ○ Stubborn teammates who cannot see opposing opinions as potentially valuable can create a defensive culture. One player informed me that a football coach furious at offsides penalties required all offensive plays to be run on the second hut. Players complained to the coach, informing him that this was giving the defenders an advantage as the defensive line was beginning to simply ram the offensive line on each second hut. Nevertheless, the coach—furious at the penalties—stubbornly insisted on the same count each time. The problems transcended the linemen's disadvantage and were corrosive to the culture of the team.

The late John Madden once remarked that "winning is an excellent deodorant." When you are winning, some of the problems that Gibb lists are overwhelmed by the esprit de corps that comes from victory. Madden, once a head coach of the Super Bowl-winning Oakland Raiders, went on to comment that when a team is losing, there is no deodorizer that works because "everything stinks." Nevertheless, all things being equal, what is likely to yield a positive nonsummative result is the existence of supportive culture criteria and the absence of defensive culture elements.

© UPI/Alamy Stock Photo

The late John Madden once remarked that "winning is an excellent deodorant."

FUNCTIONALISTS AND INTERPRETIVISTS

Some writers described as functionalists assume that culture is a direct function of communications from head managers—in sports general managers, coaches, athletic directors. Functionalists believe, for example, that signage reading "There's no I in team", orientation speeches from an athletic director, and *this is how we do it here* messaging from coaches can engineer culture.

Another group, interpretivists, suggests that the organizational culture is the residual of all communications, regardless of how official they may be. The interpretivists interpret the culture of an organization by observing communication patterns, much like an ethnographer studies groups. They might listen to conversations in the locker room, examine both formal and informal e-mails, study, and even linger in the cafeteria in an attempt to understand the culture by observing communication patterns. An interpretivist would argue that general managers could create bumper stickers that read "Trust the Process," but these signs, metaphorically, would have to stick. If they did not, if informal communications by players, reporters, coaches indicated that the stickers were for the optics, then the culture would not be affected by the postings.

Test Yourself: Apply the Principles

Think about a team that you were on at any level. It could be Little League, youth soccer, high school varsity, a club team, or any organized team.

- On a scale of 1–5, with 1 being *not at all* and 5 *very much so*, do you consider players and coaches on that team
  - Condescending
  - Stubborn
  - Manipulative
  - Indifferent
  - Overly Critical
- Was the culture on that team driven by "management" or by the communication of all members of the team, including "management"?
- Were your teammates and coaches appropriately supportive?
- Were communications typically credible?
- Were there credible messages emphasizing excellence?

Leadership and Coaching

THEORY X AND THEORY Y

Douglas McGregor articulated two contrasting sets of principles which he called Theory X and Theory Y. If a coach subscribed to Theory X, she or he would have certain assumptions about players that are antithetical to the assumptions held by a coach who believed in the principles of Theory Y. In the table below, readers can see the contrasting principles of these theories.

- **Theory X Assumptions**
  - People dislike work and avoid work when possible.
  - People are not ambitious and prefer direction.
  - People do not seek responsibility and are not concerned with overall organizational needs.
  - People must be directed and threatened with punishment to achieve organizational productivity.

- **Theory Y Assumptions**
  - Under the right circumstances, people will view work as natural as play.
  - People are ambitious and prefer self-direction.
  - People seek responsibility and feel rewarded through their achievements.
  - People are self-motivated and require little direction.
  - People are creative and capable of organizational creativity.

A coach holding Theory X assumptions would believe that players tended to dislike practice and were inherently not ambitious, essentially lazy. Given a choice between hard or easy practices, Theory X holds that players would nearly always choose easy practices. The theory assumes that players actually prefer direction as opposed to self-direction. With nothing to do, Theory X proponents believe that players would be content—and would only perform industriously for increased playing time, other external rewards, or for fear of punishment.

A coach who believes in Theory Y assumes that under the right conditions, players will be industrious and not lazy and actually would prefer meaningful work to being idle or doing easy drills. A Theory Y coach believes that given nothing to do, athletes would seek out activities that would improve their game.

If you were a coach of a team, would you have a Theory X orientation when you first meet with your players or Theory Y? Would you assume that without strong direction, the players would default to lazy behavior and therefore feel that you would have to prod them with threats that they might lose their scholarships or jobs if they do not perform? Or would you assume that players inherently want to excel, and your job is to create the environment that will serve as a foundation for excellence?

Frederick Taylor was a management theorist associated with what is called Classical Theory. His name is so closely associated with Classical Theory that sometimes Classical Theory itself is called Taylorism. A primary tenet of his approach is called Scientific Management. Taylor believed that any job can be studied to determine "the one best way" to do the job. The goal of leadership then is to determine the best way and to tell others how to do the job. In a coaching context, this would mean that a coach's job would be to study how to prepare to play, how to play against specific opponents, and clearly communicate how to execute the game plan.

Taylor also believed in two principles closely aligned with Theory X. He called these principles natural and systematic soldiering. Natural soldiering means that people are naturally lazy, naturally inclined to operate like soldiers who have to be told what to do and when to do it.

"There is no question," he wrote, "that the tendency of the average [person] is toward working at a slow easy gait (Taylor, 2014, p. 6). More insidious, he claimed, was the principle of systematic soldiering. Taylor argued that the anomalous individual who was, in fact, industrious would observe the natural soldiering of peers and either learn or be coached to work at "a slow easy gait." This he called systematic soldiering.

Should a coach assume that Taylor was correct? That without strong communicative messages players would not work hard. Frank Deford wrote a *Sports Illustrated* article called "The Toughest Coach That Ever Was" about a football coach named Bull Cyclone Sullivan. (Deford 1984, pp 44-61) Sullivan was indeed tough. Once, to convince defenders of the importance of holding their ground, he placed a defensive line on the slope of a pond. Then he had the offensive line attempt to knock the defenders into the water. That, he assumed, would teach the defenders to keep their ground.

Are players motivated by such approaches? Does fear inspire players to shed a tendency to be less than industrious? A former student, a student-athlete, read the article about Bull Cyclone Sullivan and commented: "I'd kill to play for a coach like that." Other student-athletes in the class were less supportive of that style. Would you like to play for a dedicated but tyrannical coach?

In large part, the book *Organizational Communication Imperatives* is a comparison of leadership styles. The leadership style of Dr. Wernher von Braun, who led NASA's Marshall Space Flight Center (MSFC) in the 1960s, is juxtaposed with that of Dr. William Lucas, who headed the center in the 1980s. Lucas was at the helm when the Challenger exploded on January 28, 1986. The book underscores the point that the leadership styles significantly affected internal communication and success at the center. Whereas von Braun was encouraging, supportive, and engaging, Lucas was aloof and critical. Excerpts from interviews with Lucas's subordinates are revealing. "Lucas wanted information filtered. His communicative style was intimidation." "Lucas was a dead fish. Cold, vindictive, he would embarrass people publicly." "I feel bad about saying this, but people were afraid to bring bad news to Dr. Lucas for fear that they would be treated harshly" (Tompkins, 1993, pp. 163-164).

In your experience, are there more coaches and general managers like Von Braun or more like Lucas? Can Lucas-type coaches be winning coaches? Winning general managers? Can Von Braun-like coaches be winning coaches, winning general managers?

"Player only meetings" suggest that Theory Y principles have merit.

Classical theorists could not explain the phenomenon of player-only meetings when teams perform poorly. If players require direction, why do they meet independently to improve?

In the 2016 World Series, the Chicago Cubs looked like they were finally going to break a more than century-old drought. They went into the bottom of the eighth leading 6-3 but then proceeded to give up three runs which allowed Cleveland to tie the game. All of the momentum that the Cubs had was now gone. After a scoreless ninth inning from both sides, it began to pour in Cleveland. Consequently, there was a rain delay. During the delay, the Cub players decided to have a players-only meeting to regroup. Cub player Jason Heyward led the meeting, which some claim was instrumental in their eventual 8-7 victory. Regardless of how influential it was, the fact that Heyward and the Cub players wanted to meet is an indication of Theory Y principles and not Theory X.

Steve Kerr was the coach of the 2017–2018 NBA champion Golden State Warriors. During a game in the spring of 2018, Kerr allowed his players to run their own time-out huddles. The coach was asked about the unusual approach: "It's their team. . . As coaches, our job is to nudge them in the right direction, guide them, but we don't control them. I thought they communicated really well together. . . it was a good night for the guys."

Of course, you are more likely to have a "good night for the guys" if Kevin Durant, Stephen Curry, and Klay Thompson are three of the guys. But there is the possibility that teams with such talent, if coached by someone who believes in Theory X, could underperform and become a contrary group as opposed to a supportive one.

© Kathryn Beckman Kirsch/Shutterstock.com

THE HAWTHORNE STUDIES AND TEAM COMMUNICATION

The Hawthorne Studies may be the most well-known study ever conducted in the field of management. They were so called because they were conducted in the Western Electric Hawthorne plant in Cicero, Illinois. The studies were conducted in order to examine and test certain principles of Classical Theory. The idea was to assess how workers would react to varied physical conditions in order to identify the optimal physical environment for productivity. Ironically, the findings of the studies compelled advocates of Classical Theory to reconsider their positions. In the final analysis, instead of serving to support and solidify Classical principles, the Hawthorne Studies actually were a catalyst for the development of an alternate and contrary theory called Human Relations Theory. The studies were significant because they served to change, and change radically, attitudes about how/why people performed. Also, the Hawthorne Studies were noteworthy because they altered the perspective theorists had about the importance and nature of communication as an element of efficient leadership.

There were four parts that were identified as segments of the studies. The first is the most famous and the one that is likely to be familiar to readers who have studied organizational behavior previously. In this phase, workers were observed while researchers varied lighting intensity. The assumption of the theorists was that increased lighting would increase productivity. If the lighting was better, people who did piece work would be better able to do their work and produce more. As expected, when lighting was increased, performance increased. However, to the surprise of the researchers, as lighting was decreased, worker performance remained higher than normal, even when the lighting became very dim. Production only went down when the lighting became so low that the participants complained and said they could not see what they were doing (Roethlisberger et al., 1949, p. 17). In the control group, where lighting remained constant, productivity also went up. The results were, well, illuminating and the variable, apparently, was not illumination. There had to be some other factor that compelled people to be more productive. The researchers agreed that this motivator was related to observation, change, and implicit recognition.

The second phase of the Hawthorne Studies, referred to as the "relay assembly" studies, began in 1927. In this phase, work conditions such as hours, coffee breaks, pay incentives, and the quality of food provided was varied. The objective of this component was consistent with the first. The assumption would be that if pay incentives went up; coffee breaks were increased in terms of frequency and duration, and if working hours were more attractive, then productivity would increase accordingly. The idea, consistent with Scientific Management and Classical Theory, was to discover the optimal conditions. As with the studies based on illumination, varying conditions did *not* have a direct effect on productivity.

The Hawthorne Effect is a phrase used to describe the results of these two parts of the study. In brief, the Effect refers to the fact that people tend to alter their behavior when they are observed. The motivational variable was the attention, as opposed to the altered conditions. It also made researchers acknowledge that a certain type of communication was an important factor for leaders. If observation and recognition were motivating factors, then wouldn't leaders need to be able to communicate more than just the best way to do a job? As applied to coaches and communication that affects performance, would coaches have to genuinely recognize the contributions of players in order to motivate them? And wouldn't coaches have to credibly communicate criticism to those who were not similarly industrious?

The third component of the Hawthorne Studies involved conducting interviews. Over twenty thousand were questioned about their attitudes toward work, co-workers, management, and the organization. The results of this phase of the study revealed not only that interviewees had concerns but also that they enjoyed the opportunity to express themselves about various issues. The interviewees seemed to enjoy being able to "vent" during the interviews. The findings from this third phase appear to contradict other beliefs of the Classical theorists. The Classical theorists were inclined to believe that communication in organizations need only go downward from management. The principle of Scientific Management was simply to discover the best way to do a job and then tell people how to do it. The third part of the Hawthorne Studies seemed to indicate that there might be some value in allowing for an opportunity to communicate upward and to initiate communication with leaders.

The last part of the Hawthorne Studies is called the bank wiring phase. Researchers observed workers and found that they established informal rules and norms that they abided by in order to complete their tasks. These norms were not necessarily consistent with the formal guidelines and procedures established by leaders. This again contradicted notions of the Classical Theory. Classical theorists assumed employees received the only consequential messages from downwardly directed formal messages. Apparently, the real rules might be established informally by social peer-related pressure and governance, communicated horizontally from worker to worker.

What do the Hawthorne Studies, McGregor's, and Taylor's theories have to say about the role of communication in creating team cohesion? There are a number of conclusions.

- Communication about rules and policy is not the only significant message. Communication reflecting recognition of performance is important. These messages have to be credible, or they are meaningless, but if they are perceived as credible, they can motivate players to excel.

- While some players may need to be prodded to perform, others in a supportive culture will naturally be inclined to excel. Teams can and have demonstrated the potential for self-motivation.

- Coaches will always have to accept ultimate responsibility for decision-making. However, players can have meaningful input and desire to be heard. Coaches would be wise to, on occasion, genuinely listen to player ideas while clearly informing players that the final decision rests with the coaching staff.

- Players who are committed to excellence and take responsibility for encouraging teammates are very valuable to team success.

- Communication, from a constitutive perspective, can shape relationships that will affect the nonsummative result.

THE JACKASS FALLACY

Harold Levinson (1973) wrote a *Harvard Business Review* article which he called "Asinine Attitudes Towards Management." In it, he refers to something called *the jackass fallacy*. He said that what precludes healthy communication in organizations is the default assumption that Theory X principles are correct and, as applied to sports teams, players are essentially jackasses that have to be led. Levinson's point is that such a default tendency is not only inaccurate but also corrosive. If coaches default to this notion, it is inevitable that there will be problems.

CRITICAL THEORY AND MANUFACTURED CONSENT

Critical Theory refers to assumptions about the misuse of power. Critical theorists assume that communication can be used as a tool for abuse. For example, critical theorists would argue that coaches who consistently and indiscriminately ridicule athletes are abusing their authority and using communication as a tool for abuse.

The phrase *manufactured consent* is used by critical theorists to describe the phenomenon of buying into subjugating communicative behaviors. For example, if players believe it is not a problem for coaches to scream at them incessantly, this may be because consent has been manufactured such that athletes believe that the constant criticism is being done for their own good. Their consent to behavior that in other contexts might otherwise be considered reprehensible had been manufactured. Of course, sometimes coaches may have to be critical in order to transmit messages accurately. However, critical theorists suggest that some coaches use authority inappropriately and can bully others gratuitously, negatively affecting relationships and the constitution of the team.

Organizational Identification and Concertive Control

Buck Showalter always told me when I was a young coach in the big leagues, starting in the Yankee organization, that the best clubhouse you can have is a clubhouse that polices itself.

Brian Butterfield, third base coach for the Chicago Cubs

Organizational Identification refers to the extent to which individuals in an organization identify with its goals and values. If you are on your school's track team and you feel as if the values of the team, the way it recruits, the way you are coached, the way you and your teammates industriously prepare and perform are all exemplary, then you likely will begin to identify with the track team. Your allegiance to the team will be entwined with your sense of self.

If, on the other hand, you reject the culture that surrounds you and wonder if you belong on such a team because, for example, the coach recruits deceptively or makes racist remarks behind certain players' backs or because you feel manipulated by bogus slogans that seem conceived to manipulate—then you will likely not identify. It makes sense that persons who have low levels of organizational identification would seek to play elsewhere or at least prepare less passionately than those who respond positively to the organization's culture and identify with it. Athletes may learn the culture, reject it, and say to themselves, "I don't belong here and I need to find a better fit. This culture is inconsistent with who I am. These people are all insensitive. If I stay here longer, I will become insensitive."

In essence, identification occurs when a person has been socialized to the extent that they consider that "the way they are is the way I am." The track athlete, in a supportive environment, will not say, "*They* play for championships," but rather, "*We* play for championships." Bullis and Tompkins have said that identification occurs when "the organization becomes as much a part of the member as the member is a part of the organization" (Bullis and Tompkins, 1989, p. 289).

Tompkins writes about how he began to think about organizational identification after a period of consulting at the Marshall Space Flight Center in Huntsville, Alabama.

… As I began my long drive home from Huntsville to Detroit, I realized that I had entered a state of identification with the organization. I felt a part of it, a sense of belonging, and had persuaded myself that we had common interests: What was good for the space program was good for me. There was an inherent emotional component, positive in nature, a symbolic satisfaction in my relationship with the organization… The organization became part of me … (P. Tompkins, 2005, p. 62)

Tompkins and Cheney have written extensively about organizational identification and a concept they call concertive control. Concertive control occurs when teammates work "flexibly in concert to solve problems and get the work done" (P. Tompkins 2005, p. 193). When high levels of concertive control exist, players do not practice simply to comply with a coach's directive; they practice because they have bought into the goals of the team, identify with the team, have themselves established rules and norms to guide their own activities, and make decisions consistent with the team's cultural values. Players do this because the organization's cultural values have, in fact, become their own. As Gossett described it, "personal identities are joined with [the] organization and thus make organizationally apparent decisions without the need for direct managerial oversight" (Gossett, 2006, p. 383).

Bureaucratic control means that the organizational structure is the most powerful control mechanism. Administrative control means that players are controlled because of the leaders, in particular, their coaches or general managers. The presence of concertive control is different and not insignificant. As opposed to bureaucratic or administrative control, with concertive control, players have assimilated to the extent that they are self-motivated, self-directed, and desire to perform in the best interest of the team with which they identify.

A great deal of ink and air time is given to culture in sport. Players transfer to clubs "because of the culture", coaches recruit players who "align with our values", and culture seems to be portrayed as the point of difference across a whole range of performance measures. And rightly so-when you are part of a great team, it feels different.

John Alder, "Culture and Coaching: The Shadow of Team Values."

Fair or Foul   Questions of Ethics

A coach who, in her heart of hearts, believes in Theory X tells her team that she believes in Theory Y. That is, she believes that athletes are inherently lazy and therefore need to be (a) directed, (b) admonished, and (c) threatened with lack of playing time in order to get them to perform. Nevertheless, she begins on the first day of practice by saying that she "believes in you." She says that she believes that players "desire to win and will work hard to win as a team, and even if she was not at practice, she would see athletes practicing hard on the ice."

If this is stated as a ruse, and the coach does not believe it but rather hopes it will get players to trust her more and accept her admonishments and threats, is that fair or foul? For the sake of this exercise, assume the coach has been able to motivate players with this ploy in the past.

Four Cs

Let's summarize this chapter by reviewing four interdependent factors that affect nonsummativity.

Culture. The organization's culture can have an effect on performance. Teams should strive to meet the criteria for supportive cultures and be vigilant about avoiding the characteristics of defensive cultures. Communication is a factor in establishing culture. What results as the team's culture is the amalgam of all communication that takes place within the system that is a team.

Coaching and Leadership. Lombardi's claim that coaches who know Xs and Os are "a dime a dozen" is likely an exaggeration. Knowing the game is essential to coaching in the same way that knowing a business is vital for any person who leads a corporation. However, knowledge and the ability to relay what you know are distinct. Moreover, as it relates to sports communication, awareness of what motivates and demotivates athletes is central to a coach's success, as is the willingness to communicate to so motivate.

Character and Commitment. Sam Walker's book *The Captain's Class* argues exhaustively that what separates the truly great teams from others are the captains who lead the teams. He argues that teams need captains who are persistent, willing to do thankless jobs, have a democratic communication style reflected in both verbal and nonverbal behaviors, and are committed to team, as opposed to individual performance (Walker, 2017, p. 91). These same requirements for excellence apply to all players, staff members, and coaches on a team.

Constitutive Communication. Successful teams understand that communication is not simply a transmission phenomenon. Communication shapes relationships. When people are labeled "good communicators," this does not just mean they can get their messages across—although this is essential. It means they know that how they get their messages across will be a factor that creates the evolving entity that becomes the team.

Anna Katherine Clemmons wrote an article about Virginia basketball in the early months of the 2017–2018 season. The article was titled "The Whole Package." The subtitle "Without a Dominant Veteran Superstar, The Men's Basketball Team Has Succeeded By Exceeding the Sum of the Parts."

The article explains how Virginia had been far more successful than initially expected. After an away win at powerhouse Duke University, head coach Tony Bennett was asked about the team's surprising accomplishments. He said it was about "…the whole being greater than the sum of the parts… We have really good parts, and there's talent… But there's a synergy, or a chemistry, that when they're right, is making them even better" (Clemmons, 2018, p. 61).

Ironically, after the excellence of the season and a number one ranking in the NCAA tournament, Virginia was defeated by another team that also illustrated the potential for the whole being greater than the sum of its parts. In the first round, the University of Maryland, Baltimore County—a school from the relatively weak America East conference, not only beat but overwhelmed Virginia.

Both teams' performances throughout the season support the principle that interpersonal and coaching communicative behavior—and the residual culture from that communication—can be a powerful variable affecting team success.

Chapter Conclusion—Take-Aways

- Teams can be greater than the sum of the individual talent on the team. Outstanding talent does not guarantee that a team will excel. This phenomenon is referred to as nonsummativity: The whole is unequal to the sum of its parts.
- Factors that affect team cohesion and success are
    - Interpersonal conflict
    - Emotional intelligence
    - Team climate and culture
    - Coaching and leadership
    - Organizational identification
    - Concertive control
    - Character
- Team culture is dependent on a number of communication factors
    - Constructive vs. condescendingly critical evaluation
    - Honest vs. deceptive or manipulative behavior
    - Empathic vs. indifferent attitudes toward teammates, coaches, and players
    - Appropriately flexible behavior vs. intransigent posturing
- Team success is based in large part on understanding both the constitutive and transmission value of communication.

QUESTIONS

- How does the principle of nonsummativity apply to sports teams?
- In your experience, what are the keys to positive nonsummative results?
- Assume a coach has a team with two superior talents without whom the team cannot be victorious. Should the coach treat these players differently than the other athletes on the team?
- How would you describe concertive control to a person who was unfamiliar with the phrase? If it is possible to have concertive control, does that mean there is no such thing as "natural soldiering?" Explain your reasoning.

Practitioner Perspective

Hilary Witt

Courtesy of UNH Athletics

Head Coach University of New Hampshire
Women's Ice Hockey

Hilary Witt has been the head women's ice hockey coach at Yale University, an assistant coach for Team USA, and is now the head coach of the University of New Hampshire.

While at Yale, she was named the ECAC Women's Coach of the Year and became the school's all-time coaching leader in wins. She is a member of the Massachusetts Hockey Hall of Fame.

AZ. How significant is communication to your success as a Division I hockey coach? In what ways?

HW. I have found throughout my career, when I have effectively communicated, it directly affected our team success and relationships in a positive way. On the flip side, I would say nine out of ten times when things are not going well, it is directly tied to a lack of communication.

I have learned that you have to communicate with each individual differently. Some players want direct and blunt feedback. Some players need a softer tone. Often times just asking a player how they are doing and letting them know you care can make a difference in how they perform.

I also feel honest communication is the most important part of being a coach. Sometimes the truth hurts when talking about playing time or off-ice behavior, but the only way to help players be the best they can be is by communicating with them and being honest.

AZ. As a head coach, I imagine you have several audiences. That is, I know you have to interact with players. How important is it to communicate with fans? The athletic director? Your assistant coaches? Other head coaches at UNH? Other coaches in the league? Media Sources? Parents of Players? Faculty? Alums? Potential Donors? Community Members?

HW. Fans: I think it's important to recognize the fans. They are spending their time and money to support our team, and I really appreciate that. A handshake and a smile go a long way. When I have the opportunity to talk with them, I really try to listen more than anything else.

Athletic Director: It's vitally important to communicate with the Athletic Director. He or she has a lot on their plate, so hearing from the Head Coach is important for them to stay up to speed on what is happening with my program. I feel it is my job to advocate for my athletes. Sometimes I have to ask for more from the Athletic Director, and it's also really important to let them know how much I appreciate it.

It's also important for me to keep them updated on what is happening in our sport overall, with rules, recruiting, staffing, resources, and more.

Assistant Coaches: Communicating and learning from assistant coaches is so important. Much like the players, I feel like I have to be aware of how I communicate with each coach because they are very different.

Assistant coaches have opinions, and they should. Some are really good at communicating them, and some need you to pull it out of them a little more. Sometimes they say things I don't want to hear but need to. It is important for me to have assistants who aren't afraid to communicate, and I understand at times, that is difficult.

Other coaches at UNH: UNH is such a special place because the coaches support each other so much. I think it's important to communicate with each other to show that support and to learn from one another. I like going to their games and chatting with them about how it went. You can learn so much from other coaches, and I would be doing myself a disservice if I didn't interact with them.

Other Coaches in the League: Hockey is such a small sport, so the coaches spend a lot of time together on the road recruiting, at games, and at meetings, so we communicate a lot. I think it shows sportsmanship, helps our game grow, and teaches our players respect.

Media Sources: I never turn down an opportunity to talk to the media about our team. Exposure is key for our game, and when someone wants to talk about the great things our players are doing on and off the ice, I welcome that.

Parents of players: When it comes to our players, my first choice is always to communicate with them directly. I feel my job is to help teach and prepare them to advocate for themselves. That being said, when I see the parents at a game, it's always nice to chat with them. They are our biggest fans, and I really appreciate everything they have done to help their children reach their goals.

Faculty: Some of my biggest supporters as an athlete were faculty members. It means a lot to student-athletes when a faculty member takes interest in what they are accomplishing on the ice.

It's nice to see them in the rink on the weekend. I think it's very important to let them know how much I appreciate the support they give my athletes.

I also think it's important for them to know how much I respect their academic expectations of my athletes. I work with our academic advisor to communicate with faculty about a student's progress in the classroom.

Alums: One of the things I have learned over the years is that alums care about the program if the program cares about them. They gave their heart and soul to their team when they were a player, and they like to talk about their experience, and I think it's so important for someone in my position to listen to their stories.

I try to celebrate the past and teach my current players about those who came before them.

Potential Donors: I always want our program to compete at the highest levels, so anytime I can help my program by fundraising, I attempt to do that. Communicating my vision for the program and appreciation for what people are willing to give is key to that goal.

Community Members: Community members are oftentimes our biggest fans. It's always nice to represent my program in the community and to get to know people. Everyone is busy, so when people take the time to support you, I feel like showing appreciation and taking the time to have a conversation is important.

AZ. How can successful interaction with these audiences affect the success of your program?

HW. I believe that representing my team in a positive, respectful, and humble way is the best way to teach my student-athletes to do the same. By treating people with respect and listening to them, I can become better, and my team can. Each of the audiences mentioned could have a positive or negative impact on a student-athlete. I always want to put my players in the best position to succeed in hockey and in life. By communicating effectively with each audience, I can help my student-athletes. Every player wants to play in front of fans, so by communicating with them, letting them know how much we appreciate their support, and listening to them encourages them to come back.

Communication and relationship building with alums and donors has enabled us to make upgrades to our locker room. Convincing student-athletes that communicating with faculty is vital to their success can sometimes be challenging, but once they realize how much it helps, they are so much more comfortable in the classroom. When they are confident in the classroom, they tend to be confident on the ice. As a coach, I need to respect and communicate with each of these audiences so I can hold my players to the same standard.

AZ. How has new media affected communication with various audiences?

HW. Social media has made communication better in some ways and worse in others. It is great to be able to tweet about positive stories on our players and to market our sport, but there is also an obsession with it. It would be nice to actually talk to a person rather than text. It is so hard to read sincerity, sarcasm, and tone with a text. The actual message can be so distorted, and it can cause an issue that doesn't exist. Aside from a logistics message or some sort of congratulations, I avoid any conversation over text or social media with my players, and I don't let them communicate with me over text aside from those areas either. I don't want them avoiding conversation or conflict.

AZ. In what ways did COVID make it difficult for you to communicate with the various audiences.

HW. Covid required everyone to think outside the box and communicate in creative ways. With information and protocols changing by the day, communicating with student-athletes and their families became vitally important. At times it became frustrating because just as a plan was communicated, a policy or guideline changed. It was a very confusing time. It became vitally important to not only deliver information in a timely manner but also incredibly important to listen and receive information in a timely manner to have the most updated protocols.

AZ. Did the fact that you were forced to use, for example, Zoom technologies bring about anything positive.

HW. Having the ability to use Zoom and other virtual meeting technology was not only important to deliver information but to also connect face to face. Texting and calling are often times the most convenient ways to communicate, but I feel face-to-face interaction is always the best way to communicate because so much of delivering and receiving a message is through tone and non-verbal cues. Zoom enabled us to do that during the pandemic.

AZ. Did you become aware of some positive features of the new technology that, had it not been for the crisis, you would never have known?

HW. I absolutely feel Zoom had a positive impact on quality of life during a stressful time but also an outlet from being quarantined. The pandemic was stressful for everyone, and having the ability to connect and be productive through Zoom was and is important. Although communicating through Zoom with college students is not ideal 100% of the time.

AZ. What are your biggest communication challenges?

HW. One challenge is remembering to check in on people during our most busy times. I have a lot of players, but I have to remember to communicate with them about topics other than hockey, so they know I care because I do. The same goes for my staff and the people who work so hard for us to be successful. Life gets busy, but I need to remember to listen and to take the time to check in. The other challenge is access. Players are on their phones all the time. Sometimes I wish they had a little time to reflect after a game before they jump on their phone.

I feel like opinion is based on perception. If you don't communicate effectively, that perception can be based on very skewed information, which then can form negative opinions. That can be very bad for a team. I believe honesty is the best policy, and communicating that effectively-that is the key to success.

AZ. Any particular anecdote about communication challenges you want to relay?

HW. I got injured when I was a senior and had never missed a game until that point in my career. I was devastated. I was sort of moping around the locker room and training room while everyone else was preparing for the game. I felt bad for myself, and then another senior spoke up and said: "Knock it off, it isn't about you, and the team is trying to get ready to play." I was shocked that, as a senior captain, I was behaving that way. I didn't even realize it. I was so grateful that she had said something. She was the same teammate who was there for me and helped me through the injury, but in that moment, she had the courage to say something when her friend and teammate was hurting the team. That moment has stuck with me for the last 18 years. Had she not communicated with me, I would have become a bigger distraction. As a coach, I wish more players had the courage to do that.

First Person — Theory X and Y and Sports

Theory X holds that people are basically lazy, do not naturally seek out responsibility, and are motivated to perform only by monetary rewards.

Theory Y believes that people are not inherently lazy, will, under the right conditions, see work to be as much fun as play, and therefore have a natural desire to seek out responsibility.

Given the choice of doing nothing or doing something, Theory X suggests that people would delight in doing nothing. Theory Y believes that people would be frustrated by doing nothing.

Can anyone who watches sports ever believe in Theory X?

Consider the conference championships that precede the NCAA Division I women's and men's basketball tournaments. In many conferences, only one team, the winner of the conference tournament, will advance to the Big Dance.

Players who win jump out of their skins at the end of the final game, thrilled that they were victorious. Losers weep. Winners hoist coaches and hug each other. Losers plod off despondently.

Ninety percent of the players who compete in these tournaments will never play professionally. They will not play for money. They play for something else. And that is, to excel, to be recognized in their own heads and in the heads of the people who support them. The need for recognition can have its own dangers, but believing that people only perform for monetary rewards is shortsighted.

It's not just college basketball. A professional baseball player earning millions of dollars hits a key homer, and the dugout explodes with joy. This was clearly apparent after the Field of Dreams White Sox-Yankee game in the summer of 2021. It could be a meaningless game in the middle of the season; players race out to congratulate the millionaire who has achieved nothing monetary because of the hit. It's all smiles as Gatorade is dumped on the hero's head. Theory X cannot account for this reaction.

The past; the present; the by-and-by
The proof is there for Theory Y.

Chapter 6

Sports Communication and Social Issues

© UPI / Alamy Stock Photo

Chapter in a Nutshell

Sports can have a powerful effect on society. In this chapter, we explore how the intersection of sports and communication has affected our world and why it will continue to do so.

Specifically, at the end of the chapter, students will be able to:

- Identify several events that reflect the influence sports communication has had on society.
- Describe how sports communication has affected gender, race, and politics.
- Identify organizations that have as their mission examining sports and society.
- Analyze how sports and communication have affected their own political and cultural attitudes.

Sports Communication Prompts

- Below you will see statements pertaining to some aspect of communication and sports. For each item
    - Decide whether you agree or disagree with the statement.
    - Explain your rationale for the position.
    - If possible, support your position with examples.

1. The *Sports Illustrated* Swimsuit issue and *ESPN The Magazine* Body issue are demeaning to women. The magazines should discontinue publishing these issues.
2. Women's sports would be more popular if they enjoyed the same media exposure as men's sports. The main reason why the WNBA has not taken off is because there is not enough media attention given to the games.
3. Colin Kaepernick is a pariah because he nonverbally communicated his perspective. What he did is within his First Amendment rights. However, the fact is he could not get a job not because he did not have the talent but because he expressed a controversial viewpoint.
4. If a man can coach a women's basketball team, then a woman can coach a men's basketball team.
5. Physical attractiveness should not be a criterion when selecting a male or female television broadcaster.
6. Athletes have an obligation to use their platforms and be spokespersons for important societal causes.

Sport has the power to change the world. It has the power to inspire; it has the power to unite people in a way that little else does. It is more powerful than governments in breaking down racial barriers. It laughs in the face of discrimination.

Nelson Mandela

I think it's important to speak up because as I continue to gain success and followers in my sport, I also have a platform which I can speak on and I'm speaking for others who might not have the opportunity.

Breanna Stewart

Sports is the best means of communication between people from different religions and countries.

Yao Ming

Sports, Communication, Activism, and Culture

The worlds of sports, communication, and social change are regularly intertwined. Consider indications of these interconnections which surfaced in the third decade of the twenty-first century alone:

- *Inside the NBA* broadcaster Kenny Smith, a former star college and professional basketball player, removed his microphone and walked off the TNT set in protest of the shooting of Jacob Blake. The Milwaukee Bucks scheduled to play the Orlando Magic in a playoff game went on strike because of the incident, and their playoff game was postponed. Other sports leagues stopped play and postponed regularly scheduled contests.

- An unexciting meaningless college football game made national news. The score was Missouri 21-Vanderbilt 0 at the beginning of the second half, and the final score was Missouri 41- Vanderbilt 0. Nevertheless, a story about this non-contest appeared in the *New York Times* front section the next day. The coverage in the Times and throughout the country was because a woman named Sarah Fuller kicked off for Vanderbilt to start the second half. It was the first time a woman had ever played in a Power Five football game. When interviewed about the event, Fuller commented, "All I want is to be a good influence to the young girls out there because there were times that I struggled in sports" (Kicking Down, 2021). The kicker inscribed the words "Play Like a Girl" on the back of her helmet.

- The 2021 Major League baseball game scheduled to be played in Georgia was moved to Colorado. The reason: the state of Georgia had approved a very controversial law called the Election Integrity Act. Many felt that this legislation was a deliberate attempt to reduce the numbers of African Americans who could vote. The commissioner of major league baseball, Rob Manfred, made a statement when announcing the changed venue: "Major League Baseball fundamentally supports voting rights for all Americans and opposes restrictions to the ballot box." https://www.npr.org/2021/04/02/983970361/mlb-moves-all-star-game-from-atlanta-over-georgias-new-voting-law

Issues related to race, politics, and gender have been influenced by sports and sports communications. Athletes, coaches, leagues, television and film producers, and even fans have utilized their platforms in attempts to effect social change. Some believe that athletes not only have the right to use their platform to advocate for social justice but also the responsibility to do so. Megan Rapinoe, for example, makes this point throughout her book, *One Life* (Rapinoe, 2020). William Rhoden argues similarly in, *Forty Million Dollar Slaves* (Rhoden, 2006). Etan Thomas, a former Washington Wizards basketball player, extends the point in his book *We Matter: Athletes and Activism*:

> Today, there is a new resurgence of the athlete-activist we love and hold in high regard. They are courageous, high profile, have access to millions with a push of a button because of social media, and they are ready and willing to risk fame, fortune, and endorsements and endure criticism to stand up for what they believe in. (Thomas, 2018, p. 7)

In her book, *One Life*, Megan Rapinoe argues that athletes should use their platforms to advocate for social justice.

Thomas's depiction of contemporary activism reflecting a "new" resurgence could be debated. While the number of athletes who've spoken out on social and political issues may ebb and flow, there have always been sportspeople who've understood the power of their platform for both conservative and liberal causes.

All-time NBA star Wilt Chamberlain declared his support for Republican presidential candidate Richard Nixon in 1968. Shortly after pitching successfully in the 2004 World Series, Curt Schilling campaigned enthusiastically for Republican George Bush in the incumbent's bid to win reelection that November. Soccer great Abby Wambach was a vocal supporter of Hillary Clinton in 2016. Former Indiana University basketball coach Bobby Knight and Dennis Rodman—an unlikely tandem—were among those who strongly endorsed President Trump during the 2016 campaign. In December 2017, Auburn University alumnus and basketball Hall of Famer Charles Barkley spoke forcefully for Democrat Doug Jones at a political rally held on the eve of an Alabama Senate special election. Former NFL running back Herschel Walker endorsed President Donald Trump in his reelection campaign in 2020. Tennis champion Martina Navratilova supported Joe Biden.

It's not just about political campaigning. Sportswomen and men have used their microphones to communicate in support of social change in various ways. Steve Tignor (2015), a writer for *Tennis* magazine, commented that Arthur Ashe was able to "use tennis to inspire social change." Sportswriter Frank Deford contends that Ashe's decision to play at the 1973 South African Open was a factor in changing the sinister policy of apartheid. "After Arthur came there as a competitor … something of a rent had been opened in the curtain of apartheid and after that it simply wasn't possible to close it all the way again" (Deford, 2012, p. 302).

Vera Caslavska, a gymnast from what was then Czechoslovakia, sent a courageous message to the Soviet Union in 1968. St. Louis Cardinal Curt Flood spoke out bravely against the oppressive reserve clause in major league baseball, an issue that transcended sports. Muhammad Ali was vocal in his opposition to the Vietnam War. In protest of the Trayvon Martin killing, LeBron James tweeted a photo of his Miami Heat team where all players bowed their heads and wore "hoodies."

Billie Jean King has been an outspoken critic of gender inequalities in sport and elsewhere. Her actions off the court and on have had a discernible effect on our world. King's biographer, Susan Ware, wrote that King used "her celebrity and fame as a bully pulpit to bring her feminist-tinged brand of tennis to a wide national audience" (Ware, 2011, p. 39). In the wake of the 9-11 attacks, Muslim basketball player Hakeem Olajuwon spoke out about how the terrorists did not represent the principles of Islam. Olympic snowboarder Cheryl Maas emphatically opposed Russia's anti-gay policies and forcefully expressed her disapproval of Sochi hosting the 2014 winter games. In late November of 2021, NBA center Enes Kanter legally changed his name to Enes Kanter Freedom and vowed to continue to speak out against international governments that deprive citizens of freedoms-regardless of how his messages might negatively affect his career.

Several athletes have used their sports fame to win congressional elections, putting themselves in a position to speak even more loudly in support of their political and social philosophies. Major league baseball pitcher Jim Bunning became a Republican senator from Kentucky. Princeton and New York Knick basketball great Bill Bradley won a New Jersey Senate seat as a Democrat. University of Oklahoma quarterback J.C. Watts was elected to be a Republican congressman from Oklahoma. The aforementioned Herschel Walker is currently a candidate for a 2022 United States Senate seat. There are at least a dozen more ex-athletes who, because of their sports visibility and popularity, were able to become political legislators and, consequently, spokespersons.

© REUTERS/Alamy Stock Photo

Former Georgia running back Herschel Walker ran for a United States Senate seat in 2022.

There are those who believe that athletes are just that, only athletes, and should not use their sports-derived platforms to communicate about issues beyond those that relate to the games they play. A contentious 2018 debate ensued when a broadcaster, Laura Ingraham, reacted to political statements made by NBA players LeBron James and Kevin Durant. Both had been critical of President Trump.

Ingraham said:

Unfortunately, a lot of kids—and some adults—take these ignorant comments seriously. Look, there might be a cautionary lesson in LeBron for kids: This is what happens when you attempt to leave high school a year early to join the NBA. And it's always unwise to seek political advice from someone who gets paid a hundred million dollars a year to bounce a ball. Oh, and LeBron and Kevin: You're great players but no one voted for you. Millions elected Trump to be their coach. So keep the political commentary to yourself or, as someone once said, shut up and dribble. (Curtis, 2018)

These remarks, as one might suppose, did not put an end to the public discussion and, predictably, ignited the discourse. James responded that he would not just shut up and dribble. His fellow players encouraged him to remain vocal. Charles Barkley hosted NBC's *Saturday Night Live* shortly after the Ingraham remarks. In his opening monologue, he said:

I'm an athlete, and athletes have been speaking a lot this year. They've been kneeling during the anthem, refusing to go to the White House … this country has a great tradition of athletes speaking their minds. Muhammad Ali changed the way people thought about Vietnam. Jim Brown had people thinking about race… At the end of the day, athletes are the only ones speaking out in their communities… .:[To James] Keep on dribbling and don't *ever* shut up. (Mandell 2018)

Ingraham did not herself shut up as the war of words escalated. She responded to criticism by saying that her comments were not inappropriate and asserted that they were consistent with her prior messages:

In 2003, I wrote a *New York Times* bestseller called '*Shut Up & Sing*' in which I criticized celebrities like the Dixie Chicks and Barbra Streisand who were trashing then-President George W. Bush. I have used a variation of that title for more than fifteen years to respond to performers who sound off on politics. I've told Robert DeNiro to 'Shut Up & Act,' Jimmy Kimmel to 'Shut Up & Make Us Laugh,' and just this week told the San Antonio Spurs' Gregg Popovich to 'Shut Up & Coach.' If pro athletes and entertainers want to freelance as political pundits, then they should not be surprised when they're called out for insulting politicians. (Curtis 2018)

As is apparent, some have debated whether sportspeople should use their platforms. But no one can debate that they have. And it's not just athletes but also the actions, behaviors, and communications of those who have written books about sports, made films about sports, coached athletes, and established leagues that reflect the interconnected nature of sports, communication, and social change.

David Maraniss's book on the 1960 Olympics is subtitled "The Olympics that Changed the World." One could certainly make the case that those games—the first Summer Olympics to be commercially broadcast—had a powerful effect. Maraniss writes, "In sports, culture, and politics—interwoven in so many ways—one could see an old order dying and a new one being born" (2008, p. 11).

The award-winning documentary "Hoop Dreams" follows the lives of two young men hoping, quixotically, to emerge from poverty and become wealthy professional athletes. Like Darcy Frey, the author of *The Last Shot*: *City Streets, Basketball Dreams,* the producers of *Hoop Dreams* make a persuasive case, however indirectly, that the notion that professional sports is a realistic ticket to a sweet life of affluence is more likely than not, and more often than not, illusory and insidious.

ESPN's *Nine for IX* series celebrates forty years of Title IX. It includes, appropriately, nine documentaries about women in sports. Ava DuVernay's *Venus Vs.* is one of these nine. The documentary follows Venus Williams's successful efforts at obtaining equal pay for women Wimbledon champions. Several commentators in the documentary, including Billie Jean King and *New York Times* tennis writer Christopher Clarey contend that Williams's victory off the court had an effect on leveling the playing field for women in other domains beyond athletics.

The aforementioned Gregg Popovich, the San Antonio Spurs' very successful basketball coach, has very vocally

© Neale Cousland/Shutterstock.com

Tennis champion Venus Williams spoke forcefully for equal pay for women at Wimbledon.

challenged political cowardice. There is nothing equivocal about, "The people who work with this president should be ashamed because they know better than anyone just how unfit he is, and yet they choose to do nothing about it. This is their shame most of all." (Gartland 2017).

Visionary Rube Foster founded the first Negro National League in 1920 and had a goal to use professional baseball as a mechanism for economic and political liberation. In the midst of pervasive racism and exclusion, Foster's league "created a universe in which the black presence was accepted, nurtured and celebrated" (Rhoden, 2006, pp. 97, 110).

© The Picture Art Collection/Alamy Stock Photo

Andrew "Rube" Foster was known as the "father of Black Baseball" (Rhoden, 2006, page 100).

Professional and collegiate sports leagues have created dedicated entities to address important social causes. NBA Cares is one such entity. Its NBA Voices program has in its stated mission: "... to address social injustice, promote inclusion, uplift voices and bridge divides in our communities ... to bring people together and use the game of basketball to demonstrate the importance of equality, diversity and inclusion" (NBA Voices https://voices.nba.com/about/).

In addition, sports organizations not affiliated with leagues, teams, or particular athletes, have spoken out about social issues. The Center for Sport and Society at Northeastern University is one such organization. The National Consortium for Academics and Sport is another. The Institute for Sport and Social Justice (ISSJ) is a third. On the home page of the ISSJ website, one reads that the institute is about "Changing Lives through the Power of Sport."

The international organization *Sport Matters* claims that it is using the power of sport to change the world. Its website reads that it is "dedicated to making a difference in people's lives using the power of sport as a tool for development in Australia, the Pacific, Asia and Africa."

Media powers have used their very influential platforms to address sport and social issues. ESPN's former website, The Undefeated, explored the intersection and influences of sports and culture. In the Spring of 2022 ESPN rebranded the site as Andscape-a "reimagination, expansion and diversification of The Undefeated's former platform." The Undefeated took its name from the words of the poet Maya Angelou:

You see, we may encounter many defeats, but we must not be defeated. It may even be necessary to encounter the defeat, so that we can know who we are. So that we can see, oh, that happened, and I rose. I did get knocked down flat in front of the whole world, and I rose. I didn't run away – I rose right where I'd been knocked down. And then that's how you get to know yourself. You say, hmm, I can get up! I have enough of life in me to make somebody jealous enough to want to knock me down. I have so much courage in me that I have the effrontery, the incredible gall to stand up. That's it. That's how you get to know who you are. (Schnall, 2009)

© dpa picture alliance / Alamy Stock Photo

Willie Mays receives the Presidential Medal of Freedom from President Obama. The president had told Mays, "If it hadn't been for folks like you and Jackie [Robinson], I'm not sure that I'd ever get elected to the White House."

Test Yourself: Apply the Principles

- You are the sports editor of a local newspaper. Does your sports section need to address how genuinely professional teams follow rules obliging them to interview people of color when there are coaching openings? Does your answer depend on the demographics of your readership? If the answer to the second question is yes, why do the demographics matter?

- You are the general manager of a dedicated sports station, e.g., The Tennis Channel. Does your network have the responsibility to schedule programming that examines social justice issues?

- You are a college basketball coach. Does your job require discussing with your players the historical injustices done to Black athletes that prevented them from participating in the past?

HBO's *Real Sports* with Bryant Gumbel is an example of a network dedicating a sports program to issues that transcend sports and one that explores the effects of sport and society. Visit the website for AWSM (pronounced "Awesome") for the "Association for Women in Sports Media." It is apparent that the site's content and existence are not solely or primarily about techniques for efficient sports broadcasting. One of AWSM's articulated objectives is to "serve as a watchdog, promoting fair portrayal of female professionals in sports media, encouraging diversity, positive workplace environments and equal access to opportunities" (awsmonline). It is http://awsmonline.org/we-are-awsm.

Even when sportspeople do not intend to address and affect politics, culture, and international relationships, sports and related communication have had effects.

The bizarre end to the 1972 men's gold medal basketball game reflected the nature of the Cold War and did nothing to thaw international tensions. The U.S. players on that basketball squad declined then, and still decline, to accept their silver medals because of the peculiar way that game concluded.

The movie *Invictus* and the documentary *The Sixteenth Man* describe how a national rugby team became a unifying factor in the healing of South Africa after apartheid. President Nelson Mandela understood that "sports has the power to change the world." The Springboks, the national rugby team, had been, before Mandela's release and presidency, a symbol of the cruel apartheid system. Yet, the Springboks, with the support of Mandela, became a remarkable vehicle for social change. The back of the team bus displayed a healing slogan: *One Team, One Country*. After the upset victory of the Springboks in the 1995 World Cup, Blacks and whites cheered together in the celebratory crowds.

The appropriately named *Miracle on Ice* in the 1980 Winter Olympic games provided comfort and relief to many Americans who had endured months of reports about how a handful of Iranian students had captured more than fifty Americans and held them hostage for months. According to *a Sports Illustrated* piece:

> When the score of the U.S.–Soviet game was announced at a high school basketball game in Athens, Ohio, the fans—many of whom had probably never seen a hockey game—stood and roared and produced dozens of miniature American flags. In a Miami hospital, a T.V. set was rolled into the surgical intensive care unit; doctors and nurses cheered on the U.S. between treating gunshot wounds and reading X-rays. In Atlanta, the manager of the Off Peachtree restaurant, concocted a special drink he called the Craig Cocktail, after U.S. Goalie Jim Craig. What's in a Craig Cocktail? "Everything but vodka." Impromptu choruses of "The Star-Spangled Banner" were heard in restaurants around Lake Placid, while down in the U.S. locker room—the players leather-lunged their way through "God Bless America!" (Swift, 1980, p. 18).

Seventy million people in a nation that was then less than twice that size listened on the radio to boxing great Joe Louis defeat the German Max Schmeling in their 1938 rematch. It was one of the rare events that, at that time, brought white and black people in America together. Hitler had held up Schmeling as a symbol of Aryan supremacy after the German fighter defeated Louis in their initial bout. In the rematch, Louis knocked out Schmeling in the first round, causing wild celebrations, particularly in Harlem but also throughout the United States. (*Goodman 2013*)

In the following pages, several events are described that reflect how communication and sport have been symbiotic partners that have affected our culture, society, and in some cases, the evolution of history.

Handshakes and Flashbulbs

That's when I first felt that this was more than a basketball game. I couldn't believe how many flash-bulbs went off, when all I'd done was shake his hand.

Jerry Harkness, Loyola Rambler 1963 captain, referring to shaking the hand of Mississippi State captain Joe Dan Gold.

Mississippi State University's 1959, 1961, and 1962 basketball teams were great. Unusually so. In each of those three years, Mississippi State won the Southeastern Conference. The 1959 and 1962 teams lost only one game each season.

As Southeastern Conference champions, the three teams were entitled to participate in the NCAA basketball tournament, what we now refer to colloquially as March Madness. However, none of these three Mississippi State teams participated. They were prohibited from doing so. The State of Mississippi then had what was referred to as an unwritten rule. That unwritten rule prohibited teams from Mississippi from playing athletic contests against opponents that had integrated teams.

It may be difficult for those who have come of age in the first decades of the twenty-first century to believe that there ever was any such unwritten rule. However, in 1963 no school in the Southeastern Conference had any Black players on any team roster. The 1954 Supreme Court case, Brown vs. Board of Education, had ruled unanimously that separate but equal education was inherently unequal. Nevertheless, in the South, segregation prevailed for years after the decision. Ugly confrontations in Arkansas and Georgia preceded ugly confrontations in Mississippi when there were attempts to integrate. In the fall of 1962, James Meredith became the first African American to attend the University of Mississippi. It was not a simple matter. There were bloody protests that were inflamed and not doused by the sitting governor.

Each of the years when Mississippi State was eligible to advance to the tournament, there was discussion and grumbling about whether the team should be allowed to participate. Regularly, Mississippi newspapers came out in favor of denying participation. An editorial comment in the February 19, 1959, *Jackson Daily News* was typical:

Agitators are already at work creating an issue which places the entire state in an uncomfortable position of being asked, once again, to reiterate its stand on segregation. The situation isn't raised by thinking citizens but those emotionally aroused by the beat of athletic passion goaded by clapping hands and the muffled yells of hoarse throated rabid fans basking in the exuberance of momentary glory … The issue is: Will Mississippi forsake long established, well considered policy for the sake of an empty promise of another swallow of shallow bouncing, round ball glory? (Veazey, 2012, p. 36)

Once again, in 1962–1963, Mississippi State was the Southeastern Conference champion and eligible to play in the tournament. This time, the president of the university, Dean Colvard, and the head coach, Babe McCarthy, were determined to let the players compete. Colvard announced that he was supportive of the team's participation. And the state's Board of Trustees of Higher Learning voted 8-3 to allow the team to play despite the unwritten rule.

However, two Mississippi state senators were able to persuade a judge to issue an injunction that would forbid the team from leaving the state. Colvard and McCarthy literally snuck out of Mississippi, so neither could be served with the injunction. According to the documentary *Game of Change*, Colvard actually found McCarthy at a hamburger restaurant, told him to get in the car, and lay on the floor of the backseat to avoid detection. Eventually, they both left the state. The players escaped the next morning. Their getaway plan was something that could have been constructed by a mystery novelist. The team sent the second string to the airport, assuming these players might be stopped while the first team would depart on another plane. That ploy proved not to be necessary when the sheriff who would be delivering the injunction told a staffer that it was his coffee break time-a code to inform the team that nobody would be around to stop the plane from leaving. Both units eventually departed, met up with Coach McCarthy in Nashville, and flew on to East Lansing, Michigan, where they would play the integrated Loyola University of Chicago Ramblers.

The Ramblers would eventually win the entire tournament, but for most observers of sport and society, it was the game between Mississippi State and Loyola—not the championship game—which was the most meaningful contest. Before the game began, captain Joe Dan Gold of Mississippi State and captain Jerry Harkness of Loyola met at midcourt. Said Harkness over fifty years later, "I will never forget that time shaking his hand, the warmth was there—almost to say, 'I'm here and I'm glad to be here.'" So many flashbulbs went off when the two shook hands. The photograph that captured the event would be in newspapers and magazines across the country. "I can't remember one basket," said Harkness, "but I can remember the handshake."

When the team flew back to Starkville, they did not know what to expect. The players could see a crowd on the ground awaiting the landing. On the plane, one player said to another, "I don't know if they are here to welcome us or send us back." The reception they received was overwhelmingly positive. The players were cheered and embraced when they deplaned despite having lost to Loyola. Jack Cristil was the long-time radio announcer for Mississippi State. He claimed that this one game "probably did more to help the segregation situation and integrate it than any other one event, because people could relate to it" (Veazey, 2012, p. 118). President Colvard's son said the game "changed so many people's minds in Mississippi and elsewhere." (Harkness et al *Game of Change* 2008).

March 1963: Loyola player Jerry Harkness extended his hand to Joe Dan Gold before the tip-off. The handshakes between Mississippi State vs. Loyola players proved to be a powerful moment in college basketball history.

The result of the "Game of Change" was not, of course, immediate tolerance and elimination of racial tension. An underground newspaper rag printed up by redneck students reported the final score of the game using repulsive epithets. In June of that same year, Medgar Evers was murdered in Jackson, Mississippi, by a white supremacist. One year later, three young civil rights workers were found buried in the mud near Philadelphia, Mississippi. Nevertheless, despite racial hatred that has never fully dissipated, the March 15, 1963, game was meaningful. In documentaries produced about the event and in books written, the players, students, and citizens of Mississippi comment that the event was a catalyst for civil rights in a state that had been deservedly notorious for denying them.

Mexico City

At the 1968 Olympic games in Mexico City, two sprinters from San Jose State University won medals in the 200-meter race. Tommie Smith won the gold and John Carlos the bronze. Something unexpected happened at the awards ceremony. Instead of typical foot attire, both Smith and Carlos wore only black socks. Instead of looking at the flag, both athletes bowed their heads during the anthem. Instead of hands by their sides, Smith raised his right arm and made a fist with his hand. Carlos raised his left arm and also made a fist. Carlos wore beads around his neck, which he claimed subsequently were meant to symbolize and protest lynchings that had taken place in the United States in the late nineteenth and early twentieth centuries.

The previously mentioned Czech gymnast, Vera Caslavska, protested similarly. Two months before her nonverbal protest, the Soviet Union had sent tanks into Czechoslovakia to thwart any attempts by the Czechs to distance itself from the then Soviet bloc. Caslavska won two medals in Mexico City. On both occasions, when accepting her medals, she bowed her head and turned to the right. ABC sportscaster Jim McKay was covering the Olympics. At the second medal ceremony for Caslavska, McKay said, "She has turned her head to the right and down, just as she had at the last ceremony. This does not appear to be an accident." (Hoffer, 2018 page 225)

Richard Hoffer, a sports journalist, is the author of *Something in the Air*—a book about politics and the 1968 Olympics. Regarding Caslavska's nonverbal message, Hoffer writes:

> It was a slight gesture, but as remarkable as a fist in the sky. A modest bow, but as furious as a punch in the face. It was just a quiet glance downward, but also, thanks to this new and lively medium, a wild and desperate shout, bouncing off Intelsat, heard loud and clear in 400 million homes. (Hoffer, 2018, p. 225)

George Foreman is known primarily in the first decades of the twenty-first century as a pitchman for his line of grill products and for encouraging aspiring inventors. In October of 1968, Foreman was a gold medalist at the Olympics—the winner of the heavyweight boxing division. When the final bout was over, Foreman walked around the ring waving a small American flag.

What is interesting for those who study sports communication is that the common interpretation of Foreman's flag-waving is, actually, incorrect. Most people thought that Foreman was waving a flag to counter the Smith and Carlos Black power protest that took place days earlier. This, according to Fore-man, was not the case. Foreman was upset that at a previous bout in the competition, an American featherweight, Albert Robinson, had clearly been winning but had been suspiciously disqualified by a Soviet judge for a phantom head butt. With his flag-waving, Foreman was commenting on the cheating by the judge, not making a political statement repudiating Smith and Carlos. As Foreman said, "I was thinking, gotcha, to those judges. That's all. The international rules of boxing were, cheat America. I wanted to show those judges, make sure they knew who I was, what colors I was wearing. So I waved that flag. 'Gotcha'" (Hoffer. 2018, p. 232).

George Foreman waves the flag at the 1968 Olympics.

© Bettmann/Contributor/Getty

Students who examine communication from a transmission perspective would correctly analyze Foreman's communication as ineffective since it was misinterpreted. There were, however, mainstream benefits to Foreman because of the misinterpretation. He was invited to the White House by President Johnson and met with the press. On that occasion, Foreman said, "I'm glad to be an American. I don't have no disrespect for the flag." Murray 1990 https://www.latimes.com/archives/la-xpm-1990-01-11-sp-418-story.html

George Foreman was hardly a political spokesperson. In his youth, he had been something of a ne'er do well, not always behaving on the right side of the law. However, because of how his flag-waving communication had been misinterpreted, his relationships with white audiences had been reshaped, and he was seen as a responsible citizen by those who found the Smith and Carlos behavior to be reprehensible. His relationships with Black audiences suffered as he was seen as an opponent of an important social cause. In his book, *Souled Out? Newsday* reporter Shaun Powell wrote, "[Foreman] swiftly became, in the eyes of a good many, the definition of a sellout … His attempt to heal the wounds caused by the strife of the 60s was viewed as brave by some in white society but cowardly by a good segment of black society, given the bold risk taken by Smith and Carlos" (Powell, 2008, p. 12).

Fast forward half a century. At the beginning of the 2016 NFL football season, a quarterback who had led the San Francisco 49ers to a Super Bowl in February 2013 made a political statement just as Smith, Carlos, and Caslavska had fifty years earlier.

Colin Kaepernick was the quarterback. Instead of standing before the game for the singing of the national anthem, Kaepernick took a knee. His objective was to support the Black Lives Matter movement. There had been a number of shootings of young Black men by police officers. These shootings had been challenged as hasty and irresponsible decisions. Protestors claimed that what encouraged the reckless killings was perhaps a subconscious sense by law enforcement officials that Black lives did not matter as much as white lives. Kaepernick's nonverbal message was intended to show his support for Black Lives Matter.

Kaepernick's nonverbal gesture had a polarizing effect. Instead of bringing people together in a collective cause, it exacerbated tensions. Using a transmission lens, many people did not get or want to get Kaepernick's message. Instead, they saw his kneeling as an insult to the flag and to veterans. That was not his intention, but that is how the message was interpreted. The President of the United States made critical remarks about the NFL players who joined with Kaepernick in protest. Many agreed with the president's comments and believed that Kaepernick was insulting veterans and the flag. Many disagreed, feeling that Kaepernick was kneeling to support the egalitarian foundation of the country and, besides, he was exercising a first amendment right.

San Francisco 49ers players Eli Harold and Colin Kaepernick kneel during the national anthem.

© Abaca Press / Alamy Stock Photo

Kaepernick's intention to bring about awareness of racial inequality resulted in his being essentially excommunicated from the league. He was unable to get hired even as a backup on a professional team after being released by the 49ers. Similarly, in the early years after the 1968 Olympics, Smith and Carlos became pariahs. Now both are seen more positively. In 2008, Smith and Carlos received the Arthur Ashe award for courage at the ESPY awards. It will be interesting to see how Kaepernick is perceived years from now. However, it is clear that Kaepernick, Smith, and Carlos used their platforms to speak for social change.

Battle of the Sexes and Beyond

Nothing has done more for gender equity in sports than Title IX. The discourse about Title IX, the debates that led to the implementation protocol, and the thirty-seven words themselves leveled the playing field in ways that go beyond sports. A second powerful driver of gender equity was a televised 1973 tennis match that has been called The Battle of the Sexes. It was a media spectacular that riveted live and television audiences. The match and hoopla before and after it had social repercussions that, at the time, would have been very difficult to predict.

SPORTS COMMUNICATION AND TITLE IX

After all the years of bad uniforms and bake sales, I was suddenly in the middle of a gold rush .... I no longer had to be a jack-of-all-trades administrator, no more making out schedules for the tennis team, no more ankle taping.

Tennessee coach Pat Summitt on the effects of Title IX
(Summitt, 2013, p. 121)

When we think about the progress women's sports has made in America it's worth remembering that Title IX ...was enacted in 1972. (DiCaro, 2021, p. 191)

Those who went to high school in the 60s may not recognize the gymnasiums of their youth. Michael Messner, an author who came of age at that time, described a visit to his high school in his book *Taking the Field: Women, Men, and Sports*. Messner's dad had coached basketball at the school for many years, and Messner himself had played basketball there. When he returned to the school, he noticed a number of changes.

When he attended, there had been a "girl's gym" and a better-equipped boy's gym. No longer. The old boy's gym had been replaced and was now called "the new gym." What had been the girl's gym was now called the old gym. The new gym, like its predecessor, had tiles on the outside of the building, each of which displayed images of athletes. Unlike its predecessor, the tiles in the new gym depicted female athletes as well as male athletes.

After his visit, Messner paged through the sports section of his own yearbook and juxtaposed it with an annual produced thirty-one years later. The sports coverage in the newer yearbook was far different than what had appeared in his own. In the new book, stories and photos of women's teams shared the pages with the men's; the women's teams wore uniforms that looked to be of similar quality as their male classmates'; there was meaningful text describing the women's teams; some of the athletic teams were coed (Messner, 2002, p. xi).

I attended high school nearly at the same time as Messner. My experience is similar. When I was in school, sports was for the boys. My yearbook included twenty-six pages dedicated to athletics. Four of these pages include pictures of women. Two of the four are pages of cheerleaders and twirlers. Photos of female athletes and teams appear on only two of the twenty-six sports pages. There was a women's swim team, a synchronized swimming team, and a basketball team. That is it. Men played football, basketball, baseball, lacrosse, cross-country, track, bowling, golf, tennis, and wrestling. I can never remember a women's sporting event advertised. Nearly every one of our men's basketball games was jammed with spectators. If you did not go to the basketball games, you watched the wrestlers or the outstanding men's swim team. I attended many sporting events and did not even know we had a women's basketball team before I leafed through the yearbook. My school was nearly split in terms of gender. Nevertheless, there were two sports for women and ten for men. If one looked through our annual, one would think that the primary sports activity for women was cheering for the men.

As Susan Ware writes in *Game, Set, Match,* prior to Title IX, women athletes were, at best, marginalized. Women's sports received a tiny percentage of the overall sport's budgets. It was not atypical for women's teams to hold something akin to a bake sale to pay for their own uniforms and travel costs. The athletic facilities for women and access to them were relatively inadequate. Typically women's teams were allowed to practice only when the men's teams were through—early in the morning or late at night (Ware, 2011, p. 8). Kelly Belanger reports in *Invisible Seasons* that as late as 1978, Michigan State University's women's basketball team held a bumper sticker sale to support out-of-state travel (Belanger, 2016, p. 135).

The specific budgeting disparities between men's and women's sports were staggering. Ware identifies a school system in New York that had budgeted $90,000 for men's sports and $200 for women's. In a percentage upgrade, a Pennsylvania school district budgeted close to $20,000 for sports, and only $160 of that went to support the lone women's team (Ware, 2007, pp. 44–45).

At the time of its passage, Title IX of the Education Amendments Act of 1972 was not considered something that would revolutionize equal opportunities for women athletes. The language of the law is relatively simple:

> No person in the United States shall, on the basis of sex, be excluded from participation in, be denied the benefits of, or be subjected to discrimination under any education program or activity receiving Federal financial assistance.

Few anticipated how those thirty-something words would affect sports and society. Title IX compelled schools to support women's sports and athletes the same way as they supported men's. If a school system provided $90,000 to men's sports and $200 for women's, there were clearly, inequities, and that would have to end.

Enforcing Title IX was not and has not been an easy matter. Once athletic departments and organizations, including the NCAA, realized the possible implications, the debate about how to comply with Title IX became robust and contentious. Opponents plaintively described doomsday scenarios that would be the result of implementation. Head coaches from the Universities of Nebraska, Michigan, Alabama, and Texas testified at congressional hearings voicing their concerns. Senators made speeches on the Senate floor suggesting that implementation of Title IX could result in the demise of college football and urged that the law exclude revenue-generating sports. Athletic directors charged that the result of Title IX would, inevitably, be a reduction in the quality of men's teams. Parents wailed that their son's opportunities would be diminished or eliminated.

Any time there is change, there is fear and pushback. But those who can be dispassionate have to marvel at the changes because of Title IX. In 1972, one out of twenty-seven women played sports in schools. Now it is more than two out of five. Four percent compared to 43%. The number of women athletes has increased dramatically since the early 1970s. Between 1972 and 2019, the number of women competing in high school sports jumped from under 295,000 to nearly 3.5 million—more than 1000% (Axon, 2018, p. 19).

Wimbledon has sent me a message: I'm only a second-class champion

Venus Williams

June 26, 2006

Have you ever been let down by someone that you had long admired, respected, and looked up to? Little in life is more disappointing, particularly when that person does something that goes against the very heart of what you believe is right and fair.

When I was a little girl, and Serena and I played matches together, we often pretended that we were in the final of a famous tournament. More often than not we imagined we were playing on the Centre Court at Wimbledon. Those two young sisters from Compton, California, were "Wimbledon champions" many times, years before our dreams of playing there became reality.

There is nothing like playing at Wimbledon; you can feel the footprints of the legends of the game—men and women—that have graced those courts. There isn't a player who doesn't dream of holding aloft the Wimbledon trophy. I have been fortunate to do so three times, including last year. That win was the highlight of my career to date, the culmination of so many years of work and determination, and at a time when most people didn't consider me to be a contender.

So the decision of the All England Lawn Tennis Club yet again to treat women as lesser players than men—undeserving of the same amount of prize money—has a particular sting.

I'm disappointed not for myself but for all of my fellow women players who have struggled so hard to get here and who, just like the men, give their all on the courts of SW19. I'm disappointed for the great legends of the game, such as Billie Jean King, Martina Navratilova and Chris Evert, who have never stopped fighting for equality. And disappointed that the home of tennis is sending a message to women across the world that we are inferior.

With power and status comes responsibility. Well, Wimbledon has power and status.

The time has come for it to do the right thing by paying men and women the same sums of prize money. The total prize pot for the men's events is £5,197,440; for the women, it is £4,446,490. The winner of the ladies' singles receives £30,000 less than the men's winner; the runner-up £15,000 less, and so on down to the first-round losers.

How can it be that Wimbledon finds itself on the wrong side of history? How can the words Wimbledon and inequality be allowed to coexist?

I've spent my life overcoming challenges and those who said certain things couldn't be achieved for this or that reason. My parents taught me that dreams can come true if you put in the effort. Maybe that's why I feel so strongly that Wimbledon's stance devalues the principle of meritocracy and diminishes the years of hard work that women on the tour have put into becoming professional tennis players.

I believe that athletes—especially female athletes in the world's leading sport for women—should serve as role models. The message I like to convey to women and girls across the globe is that there is no glass ceiling. My fear is that Wimbledon is loudly and clearly sending the opposite message: 128 men and 128 women compete in the singles main draw at Wimbledon; the All England Club is saying that the accomplishments of the 128 women are worth less than those of the 128 men. It diminishes the stature and credibility of such a great event in the eyes of all women.

The funny thing is that Wimbledon treats men and women the same in so many other respects; winners receive the same trophy and honorary membership. And as you enter Centre Court, the two photographs of last year's men's and women's champions are hung side by side, proudly and equally.

So why does Wimbledon choose to place a lesser value on my championship trophy than that of the 2005 men's winner Roger Federer? The All England Club is familiar with my views on the subject; at Wimbledon last year, the day before the final, I presented my views to it and its French Open counterparts. Both clearly gave their response: they are firmly in the inequality for women camp.

Wimbledon has argued that women's tennis is worth less for a variety of reasons; it says, for example, that because men play a best of five sets game, they work harder for their prize money.

This argument just doesn't make sense; first of all, women players would be happy to play five sets matches in grand slam tournaments. Tim Phillips, the chairman of the All England Club, knows this and even acknowledged that women players are physically capable of this.

Secondly, tennis is unique in the world of professional sports. No other sport has men and women competing for a grand slam championship on the same stage, at the same time. So in the eyes of the general public, the men's and women's games have the same value.

Third, athletes are also entertainers; we enjoy huge and equal celebrity and are paid for the value we deliver to broadcasters and spectators, not the amount of time we spend on the stage. And, for the record, the ladies' final at Wimbledon in 2005 lasted forty-five minutes longer than the men's. No extra charge.

Let's not forget that the U.S. Open, for thirty-three years, and the Australian Open already award equal prize money. No male player has complained—why would they?

Wimbledon has justified treating women as second class because we do more for the tournament. The argument goes that the top women—who are more likely also to play doubles matches than their male peers—earn more than the top men if you count singles, doubles, and mixed doubles prize money. So the more we support the tournament, the more unequally we should be treated! But doubles and mixed doubles are separate events from the singles competition. Is Wimbledon suggesting that, if the top women withdrew from the doubles events, that then we would deserve equal prize money in singles? And how then does the All England Club explain why the pot of women's doubles prize money is nearly £130,000 smaller than the men's doubles prize money?

Equality is too important a principle to give up on for the sake of less than 2% of the profit that the All England Club will make at this year's tournament. Profit that men and women will contribute to equally through sold-out sessions, T.V. ratings or attraction to sponsors. Of course, one can never distinguish the exact value brought by each sex in a combined men's and women's championship, so any attempt to place a lesser value on the women's contribution is an exercise in pure subjectivity.

Let's put it another way, the difference between men and women's prize money in 2005 was £456,000—less than was spent on ice cream and strawberries in the first week. So the refusal of the All England Club, which declared a profit of £25 million from last year's tournament, to pay equal prize money can't be about cash. It can only be trying to make a social and political point, one that is out of step with modern society.

I intend to keep doing everything I can until Billie Jean's original dream of equality is made real. It's a shame that the name of the greatest tournament in tennis, an event that should be a positive symbol for the sport, is tarnished.

Venus Williams

Three Prongs, Facilities, and Scholarships

In order to comply with Title IX, schools receiving federal financial assistance have to prove that (a) there is proportional participation in sports, (b) facilities for men and women are equitable, and (c) scholarships are available for female athletes as well as male athletes.

Proof of participation is satisfied by meeting one of three compliance "prongs." Institutions have to demonstrate either that the number of participants in women's sports is roughly proportional to the percentage of women in the school, or there has been progress and a plan toward the goal of proportional participation, or the percentage of participation reflects the interests of the students at the school.

As it relates to facilities, there can be no discrimination in terms of

- The scheduling of practice time and access to facilities
- Equipment
- Locker room space
- Housing and dining
- Publicity for sports
- Opportunities to receive
  - coaching
  - academic assistance

The days of bake sales to obtain uniforms are over unless the men's teams also have to also peddle cake to fund their programs. If schools give scholarships to men, then there needs to be scholarships given to women. Equity issues still remain, but because of Title IX, the landscape for equity in sports and beyond, as Belanger writes, has been "radically transformed" (Belanger, 2016, p. xi). In 1999, the U.S. women's soccer team won the World Cup. In 2018, the U.S. women's ice hockey team won the gold medal in the Olympics. In 2021 the United States women's basketball team won its fifth consecutive gold medal in the Olympics. How many of the athletes who participated in these games would have been discouraged from exercising their athletic talents had it not been for Title IX?

King and Riggs—A Seminal Moment

If Title IX had the greatest effect on gender equity, a close second would be the media spectacular that took place one year after the passage of Title IX and many years before Title IX would be implemented. The event was called The Battle of the Sexes. In an ESPN documentary and her memoir, sportswriter Lesley Visser described the match as "the seminal moment in the women's movement" (Stern et al, *Let Them Wear Towels; Visser, 2017, p. 17*).

The Battle of the Sexes took place on September 20, 1973. It was a tennis match that pitted a fifty-five-year-old former Wimbledon and US Open champion, Bobby Riggs, against the not quite thirty-year-old Billie Jean King—one of the best women's tennis players of all time. Years after the contest, the *New York Times* wrote about the significance of the event beyond sport.

> *In a single tennis match, Billie Jean King was able to do more for the cause of women than most feminists can achieve in a lifetime.*

"The Troubles and Triumph of Billie Jean King" (New York Times editorial May 6, 1981).

Over ninety million worldwide viewers watched the match on television. More than 30,000 packed the Houston Astrodome where it was held. To understand the enormity of these audiences, consider that in 2017 less than two million television viewers watched the finals of the US Open. The seating capacity for Arthur Ashe Stadium, where the 2017 match was played, is not quite 24,000. Millions more watched the Battle of the Sexes in 1973 than watched the US Open championship forty-four years later.

It was a much-hyped event. Riggs had boasted in the weeks prior to the match that no woman could compete with a professional male player. He spewed classic male chauvinist rhetoric. He regularly wore a tee-shirt that read, WORMS, standing for the World Organization for the Retention of Male Supremacy. He was fond of saying, "Women who can, do. Those who can't, become feminists." During the first few games of the match, he kept on his warm-up jacket with the words *Sugar Daddy* on it. Despite his bluster, King won the match in straight sets: 6–4, 6–3, 6–3. King was victorious on many levels. As Pat Summitt wrote in her memoir:

> Like every other woman in the country I pressed close to the television and screamed an exultant "Yes!" when it was over. That match was a springboard—it brought awareness to female athletes and made us relevant. From that point on, the suggestion that there were some things women couldn't do would lose ground. (Summitt, 2013, p. 79)

Bobby Riggs spews male chauvinist rhetoric before "The Battle of the Sexes".

Kathryn Jay, in *More Than Just a Game,* wrote that Riggs's pre-match jousting included barbs suggesting that women did not have the mental capacity to withstand stress. The match showed "that King, and by extension, the women she represented could concentrate and win under extreme conditions" (Jay, 2004, p. 164). "Billie Jean King's decision to play Bobby Riggs," wrote biographer Susan Ware, "was a conscious political decision. She always realized that the match was much bigger than tennis" (Ware, 2011, p. 7). In her autobiography, King herself wrote: "I wanted to show that women deserve equality, and can perform under pressure and entertain just as well as men. I think the outcome, and the discussion the match provoked, advanced our fight" (King, 2021 p. 5).

PRESENCE ON THE AIR AND IN THE BOOTH

More male sports are still broadcast than women's, but there is a presence that was certainly not there before the Battle of the Sexes and Title IX. Women's collegiate championships in softball and basketball are broadcast nationally. The WNBA draft is broadcast nationally. The 1999 women's soccer team packed the Los Angeles coliseum. ESPNW is dedicated to women's sports.

While female broadcasters are still often relegated to sideline reporting, there have been substantive changes from the time when a woman on a sports show was an anomaly or when sports reporters could not gain access to a press box or locker room. Doris Burke is an NBA basketball analyst, Suzyn Waldman is an everyday Yankee radio announcer, and Jessica Mendoza is in the booth for Sunday night baseball. In 2021 Lisa Byington became the play-by-play announcer for the Milwaukee Bucks.

The story of how women had to fight to get access into locker rooms is well depicted in the Annie Sundberg and Ricki Stern documentary, *Let Them Wear Towels*. As sportswriter Claire Smith comments in the documentary, steps taken toward equity in sports—in her case, steps taken to allow equal access for women sportswriters—"transcended sports" and were steps "that advanced the society." Still, despite Title IX and despite discernible advances, the playing field is not level. Interested readers might want to read Julie DiCaro's *Sidelined* to understand how the field remains tilted. As DiCaro writes early on in her book, "Women who work in the [sports broadcasting] industry swim in a toxic stew of gender inequality" (DiCaro, 2021, p. 2).

Fair or Foul   Questions of Ethics

When Michael Jordan was asked why he did not endorse a Democratic candidate running for office, Jordan allegedly said, "Republicans buy sneakers too." Is that Fair or Foul? In other words, is it ethical for a role model who was a star athlete to be apolitical because of the financial effects of any endorsement?

Marathon Bombing

On April 20, 2013, five days after delusional terrorists interrupted the Boston Marathon by planting bombs where innocent spectators were standing, David "Big Papi" Ortiz, a Red Sox baseball hero, walked out to the pitcher's mound at Fenway Park and made a speech.

The finish line at the Boston Marathon is not far from the entrance to Fenway Park—a little over a mile. Annually, on the third Monday of April, Bostonians celebrate Patriots Day, commemorating the battles at Lexington and Concord that began the Revolutionary War. The day is festive, especially when the weather is warm or at least sunny. Spectators line the 26.2-mile course and are three or four deep on Boylston Street, where the race concludes. It was on Boylston Street near the finish line where the bombs went off. The terrorists' behavior was especially horrific since the result of any explosion would not be any rational political statement but rather death and injury to those crowded together along the sidewalk cheering for family and friends.

The Red Sox had completed its morning game by 2:10 p.m. The bombs went off about an hour later. The Red Sox were already preparing to travel to Cleveland and were not scheduled to return to Boston until Friday, April 19.

On the nineteenth, however, the city was in lockdown as the chase was on for one of the bombers. The baseball game was canceled. The terrorist was captured on Friday night, and therefore the game on the twentieth would be played as scheduled. There was a ceremony before the game that honored the first responders and all those who had been affected by the tragedy. As part of the ceremony, Ortiz spoke on behalf of the Red Sox.

Using language not typically heard over public address speakers at a ballpark, Ortiz declared that nobody was going to divide Boston. He declared that Boston was "our bleeping city, and nobody is going to dictate our freedom."

Three days earlier, on April 17, the Boston Bruins were playing a hockey game. This game, too, had been postponed as it was originally scheduled for the day of the bombing. The words Boston Strong were projected on the ice at both ends. Before the national anthem, there was a musical and visual tribute to those who had been victimized. After that, Rene Rancourt, the usually flamboyant singer of the national anthem, appeared on the carpet. He began singing. Ten seconds into the anthem, he dropped the microphone. When he did so, all one could hear was the stirring voices of the 19,000 fans in the arena singing the anthem.

The handshake with the Loyola Ramblers, the Mexico City Salute, the discourse surrounding Title IX, the King–Riggs match, and the post bombing speech by Ortiz represent a small sample of how sports communication has affected culture, history, and society.

In 1936, Jesse Owens undermined the mad ravings of Adolph Hitler with his four gold medal performances in the Berlin Olympics. Joe Louis's aforementioned revenge knockout of Max Schmeling was a knockout blow to totalitarianism and outrageous racism. Muhammad Ali spoke out against the Vietnam War well before the chorus of antiwar protestors had begun to lather. Stripped of his ability to compete in the prime of his years, his behavior—while hardly universally celebrated at the time—is now acknowledged as a powerful and responsible catalyst for social change.

The documentary *Murderball* describes the game of wheelchair rugby and humanizes the athletes who compete in these games. The film reflects the lure of sport as the handicapped athletes strategize and compete in ways that able-bodied athletes strategize and compete. Another documentary, *Training Rules*, revealed bigotry against lesbian athletes and was instrumental in bringing awareness to the plight of athletes who feel they have to hide their sexuality.

© Entertainment Pictures / Alamy Stock Photo

Murderball is a film about paraplegics who play full-contact rugby.

Sports communication does not always have positive ramifications. After New York Knick newcomer Jeremy Lin had a sensational series of games, the MSG network showed viewers an image featuring guard Jeremy Lin's head in between the ends of a broken fortune cookie with the sentence "The Knicks' Good Fortune" on a piece of paper (Maller, 2012). For years, the Cleveland Indians have had uniform apparel that included a caricature of a Native American. It was only in 2021 when the team announced it would change the name of the franchise. Until 2020, the NFL franchise in the nation's capital was called the Redskins, with a picture of a befeathered Native American on the helmet. A major league general manager, and two NFL Today hosts, made stunning comments disparaging African Americans.

Nevertheless, the point is that sports, as the Nelson Mandela quote that begins this chapter suggests, provides a platform for communication for social change.

When Jackie Robinson broke the color line in baseball in 1947, he did much more than just integrate baseball. When Billie Jean King defeated Riggs, it was not just a matter of tennis. Jerry Harkness remembers the flashbulbs going off when he shook hands with Joe Dan Gold, and the moment was, indeed, illuminating: "When those bulbs popped and everything, and I felt the tension, I said oh, this is more than a game. This is more than a game" (Harkness et al, *The Game of Change).*

Chapter Conclusion—Take-Aways

- Athletes, sports teams, and sports media industries have a powerful microphone. Sports figures have been advocates for social change.
- Sports, and communication about sports, have affected:
  - Race relations
  - Gender equity
  - Community cohesion
  - Attitudes toward the LGBTQ community
  - International politics
  - Attitudes toward the physically handicapped
- Some sports journalists have contended that speaking out for social change is a responsibility of sports figures.
- The reaction to sports figures who have spoken out for social justice is often initially negative.

QUESTIONS

- What are the pros and cons regarding an athlete's social responsibility to use her or his microphone?
- In what way has Title IX affected your participation as an athlete in middle and high school? In college?
- Is there a distinction between the protests of Smith and Carlos and those of Kaepernick? If so, what is the distinction?
- Is it appropriate for a coach or a league to require that athletes not participate in social protests?

Practitioner Perspective

Sarina Morales

Courtesy of Jeff Willis

Sarina Morales is currently an NFL reporter for Bally Sports and a gambling host for thegameday NFL. Previously, she spent over three years covering the Los Angeles Rams as the team reporter. Ms. Morales is also a former SportsCenter anchor for ESPN. She was part of the launch of ESPN's SportsCenter AM morning show in February of 2016. I spoke with Sarina before the first edition of this text and then again on January 20, 2022 for the second edition.

AZ. You've had many exciting jobs in sports. What are you doing now since you left the Rams?

SM Right now, I work as an NFL reporter for Bally Sports. I am expected to cover other sports long term with them, but currently just the NFL. I do hits regularly, pretty much daily, on NFL matters: Breaking news; updates on factors that could affect the games. I'm also freelancing with a gambling group called thegameday.com, specifically working with their group called thegameday NFL, and I host a gambling show with them.

AZ With the gambling show, do you entertain calls from people who aspire to be winners and are looking for suggestions, or do you just speak to experts who make predictions on games?

SM A mix of both. People will join us on YouTube. On the NFL weekends, we go on before the games start and we'll field questions live. For example, a fan might ask: "What do you think about a particular parlay? Would you take the Rams on the money line?" Gambling is new for me. Learning the language of betting and discovering how and why people gamble has been an enjoyable challenge. It's a very different mindset when you're reporting on a sports story as opposed to thinking about the event from a gambling perspective.

AZ. Can you tell us a little bit about what you did for the Rams when you worked with them.

SM. What did I do for the Rams? A lot of everything. My main job was to share information about the team to the fans, and I obtained that information in many different ways. Interviewing the players one on one; Interviewing the coaches; Taking notes during press conferences; Watching practice so I can convey what's happening with the team on a daily basis.

The thing I loved the most about the job was interacting—almost every day—with these crazy elite athletes, who live on a level of competitiveness that I can't comprehend. We talked about their job and the mundane parts of their lives. What they ate for dinner, how they spent their weekend, how their kids were doing, and where they got that bruise. We had constant interactions to get to know each other, so that familiarity was there when it was time to discuss football. That built comfort for both sides in the work environment, an environment in which I needed to prove I was trustworthy.

AZ. I know you also worked for ESPN. What did you do for them, and how would you contrast working for a team as opposed to being a broadcaster for a sports network?

SM. I did work for ESPN. My first year working for ESPN was very much focused on social media. They originally hired me to help develop their content on their social media platforms—in particular, their SportsCenter social media accounts. I had pitched a number of different interviewing concepts to ESPN because I was trying to find where I could add to the already robust news machine that operated out of Bristol, Connecticut. Funny enough, one of the ideas I pitched was singing in cars with athletes. How funny would it be to get Peyton Manning singing "Africa" by Toto? For a couple different reasons, I thought this would be the ideal interview platform. I was really excited when I pitched this idea because I thought this would add different ways to relay information in sports journalism. We never got to execute it, but this was one of many ideas I pitched to ESPN in my early stages as an employee there. Fast-forward three months later, Carpool Karaoke became arguably the biggest Internet sensation since Keyboard Cat.

Tangible work I did that first year on camera was working on a segment for SportsCenter called "NOW," which featured different stories throughout the day highlighting off-color, less X's and O's and more hugs and kisses. Finding the lighter side to sports or finding the human side to athletes and those surrounding them. They were quick bits—never lasting more than ninety seconds.

Going to the college football championship my first year was a big moment for me. I pitched using the ESPN Snapchat account to give a different point of view to Media Day. By giving my phone to a lot of the players in the middle of the media frenzy, I had moments like Derrick Henry signing his autograph and adding a filter. This ended up a unique way to highlight who he was and how creative he could be at the drop of a hat. I had some of the rookies take my phone and interview each other on what it's like being part of the biggest game of the year. It was less about being a social media takeover from one player and more about the integration of a media member with young athletes taking in media day.

In my second year at ESPN, I was able to check an item off my bucket list. I was given an anchor spot on the brand new morning SportsCenter—"SportsCenter AM." It was a highly coveted spot on the four-person roster. This role entailed watching games the night before, taking notes, sending in stories we should break down in greater detail the next morning, and I personally thought I could help our content by adding color and personality, given I was the youngest member of the team and came from a social media background. I, like any young sports fan, had a dream to be on SportsCenter at one point or another—either as an athlete or an anchor, so it was a great honor to do this job. Despite waking up for work at 3 a.m., having the opportunity to influence a sports fans' morning and day—Monday through Friday—was something I never took for granted.

I worked on features and traveled for live events during my final few months at ESPN. I got to cover Opening Day for both the Yankees and Mets. I covered Derek Jeter's retirement day at Yankee Stadium. I covered the NBA Finals and rode with Draymond Green's mom to Game 5 when the Warriors won. I went to Eddie Lacy's garage sale, and I went to Minnesota and covered Prince Night. It was a little bit of everything; it was ever-changing, and it was a great experience.

The biggest difference in working as a broadcaster for a sports network and working for a specific team comes from the access you have to your specific team every day. In a lot of ways, the team reporter is an extension of the P.R. team, but you can still create great journalistic work. The access you have and the familiarity you build with the players afford you great opportunities in this respect. Reporters outside of the organization don't typically receive the same chances.

AZ What is a typical day like for you now? Has COVID affected your work?

SM COVID certainly has affected my work. When I left the Rams I, essentially, bet on myself. I had outgrown the job with the Rams. I had been there for over three seasons and wanted to challenge myself more and cover the NFL as a whole. But then with COVID, opportunities were slow to open up, and the nature of a sports journalist's work changed. For example, this [Ms Morales gestures to the background– a room in her apartment] is pretty much my studio. It's the guest bedroom in our home in L.A. I have a backdrop, ring lights. I have microphones, the whole shebang.

A typical day? Every day I wake up, have a cup of coffee, have NFL Network on, or ESPN or I'm switching back and forth, and I go through Twitter. I'm reading whatever is trending, go on my computer and start just reading news. I review something approaching 100 emails that come from all the different NFL teams—they are updates or various bits of news. And then usually around the end of the news cycle, which is 3-5 in the evening--that's when teams finish practices--I get injury reports. I might do a hit for Bally, which is just, you know a buck thirty, to two-minute hit that basically sums up: for example, here's what's going on; here's what to expect; here are the big games; here are some significant injuries that can impact your team winning or losing this weekend, that sort of thing.

On a football Sunday, I wake up at six o'clock in the morning, I do hair and makeup on my own. I would love to have gone to a salon, but they're not open at six o'clock in the morning and my studio is in my home. So, I just do my own hair, makeup, get my lights set up by seven o'clock in the morning. I'm on a pre-production call for thegameday--the gambling group--by 7:15 Pacific Time and then at eight o'clock, I'm hosting a show live on YouTube for an hour. Once that show ends at 9:00 a.m. Pacific, we do a quick wrap, figure out what's going on for the rest of the week. Then I walk my dog to get out of the house from 9:15 to 10 a.m. and get a coffee, get what I need from the supermarket. And then at 10 o'clock in the morning, I'm back. There's two TVs set up in the living room and I have one on Red Zone, one on a game that I want to focus on. And then I watch the games from 10 a.m. to 8 p.m. at night. Then I prepare for, and host a show on twitter that recaps the games I've just watched.

I think long term, post COVID, things will grow. I'll be doing more interviews. That's what I miss. That's my bread and butter. I love interviews with the players like what I did for the Rams.

AZ. When we first met, you relayed a story about how you came up to bat in a baseball game, and all the boys in the field sat down in protest. What exactly happened there? Were the coaches in support of the boys?

SM. It happened over twelve years ago, and the day is still clear in my mind. I wrote the story as my college essay because it was such a poignant moment in my life, my development, and the competitiveness and joy I take into every professional opportunity. I had just joined a new baseball team—it was the little league Mets, and as a Yankee fan, my family made fun of me for playing on that team. My mom said, "You must really love baseball to wear that jersey." It was my first game on this team. My coach, John, went out of his way to get permission to allow me to play in the league because women were not allowed to participate. Because of that, I wasn't the most popular player on the team, never mind the league.

Instead of my teammates being excited to have a good player on their team, my team was ridiculed because a lot of the other guys would say, "Look how bad they are; they had to get a girl to play on their team." That's what I was facing in this first game. My coach put me in at first base. I remember getting a guy out at first base, and a mom shouting, "You got out by a girl!" I think it was the first inning. My dad came to that game, but he didn't stand behind our team bench. He let me be on my own that game. I don't think he realized how tough it was for me in that league. I was fifteen years old, a freshman or sophomore in high school, and I was playing softball on my high school team at the same time.

Side note. I had also never played first base until that opportunity. I lied to the coach and told him I played first base because he needed a first baseman and because I just wanted to play. I didn't realize how painful this experience was going to be for me. I went up to bat—relegated to ninth in the batting order. I went up assuming nobody would expect anything out of me. So I figured I'd do well. But the other team never afforded me the opportunity to do anything. It was a nightmare. I looked around the field to see where everyone was placed. I thought maybe if the pitcher gave me one strike, I could place the pitch and get on base. You know where everyone was standing? They weren't standing at all. Everyone, in protest of me playing in that game, sat down on the field when I was batting. The pitcher lobbed me a baseball and told me this was probably the way I wanted it pitched.

All I remember is my dad screaming at the other team. I was embarrassed for him because he had a daughter instead of a son. And how many years later, I still tear up thinking about this experience. Imagine going up to bat and you're feeling pretty accomplished. You're thinking you'll show these guys they have no idea what they're dealing with here. And they didn't even let me play. For me, it was about playing baseball. For them, it was about denying me the chance. They walked me to first base. I didn't swing at any pitch. I was too embarrassed. My coach took me out of the game, and I sat on the bench without shedding a single tear. I wasn't going to let them see that from me, despite me having a big knot in my throat.

I walked home by myself from the field that day. I remember walking up six flights of stairs, and sitting in the hallway, and crying by myself because I didn't want my dad to see me weak from experiencing that moment. I was always going to have to be tougher than those guys, no matter if they could see my pain or not. I thought I was going to quit baseball that day.

AZ. I know you continued to play baseball for years. How did you get through those who tried to stop you?

SM. There's this funny thing about pride. It doesn't let me quit anything, even when I fail. I thought, "How could I end my baseball career like this? On their terms instead of mine?" So I went to practice the next day. I showed up and continued to play the game I loved. I played one more season after that, even though they didn't want me. The funniest thing I found out during the second season playing in this league, one of the pitchers on another team who played on my high school team said, "Sarina, you haven't noticed that none of us would pitch to you?" I played dumb. He said, "No one will ever pitch you a strike, because if you hit it, we look bad. If we hit you, we look bad. We'd rather just walk you every time." I was swinging at terrible pitches, and I realized, "What good is it for me to play when I'm getting worse, and not better?" So I stopped playing competitively after that second season. However, I can still hit an eighty mph pitch in the batting cages.

AZ. You had to overcome obstacles to play. Did you have to overcome similar obstacles to work as a broadcaster? Lesley Visser recently wrote a memoir, as did Linda Cohn a few years back, discussing, in parts, hurdles they had to get over that men do not. The Nine for IX documentary, *Let Them Wear Towels* speaks to some of the same points. Julie DiCaro's 2021 book *Sidelined*, argues that women are still marginalized, sidelined. Is it easier now for women to obtain work?

SM. It's easier to obtain a job in sports as a woman thanks to the pioneers like Linda Cohn and Lesley Visser, who fought so many battles to open these doors. However, there seem to be more battles once you obtain a position in this field. Just because the door is open, doesn't mean what's behind the door isn't just as bad. There's the battle of men always questioning your sports knowledge, which is ridiculous because there are many men who work in sports and don't know everything they need to know to do their jobs.

Another obstacle I don't think we talk about is the dress code and appearance standards women get saddled with in on-camera roles. I can't tell you how much money I've spent just to avoid being criticized for my looks. I hope I can call more attention to what I say rather than how I look. That doesn't seem to be a winning battle.

None of the guys I work with on the betting show are waking up an hour prior to do their hair and makeup. Producers expect women to now be hairdressers and makeup artists in addition to being sports reporters, which I think is ridiculous. I have really good friends, female writers that won't get opportunities on camera because they don't do the makeup thing, they don't do the hair thing.

J.B. Long, the voice of the Rams, would get sit down interviews with Matthew Stafford or some of the new players that came in over the team reporter, which was me, and no one thought that that was an issue. And if I brought it up, then you know, well, she's being such a diva. I'm getting perceived as the b word-- like, "man, she's difficult to work with." But if a guy speaks up like that, like, you know, "that's a good point."

Another factor is race and the color of your skin. For me, as a Latina, as a woman, it's not been the easiest. I'm a white passing Latina. I have been turned down for a job because, "We really want someone that, you know, is a little more Hispanic." I've been also turned down for jobs because they've said I'm not sexy enough. It becomes more complex the more layers you have as an identifier. It took Jessica Mendoza eight years to even be able to do Play-By-Play in the booth for ESPN, and that was such a big deal.

So, yes, things are better but there are still problems.

First Person   July 4 International Tournament

An international Little League tournament is held each year over the July 4 weekend in Nipper Maher Park, a recreation facility that is only steps from my home. I can hear the sweet noise from my deck. This year ten teams are competing, seven from western suburbs near Boston and three from Canada—two from New Brunswick and one team from Sydney, Nova Scotia—a seventeen-hour journey from Nipper Maher Park.

At just before eight this morning, I was reading the paper when I heard the familiar sound of balls and bats, infield chatter, and parents encouraging their children. I took my coffee cup and walked the two hundred yards or so to the field.

They have spruced up Nipper Maher for the tournament. Canadian and United States flags are flying near the attractive dugouts. There is a decent little refreshment stand and a table of knickknacks for purchase. An electronic scoreboard has been erected. I hear the Canadian and U.S. national anthems played before the first game.

In the 8:15 contest, a team from North Waltham is pitted against St. John, New Brunswick. A twelve-year-old girl named Amber is throwing change-ups and looks to be the winning pitcher in the sixth as the Canadian club leads 6-3. I look at the tournament bracket sheet and see that this game will be followed by a 9:30, 11:15, and 1 o'clock game. And then these are followed by games that continue until darkness.

I begin to converse with a knowledgeable parent whose daughter will be hurling in a subsequent match. He points to another field in the complex, which looks brand new to me. He tells me that due to the incredible rainstorms that have hit Boston over the last two weeks, that field is essentially underwater. He shakes his head, wondering who could have built a field with such poor drainage since the field where we are at is perfectly drained.

I walk around to the outfield and lean on a fence, watching. A boy in right field makes a good catch on a line drive with the bases loaded, and his parents are gleeful in response.

No doubt, the families represented by these children have their own aggravations, and all is not blissful in their universe. But on this day, it seems to me that they who are congregating here for an all-day marathon of baseball are happy watching their children compete amicably.

There is a seventeen-hour ride back tomorrow night for the squad from Sydney. Look at a map, and you will see that it is on Cape Breton Island, as far away as one can be from Boston and still be in Nova Scotia. It took two cronies and me four days to drive back to Boston from Sydney many years ago. It will be a joy ride for these youngsters.

Win, lose, or draw, their experience will be a joy ride. And they, as well as their competitors, will likely have learned more from the cultural exchange that occurred while they played baseball than they might have in a classroom.

Chapter 7

Ethics and Sports Communication

© dpa picture alliance / Alamy Stock Photo

Chapter in a Nutshell

In sports, as in all aspects of life, individuals are confronted with ethical challenges. This chapter describes the range of ethical issues related to sports communication and identifies methods that can be employed to deal with these challenges.

Specifically, at the end of the chapter, students will be able to:

- Describe the diverse nature of ethical challenges related to sports communication.
- Identify obstacles to ethical decision-making.
- Identify tools that can be used when making ethical decisions.
- Develop their own code of ethics for sports communication challenges.
- Apply tools and their code to ethical challenges.

Sports Communication Prompts

- Below you will see statements pertaining to some aspect of communication and sports. For each item
    - Decide whether you agree or disagree with the statement.
    - Explain your rationale for the position.
    - Support your position with examples.
1. Sportswriters who cover a local team should protect athletes who engage in minor indiscretions and not report them if they indulge in, for example, excessive drinking or rude behavior.
2. There's nothing wrong with buying media representatives lunch and even dinners in an attempt to obtain good coverage.
3. When professional coaches have post-game press conferences, it is essential that they be transparent about injuries incurred during the contest.
4. An athlete's sexual orientation should not be discussed in any media form. It is private and unrelated to sport.
5. Gamesmanship is fine. There is nothing wrong, for example, with trying to unnerve an opponent with trash talk.

Cheating to gain unfair advantages, gamesmanship ploys, the use of performance enhancing drugs, recruiting scandals, academic misconduct associated with athletes, discriminatory practices against females and African-Americans, and other breaches of principled behavior have become everyday realities in sports.

Angela Lumpkin, author of *Modern Sport Ethics* (2017) page xvii

Cheating is as much a part of the game as scorecards and hot dogs.

Former baseball manager Billy Martin

Sports do not build character. They reveal it.

Sports commentator Heywood Hale Broun

Introduction

Many recruiters make promises to prospective athletes that are exaggerations. If recruits expect these exaggerations, and recruiters consider it part of their job, are recruiters communicating unethically when they exaggerate? In the middle of a tennis match, players will occasionally request a visit from a trainer for a professed ailment. Assume an opponent has won several consecutive games. Is it ethical to attempt to break the opponent's momentum by feigning injury and calling for treatment?

There are coaches who challenge and berate officials throughout a contest. Assume this is done to intimidate referees so that subsequent decisions will be favorable. Is this ethical? Soccer players often flop to gain an advantage, and basketball players trash talk hoping to deflate an opponent's confidence. Are soccer and basketball players unethical when they communicate this way?

It is difficult to make ethical decisions in any context, and certainly, there are ethical challenges related to sports communication. Fans, teams, coaches, sports broadcasters, and athletes regularly need to make ethical choices. The examples above happen with such frequency that they may seem benign and not unethical. Are communications that have become normal consequently not unethical? Are behaviors that are not illegal therefore not unethical?

San Diego Padres manager Bob Melvin screams at the umpire and ultimately gets thrown out of the game.

This chapter examines the criteria for ethical communication behavior in sports communication contexts. We will review the obstacles to ethical decision-making and identify some tools that can be employed by those who wish to be ethical when they communicate. Before we begin this discussion, take a moment to consider the following examples of ethical challenges. They, as you will see, are detailed and more nuanced than the scenarios presented in the introduction to this chapter. For each, decide what you would do and provide a rationale for your decision.

COVERING UP

You are a head coach preparing for your season-ending football game against an in-state archrival. The game is significant for several reasons beyond the rivalry. The victor typically is able to recruit high school athletes more effectively. Alumni and other donors are less likely to contribute generously if your team is to lose. This particular year the winner will undoubtedly be invited to the FBS playoffs, whereas the loser will compete in a relatively meaningless bowl game that will yield less income and prestige.

On the Tuesday before the Saturday game, your star quarterback is arrested for shoplifting at a local convenient store. He is accused of grabbing a six-pack and a package of hot dogs from the refrigerated section and bolting from the store. Not only has he committed this particular offense, but the proprietor claims that she reported the activity in this instance only because it is the third time that this athlete has committed a similar offense in her establishment. She asserts that on one occasion, the athlete shouted a misogynistic epithet when exiting the store and did so while laughing.

The police are still officially conducting the investigation, but at this point, it is a matter of only completing the paperwork. The responses to your inquiries plainly indicate that the athlete did indeed commit the alleged offenses. You doubt if you can win the game on Saturday without this player. Your backup quarterback has taken ten snaps all season, and every single one was in a mop-up role. The backup has not thrown a meaningful pass all year.

Should you attempt to minimize the offense? Should you leak a story to the local sympathetic press suggesting that the proprietor has a dubious background even if you have no evidence to that effect? Should you call a press conference stating that until there is definitive evidence of a crime (even though you are nearly certain of the player's guilt), the player will not be suspended? Do you instruct teammates and coaches to not speak to the press about the incident regardless of what they might know? Do you contact head university administrators and claim that the investigation is ongoing because officially it is—even though you are certain the player is culpable?

In short, do you communicate to various publics that the allegations should not stop your quarterback from playing in the game?

PHYSICAL PLAY

You are a coach and have a basketball player on your squad whose main assets are his strength, pugnacity, and physical play. You are playing an opponent with an extraordinarily talented player. You have considered several ways to defend him, but figure the best way is to get in his head and also his body. You instruct your bull of a player to push the athlete around and to start talking to him as soon as the game begins. You believe that if the trash talking and physical play unnerve the star opponent, he may not perform well and, better yet, the two may get into a pushing war that could escalate. If both the star and your physical player are ejected, it will be a huge advantage for your team. The night before the contest, you make a statement to reporters suggesting that while the star opponent is a talent, he is soft and, moreover, a whiner. You hope this might prejudice the officials to allow your tough player to have his way on the court.

Would telling the player to trash talk and defend the opponent physically be ethical? Would the player be unethical for following orders and trash-talking? Would commenting to the press that the star opponent is soft be unethical?

ICE HOCKEY GREAT

You are recruiting a coveted athlete. This woman could make or break your program. She has dazzled all who have seen her play. She can skate, shoot, defend, and is just faster on ice than nearly anyone in the country, if not the world.

You know for a fact that she is considering your school and one other. You also know for a fact that the other school is lying effusively as they recruit her. They are misleading her about the academic programs, student-athlete residences, and travel accommodations during away games. The rival is blatantly lying. You are afraid that unless you embellish the truth yourself when she visits your campus that she will enroll at the other school not because she prefers it or that it is a better fit for her, but because she is persuaded by the lies.

You decide to also lie. You offer her things you know you can't deliver. You contact alums and suggest that they too conspire to communicate a bogus narrative about the school. You also manufacture—out of thin air—a story that the coach of the other team is soon to resign and take a position at another institution. You truly believe your school is a better fit for this athlete. Also, there is no major women's professional hockey league that compensates women substantively, so if you are able to get this player to sign, you will have her for four years and dominate the competition.

Is it ethical to misrepresent your school since the other school clearly is as well?

RAIN DELAY

A half-hour before your afternoon baseball game is to start, it begins to rain heavily and steadily. This had been predicted, but the skies had actually been bright for most of the morning. The morning sunshine encouraged wishful families that the rain predictions were incorrect. However, now it is coming down. You are the general manager of this minor league team and review the forecast. It is not likely to stop raining for several hours. Nevertheless, you post an announcement on the scoreboard that specifically declares that (a) there is a rain delay and (b) that the team is hopeful that the game will be played. The truth is you are not hopeful. Unless there is divine intervention, the game will have to be postponed.

Is there anything wrong with extending a rain delay so that more people will buy food and souvenirs at the concession stands at the stadium?

However, the reality is that the club makes a good deal of money from the concessions at the park. Also, the team's financial situation is not good. There is some concern that the team will have to move to another city in order to remain viable. This will mean dozens of jobs in the area. Today, if you wait one or maybe even two hours, fans will remain at the stadium and purchase popcorn and cracker jacks and sausage sandwiches and soda and beer, and all the overpriced items that are available at the concession stands.

You feel that it is your job to not only win games but to maximize the revenue for the ball club. You feel as if you have an obligation to people who could lose their jobs if the team moves. Is it unethical to wait ninety minutes before announcing via the public address system that the game is postponed when from the start you knew for certain that the game will not be played?

ILLEGAL ACTIVITIES

You are the local beat reporter for a team. You travel the country with the club, and the relationships you have with the players and management are key to your success. Without positive relationships that facilitate easy access, your ability to do your job will be negatively affected. You will not be able to write insightful stories that engage the many serious fans who follow the team's fortunes.

It is clear to you that one of the married athletes on the team is sexually promiscuous. He is not especially secretive about the relationships and sometimes appears to actually be preening, nonverbally boasting about his allure. In addition, you notice that this player drinks heavily. It is not unusual for athletes to have a beer after a game, but this player's consumption is excessive. His performance on the pitch is still very good despite the philandering and drinking. You do wonder how much better he might be if he drank less and did less cavorting.

Do you have an ethical responsibility to include in your newspaper articles information about the off-field behavior of the athlete?

WEBSITE DECISION

An NHL player has been accused of indecent exposure. No legal action has been taken regarding the accusation, and the player insists on his innocence. He claims he was just relieving himself by the side of the road. However, a sports-focused site known for sensational reporting has a photo that, out of context at least, is incriminating. They post the photo, blurring the player's midsection, but the picture is highly incriminating, nonetheless. It looks as if the player is exposing himself to passersby. The player responds on Facebook that he is being maligned. However, the narrative of indecent exposure has gotten traction despite the counterclaim.

Holding aside for a moment the potential legal ramifications, does the website have an ethical responsibility not to post the photograph even if the attention to the site is likely to increase visitors? Assume that you believe that a rival site will absolutely post the photo if you do not. Would that make your decision easier?

GUARANTEE GAMES

You know that at the end of the football season what determines invitations to the more prestigious bowl games is won-loss records.

Assume that you are the athletic director of an FBS school. You are considering contacting the director of a financially strapped FCS school. You will invite her team to travel to your FBS school and play a game in early September. If she agrees, you will write a check to her program for $350,000. Her program will receive much-needed revenue. Your team will get an almost guaranteed win. Also, you will earn money from ticket and concession sales from the 40,000 regular attendees at your games.

Is it unethical for the FBS school to schedule such an essentially non-competitive game for the win and ticket revenue? Can you justify scheduling the game because there has been a tiny percentage of these games when the FCS school has been victorious? Is it unethical for the FBS school to schedule the game for the revenue when it is a near certainty that the FCS school cannot compete with the hosts?

LET'S GO FOR LUNCH

Sports Information Directors for two local colleges are concerned that their schools are not getting the coverage they deserve in local media. They call each other and decide to invite sports reporters from newspapers, social media, and television to speak at a lunch panel ostensibly to discuss the difficulties of covering college sports.

However, the real objective of sponsoring the event is to obtain better coverage. The two Sports Information Directors intend to chat with the media representatives when they arrive about the various achievements at the schools. The two SIDs have no audience hungering for the wisdom of these media people. In fact, they are going to have to rustle up student-athletes and coaches not busy on the day of the panel to pretend to have an audience. Is it unethical to invite the reporters to this lunch panel in order to obtain better publicity for the schools?

Assume that the invited sports media are well aware that the invitation and free lunch is intended to "buy" coverage. Do these individuals have the responsibility to decline the invitation? The Society of Professional Journalists Code of Ethics clearly reads that one should "refuse gifts, favors, fees, free travel, and special treatment, and avoid political and other outside activities that may compromise integrity or impartiality, or may damage credibility." Should they, therefore, decline the invitation?

THE SPREAD

You write for the sports section of a newspaper that is published in a state where betting is illegal. In your city, there is a voracious appetite for sports news. A rival publication is barely surviving but is doing so because of its sports section. You have been reluctant to post the gambling spreads in your publication because it is against the law to bet on sports in your state. You know, of course, that people bet illegally, but your editors have decided not to encourage illegal activity. Meanwhile, your rival posts not only the spread but also the over/under—a gambling figure meaningful only to more than casual bettors. The rival publication has a column written by a pundit who offers advice on how to bet and beat the spread. After each day, the rival not only publishes the scores of games but how teams did against the spread and over/under. Your paper is losing some readership because of its stance of not posting information about betting.

Would your paper be unethical if it began simply just posting the spreads? Is the rival unethical for providing extensive betting information in a state where betting is illegal?

Obstacles to Ethical Decision-Making

If you discussed the above examples in class, you likely heard diverse opinions on at least some of these issues. You also probably listened to varied reasons that served as the rationale for choices made. It may have been surprising to hear how a classmate determined whether a behavior was ethical. It may also have been unsettling to listen to someone whose position on an important ethical issue was antithetical to your own.

It can be difficult to make ethical choices. Even for those who are genuinely concerned with doing the right thing, it can be easy to be derailed by common obstacles to ethical decision-making.

What are these obstacles?

USING INSTRUMENTAL vs. VALUE RATIONALITY

Phillip Tompkins has been mentioned in the text previously. He was the pioneer researcher who spent time examining the United States Space program. In Chapter 3, we discussed Tompkins's work pertaining to communication networks as they relate to sports organizations, and in Chapter 5, we considered his idea of concertive control on teams.

Tompkins also wrote about two contrasting approaches to ethical decision-making: Instrumental vs. Value Rationality. *Value Rationality* refers to using values as the foundation for making ethical choices. *Instrumental Rationality* refers to making choices on the basis of benefits that may accrue because of choices made. Tompkins contends that when faced with ethical decisions, people often revert to making these decisions on the basis of what material benefits that choice will bring to a person or organization.

He contends that this type of rationality is at best peripheral to proceeding ethically. He suggests that a healthier alternative is to employ Value Rationality. In other words, how you reason about what is right and what is wrong should be based on the values you hold as important, not on the basis of what financial or other benefits will be the result of the choice.

Consider some examples of what would be considered Value Rationality.

The University of Miami Athletics department has what it calls a URespect program. The stated goal is: "... to encourage positive behavior amongst our student-athletes, coaches, staff and fans with a focus on increasing awareness and a commitment to sportsmanship at all Miami Hurricanes athletic events."

The accompanying slogan for URespect is "Respect the game. Respect the fans. Respect the U."

Assume this is not simply window dressing and reflects the core values of the University of Miami athletic department. If so, then ethical decisions that the fans, coaches, administrators, and players make should be consistent with and based upon these values. The primary consideration should not be how any decision would affect the financial health or image of the institution.

The first paragraph of the University of Tennessee Athletic Department's mission statement suggests that the department values participation in intercollegiate athletics, good sportsmanship, academic excellence, the pursuit of championship performance, and a proper balance between athletics and academics. The department desires to "be a source of pride for the University's students, alumni/ ae and supporters." All very laudable objectives.

Again let's assume this statement reflects the core values of University of Tennessee athletics and has not been provided for the optics. If so, when the University of Tennessee debates ethical matters, the thinking should rest on the values indicated in the mission statement.

The obstacle is that in the throes of making difficult ethical choices, people sometimes base their thinking on what Tompkins labels instrumental factors. If your class discussed the examples at the beginning of the chapter, you likely heard some classmates describe the rationale for their decisions on the basis of instrumental rationality.

In the case of the beat writer considering whether she should report the drinking and philandering of the player, one might contend that it is ethical not to report the behavior because if she were to report the incident, her access to players subsequently and ability to function as a reporter would be compromised. If the reporter did indeed reason this way, she would be defaulting to instrumental rationality. The "ethical" choice was not based on values but rather on the material benefits of the decision.

Before a World Series game between the New York Yankees and the Atlanta Braves, there was a ceremony honoring players who had been voted to the Major League All Century team. Pete Rose was one of the honored players and was allowed to participate in the ceremony. This was news because Rose had been banned from baseball because of allegations that he was an inveterate gambler and had wagered on baseball games. Jim Gray was a sportscaster for NBC and was covering that World Series. At the conclusion of the pre-game ceremony, Gray approached Rose and asked a number of difficult questions about his alleged betting activities. While Gray contended that this line of questioning was appropriate, many others, including players competing in the World Series, believed Gray's interview was improper given the nature of the event. The next night Yankee Chad Curtis hit a walk-off home run to win Game Three. When Jim Gray approached Curtis for an interview, the player snubbed him. He commented, "I can't do it. As a team we kind of decided because of what happened with Pete we're not going to talk out here on the field."

If Gray knew that his hard questioning of Rose would lead to his inability to access players for interviews, should that have affected his decision to ask the difficult questions? If it had, Gray would have been employing instrumental rationality as opposed to following a journalist's fundamental credo, "seek truth and report it."

Simply put, if you default to instrumental rationality when you are confronted with hard questions, then making ethical decisions is problematic. If a sports organization has deliberated thoughtfully about its values and has articulated them, then these values should be the default criteria when making hard choices. Yes, in the "Covering Up" example earlier in the chapter, benching the star quarterback will cost the team the game, but your team's stated values probably do not condone theft and misogynistic speech.

Society of Professional Journalists

C⊙DE *of* ETHICS

PREAMBLE

Members of the Society of Professional Journalists believe that public enlightenment is the forerunner of justice and the foundation of democracy. Ethical journalism strives to ensure the free exchange of information that is accurate, fair and thorough. An ethical journalist acts with integrity.

The Society declares these four principles as the foundation of ethical journalism and encourages their use in its practice by all people in all media.

SEEK TRUTH AND REPORT IT

Ethical journalism should be accurate and fair. Journalists should be honest and courageous in gathering, reporting and interpreting information.

Journalists should:

▸ Take responsibility for the accuracy of their work. Verify information before releasing it. Use original sources whenever possible.

▸ Remember that neither speed nor format excuses inaccuracy.

▸ Provide context. Take special care not to misrepresent or oversimplify in promoting, previewing or summarizing a story.

▸ Gather, update and correct information throughout the life of a news story.

▸ Be cautious when making promises, but keep the promises they make.

▸ Identify sources clearly. The public is entitled to as much information as possible to judge the reliability and motivations of sources.

▸ Consider sources' motives before promising anonymity. Reserve anonymity for sources who may face danger, retribution or other harm, and have information that cannot be obtained elsewhere. Explain why anonymity was granted.

▸ Diligently seek subjects of news coverage to allow them to respond to criticism or allegations of wrongdoing.

▸ Avoid undercover or other surreptitious methods of gathering information unless traditional, open methods will not yield information vital to the public.

▸ Be vigilant and courageous about holding those with power accountable. Give voice to the voiceless.

▸ Support the open and civil exchange of views, even views they find repugnant.

▸ Recognize a special obligation to serve as watchdogs over public affairs and government. Seek to ensure that the public's business is conducted in the open, and that public records are open to all.

▸ Provide access to source material when it is relevant and appropriate.

▸ Boldly tell the story of the diversity and magnitude of the human experience. Seek sources whose voices we seldom hear.

▸ Avoid stereotyping. Journalists should examine the ways their values and experiences may shape their reporting.

▸ Label advocacy and commentary.

▸ Never deliberately distort facts or context, including visual information. Clearly label illustrations and re-enactments.

▸ Never plagiarize. Always attribute.

MINIMIZE HARM

Ethical journalism treats sources, subjects, colleagues and members of the public as human beings deserving of respect.

Journalists should:

▸ Balance the public's need for information against potential harm or discomfort. Pursuit of the news is not a license for arrogance or undue intrusiveness.

▸ Show compassion for those who may be affected by news coverage. Use heightened sensitivity when dealing with juveniles, victims of sex crimes, and sources or subjects who are inexperienced or unable to give consent. Consider cultural differences in approach and treatment.

▸ Recognize that legal access to information differs from an ethical justification to publish or broadcast.

▸ Realize that private people have a greater right to control information about themselves than public figures and others who seek power, influence or attention. Weigh the consequences of publishing or broadcasting personal information.

▸ Avoid pandering to lurid curiosity, even if others do.

▸ Balance a suspect's right to a fair trial with the public's right to know. Consider the implications of identifying criminal suspects before they face legal charges.

▸ Consider the long-term implications of the extended reach and permanence of publication. Provide updated and more complete information as appropriate.

ACT INDEPENDENTLY

The highest and primary obligation of ethical journalism is to serve the public.

Journalists should:

▸ Avoid conflicts of interest, real or perceived. Disclose unavoidable conflicts.

▸ Refuse gifts, favors, fees, free travel and special treatment, and avoid political and other outside activities that may compromise integrity or impartiality, or may damage credibility.

▸ Be wary of sources offering information for favors or money; do not pay for access to news. Identify content provided by outside sources, whether paid or not.

▸ Deny favored treatment to advertisers, donors or any other special interests, and resist internal and external pressure to influence coverage.

▸ Distinguish news from advertising and shun hybrids that blur the lines between the two. Prominently label sponsored content.

BE ACCOUNTABLE AND TRANSPARENT

Ethical journalism means taking responsibility for one's work and explaining one's decisions to the public.

Journalists should:

▸ Explain ethical choices and processes to audiences. Encourage a civil dialogue with the public about journalistic practices, coverage and news content.

▸ Respond quickly to questions about accuracy, clarity and fairness.

▸ Acknowledge mistakes and correct them promptly and prominently. Explain corrections and clarifications carefully and clearly.

▸ Expose unethical conduct in journalism, including within their organizations.

▸ Abide by the same high standards they expect of others.

The SPJ Code of Ethics is a statement of abiding principles supported by additional explanations and position papers (at spj.org) that address changing journalistic practices. It is not a set of rules, rather a guide that encourages all who engage in journalism to take responsibility for the information they provide, regardless of medium. The code should be read as a whole; individual principles should not be taken out of context. It is not, nor can it be under the First Amendment, legally enforceable.

Codes of ethics reflect the purported values of an organization. Value rationality requires that individuals faced with ethical choices make decisions that are consistent with stated values.

EMPLOYING EUPHEMISMS FOR UNETHICAL BEHAVIOR

Is trash-talking unethical?

Is it wrong for a coach to make a statement to reporters that she hopes will influence officials?

Is it unethical to feign distress and claim to need a bathroom break when a tennis opponent has won four consecutive games at love?

These scenarios were presented early in the chapter. When you first read them, did you think they were unethical, or did you consider them examples of just gamesmanship?

Gamesmanship has been described as the "Use of numerous strategic tactics to better one's position in the game or using dubious methods to secure an unfair victory while remaining within the constitutive rules of a contest" (Hamilton, 2013, p. 138).

Trash-talking is not against the rules of a contest. Neither is taking a bathroom break to stop an opponent's momentum. Both could be called gamesmanship.

The word gamesmanship originally appeared in a book published in the 1940s called *The Theory and Practice of Gamesmanship: The Art of Winning Games Without Really Cheating*. It earned enough attention to be republished a number of times and now exists in an e-book edition. From the title, it seems as if the book would be an instructional primer. It is not. The book is a humorous take describing how some people cheat by bending the rules. It is written like a "how-to," but it is more like a "let's laugh at how some people behave." There is, for example, a tongue-in-cheek reference to "limpmanship"; how one should claim to use minor injuries to disarm an opponent. "I hope I shall give you a game . . . My back was a bit seized up yesterday" (Potter 2015, p. 23).

Trash talking on the field.

Gamesmanship is a convenient euphemism. Are there some actions labeled gamesmanship that are ethical? Surely. One could make a case that there is a distinction between calling a time-out to ice a kicker and flopping to persuade a referee to pull out a red card. However, in any case, and in every case identifying a behavior as gamesmanship in and of itself does not render the behavior ethical.

Similarly, a phrase called strategic ambiguity has crept into usage over the last few decades and is also problematic. In 1984, Eric Eisenberg authored an article in *Communication Monographs* entitled "Ambiguity as Strategy in Organizational Communication." In essence, strategic ambiguity refers to purposefully being vague when communicating for some personal or organizational gain. If a coach is asked by a player if she will be getting more playing time, and the coach says, "Trust me. Hard work will get you playing time," even if the coach does not believe that this player will possibly get more playing time, then the coach is being strategically ambiguous. Eisenberg questioned the notion that open communication is inherently desirable in organizations and argued that "at all levels, members of an organization stand to gain by the strategic use of ambiguity" (Eisenberg & Witten, 1987, p. 127).

A goal of strategic ambiguity is low perceived ambiguity. This means that when communicators are strategically ambiguous, an objective is for receivers to not suspect the ambiguity but to consider the message clear. For example, the head coach protecting the shoplifting quarterback tells university administrators that the investigation is ongoing. That is literally the truth, but it implies that there is uncertainty when it really just means that the police have not finished the paperwork. If administrators "hear" the coach's message to be "we are not sure if the quarterback did it," then the low perceived ambiguity goal of strategic ambiguity has been met. If the player asking about playing time hears that there is a chance for more minutes if she works industriously, the goal of strategic ambiguity has been met.

Arguments articulated in support of strategic ambiguity seem to be contrary to ethical principles. The following are a number of examples.

- "The use of strategic ambiguity complicates the task of interpretation for the receiver" (Eisenberg, 1984, p. 236)

- "By complicating the sense-making responsibilities of the receiver, strategically ambiguous communication allows the source to both reveal and conceal, to express and protect, should it be necessary to save face" (Eisenberg, 1984, p. 236).

- "Ambiguity can be used to allow specific interpretations of policy which do more harm than good, to be denied, should they arise" (Eisenberg, 1984, p. 235).

- "Strategic ambiguity preserves privileged positions by shielding persons with power from close scrutiny by others" (Eisenberg et al., 2014, p. 35).

- ". . . strategic ambiguity is said to be deniable; that is the words seem to mean one thing, but under pressure they can seem to mean something else" (Eisenberg et al., 2014 p. 35).

Deception scholars have defined a lie as "a deliberate attempt to mislead without the consent of the target" (Frank & Feeley 2003, p. 60). If the goal of strategic ambiguity is to decrease perceived ambiguity, then by definition, that is a deliberate attempt to mislead—a lie. As such, strategic ambiguity provides a membrane of legitimacy for deception. All the research about deception suggests that most people are not adept at detecting it (Hauch et al., 2016, p. 284). "Over twenty-five years of research in behavioral lie detection has yielded one consistent finding: humans are not very skilled at detecting when deception is present" (Feeley & Young, 1998, p. 109). No person is omniscient. Even the brightest among us have been duped by people who have communicated unethically. Sissela Bok, the author of the very comprehensive book, *Lying*, argues that those who are deceived become "resentful, disappointed and suspicious . . . They see that they have been manipulated, that the deceit made them unable to make choices for themselves according to the most adequate information available" (Bok, 1999, p. 20). She comments that even those who are inclined to deceive others desire to be treated without deceit (p. 23). Further, she argues that the damage of deceit transcends the effects on the deceived and includes the erosion of societal trust (p. 24).

To be fair to the proponents of strategic ambiguity, there can be times when being strategically ambiguous is not intended to be duplicitous. It was so, for example, in the passage of Title IX in the early 70s. Susan Ware, in her book *Game, Set, Match*, describes the evolution of Title IX. "Like many laws Title IX mandate was left deliberately broad in part because if lawmakers had made it more specific it likely would have lost the consensus of support necessary for passage" (Ware, 2011, p. 48). This is an example of what proponents of strategic ambiguity call "unified diversity." This means that sometimes ambiguity can gain unified support for a concept that, if it had been explicitly defined, would not have been so supported. Another example is the phrase "academic freedom." Academic freedom is a good thing, and it is important that universities have that as a plank in their missions. However, if universities were to define what academic freedom is, or if the architects of Title IX had defined specifically the mandate of the legislation, neither would likely receive uniform support.

A more detailed discussion of the ethics of strategic ambiguity can be found in an article in the *Journal of Business Communication* by Jim Paul and Chrysti Strbiak and also in my book on Organizational Communication. The point here is that one cannot simply contend that unethical behavior is ethical by claiming that it was just an example of strategic ambiguity (Paul & Strbiak, 1997, p. 149–159; Zaremba, 2021, pp. 95–96).

RATIONALIZING UNETHICAL BEHAVIOR

When faced with an ethical decision, sometimes people justify an unethical alternative by citing a reason why the unethical option could be, in fact, correct or ethical. The Josephson Institute of Ethics at http://josephsoninstitute.org/med-5rationalizations/ identifies a number of these rationalizations. These are listed and bolded below. For each, I provide an italicized example from the cases that begin the chapter, followed by a brief explanation.

It's Necessary.
Misleading audiences about the quarterback's theft is necessary for all stakeholders involved. Without the quarterback, the team will be defeated. If the team is defeated, then we will not recruit the state's best athletes and lose income from alumni donations and prestige bowl revenue.

This rationalization suggests that an unethical alternative is appropriate because the behavior is essential. This rationalization is an example of what Tompkins calls instrumental rationality.

It's Legal.
There is nothing illegal about trash-talking as long as it is not extensive or vulgar. Therefore it cannot be unethical. There is nothing illegal about scheduling a weak opponent in order to pad won-loss records. Therefore it must be ethical.

Whether trash-talking is legal or not can be debated. Similarly, we could disagree about the morality of scheduling guarantee games. However, the legality of the acts, or any act, is unrelated to ethics. At one time, slavery was legal. It was never ethical for one person to own another anywhere, let alone in a country where the foundational value is that all people are created equal. Some unethical behavior is illegal. However, all legal actions are not consequently ethical.

It's part of my job.
My job is to recruit players that will help us win. If I have to exaggerate to do so, then so be it. That is what they pay me for.

Your legitimate job requirements do not sanction illegitimate actions. If your job is to increase ticket sales to home games, this does not condone selling seats that have obstructed views without informing the buyer of the seat. If your job is to recruit athletes, you can do this without being unethical. Deception may be a shortsighted shortcut, but your job requirements do not compel you to be deceptive.

It's for a good cause.
If we have to move to another city, that will bring the unemployment level of our town up 4%. What I am doing by not announcing the game postponement is for a good cause.

The ends rarely justify the means in sports communication or in any context. In the case of the minor league general manager, not announcing immediately that the game will be postponed could be seen as an action for a good cause. The more money the team earns, the less likely that it will have to relocate. Yet, keeping the fans there suggesting that a game will be played is a deliberate attempt to mislead without the consent of the spectators.

I was doing it for your benefit.
The fans may seem to be the victims of the delayed announcement, but keeping the team locally will mean that these same fans will be able to enjoy watching the club as they have for years past and years to come.

This can be a convenient rationalization for unethical behavior. Often people claim that what is beneficial to themselves is really in the other's interests. It's important for anyone who makes this contention to take a step back and consider whether the alleged altruism may really be self-serving. Not telling your mother that there is a surprise party for her when she asks, "Where are we going?" is altruistic. Keeping fans in a ballpark to buy hot dogs is probably not.

Fighting fire with fire.
In order to survive, we have to do what the others do. So if our rival university is lying, then we are fighting that fire with our own exaggerations.

The recruiter can rationalize deceiving the ice hockey recruit by saying that in order to survive in a world where others deceive, one is left with no choice but to deceive. If the student subsequently complains, the recruiter could contend that the school is, in fact, a better fit for her, and the recruiter was deceptive for the student's benefit. The latter is an example of the "I was doing it for your benefit" rationalization. The former attempts to justify behavior because it is retaliatory and a method for survival. It's a bogus two wrongs make a right argument.

It doesn't hurt anyone.
Inviting the reporters to speak at the conference does not hurt anyone. They get a free lunch, our students get advice, and we may obtain some positive coverage.

"No harm, no foul" is an expression used when officiating ball games. Why call a hold off the ball if the hold is not affecting play. If the reporters speak at a conference, so what? Who gets hurt? Sometimes this rationalization is conveniently shortsighted. If there is an expectation that a free lunch will bring more coverage, the reporter is in the position of making judgments about what deserves coverage and is apparently newsworthy on factors other than a dispassionate assessment of what is worthy of coverage.

There is no personal benefit.
It's not like I benefit by withholding the information about the player's philandering habits.

Unethical behaviors can be justified by claiming that the behavior did not advantage the offender. People who use this rationalization may believe that the only criterion for unethical behavior depends on whether the person who engages in it gains personally from the action. Benefits derived from behaviors are irrelevant to making ethical choices. In addition, in this example and others of its ilk, there really are advantages to the person not reporting the transgressions. She or he may continue to have easy access to the team if they do not report the behaviors.

I paid my dues.
I have this coming to me. I have toiled for a decade without a conference championship. I have the team to win it all now. If I have to wiggle about the quarterback who made an immature decision, I am entitled to wiggle.

Whether you are due something or not is unrelated to whether it is morally right to take actions to get that something.

I can still be objective the next time.
Look, just this once, we will post this photo of the ice hockey player. Sure it is not right, but we are in a battle for advertisers. Once we get the financial rewards that increased advertising will yield from this, I can go back to being ethical.

This rationalization is used to indicate that the behavior is a one-off. This is irrelevant to whether the one-off act is ethical.

Everyone does it.
Every single school in our conference schedules these guarantee games. It is fine to do this.

The person who schedules the guarantee game may rationalize the behavior by pointing, accurately, to the fact that this has been a normalized event. This particular rationalization leads to the discussion of another obstacle to ethical decision-making: the normalization of deviance.

NORMALIZING DEVIANCE

The phrase, the normalization of deviance, has been attributed to sociologist Diane Vaughan. She writes, "...repetition, seemingly small choices, and the banality of daily decisions in organizational life—indeed in most social life—can camouflage from the participants a cumulative directionality that too often is discernible only in hindsight" (Vaughan, 1996, p. 119).

Similarly, in the 2008 memoir, *Extraordinary Circumstances: The Journey of a Corporate Whistleblower,* former WorldCom vice president Cynthia Cooper comments on the subtle acceptance of unacceptable behavior. "People," she writes, "don't wake up and say, 'I think I'll become a criminal today.' Instead it's often a slippery slope and we lose our footing one step at a time" (Cooper, 2009, p. 1).

Unethical behaviors in sports communication contexts are often the result of people losing their footing one step at a time. The college coach who protects the quarterback may be able to cite many examples when colleagues danced disingenuously with the press to avoid negative publicity. The SID who invites media representatives to a luncheon panel can point to a dozen schools where this type of event regularly occurs. The newspaper editor who publishes the over/under could report that nearly every newspaper in the land includes the point spread for games. Both the recruiter and the recruits are aware that deception is the convention and not the aberration.

And for eighteen years, a policy of encouraging athletes to take bogus classes at a major university can become normalized. A practice of admitting non-athletes into prestigious institutions as if they are athletes can become normalized. A policy of paying the parents of high school recruits in order to persuade them to attend your school can become normalized.

The normalization of unethical communication behavior can intoxicate leagues, players, coaches, and teams. Like any intoxicant, the effects are insidious because the disoriented organizations and people operate under a dangerous illusion: the illusion that unethical behavior is necessary and somehow benign.

Deviant behavior is deviant regardless of how normalized the deviance. Since at least 1951, basketball point-shaving scandals have occurred with regularity. Lance Armstrong, Marion Jones, Ben Johnson, and Mark McGuire are four of the many athletes who have admitted to using banned substances to enhance athletic performance. In Chapter 3, we discussed the academic fraud at the University of North Carolina. Similar incidents have been exposed at other universities as well. It is known that recruits in the past have received illegal benefits at several schools, including USC, the University of Kentucky, and the University of Massachusetts. Ethical decision-makers have to be vigilant and not assume that normalized behavior is condonable. The tragic case of the Duke University lacrosse players who were accused of sexual molestation might be a good example to consider. The district attorney suppressed exculpatory evidence that would have exonerated the athletes. Regardless of how normalized suppressing evidence might be, the action of the district attorney and any conspirators is ethically (and in this instance legally) reprehensible.

Lance Armstrong is one of many athletes who have admitted to using banned substances to enhance performance.

Sissela Bok concludes her very comprehensive book entitled *Lying* with the following words: "Trust and integrity are precious resources, easily squandered, hard to regain. They can thrive only on a foundation of respect for veracity" (Bok, 1999, p. 249).

If duplicity is normalized, and an organization has become accustomed to little "respect for veracity," then ethical decision-making is nearly impossible and repercussions not insignificant.

Recurring Counsel

When seeking advice on what constitutes ethical communicative behavior, the following counsel recurs:

1. **Be truthful.** Employ the academic definition of lying: "A deliberate attempt to mislead without the consent of the target."
2. **Do not**
   - Omit key information in an attempt to mislead stakeholders.
   - Clog your message with bogus or misleading statistics designed as a red herring to divert stakeholder attention.
   - Employ euphemisms as a means of justifying unethical communication.
3. **Assume a golden rule approach.** That is if you were the receiver, what would you need to know to be informed about the situation?

4. Respond to stakeholders. That is, respond to questions from external and internal stakeholders who seek information.

5. Use value-based rationality when making decisions. Avoid instrumental rationality.

6. In the game context, observe rules of sportsmanship. A player, coach, or team should not "seek to gain an advantage over opponents by means of a skill that the game was not designed to test" (Markula Center for Applied Ethics).

7. Be respectful of opponents, teammates, and officials.

8. Take responsibility. That is, do not blame officials, a player, the weather, or external factors for a situation.

9. Be responsible to the greater society beyond your organization.

10. When reporting on events, be dispassionate and true to your professional responsibilities.

Fair or Foul | Questions of Ethics

Is it ethical to:

1. Fake an injury during a game in order to buy time to rest?

2. List players as injured on an injury report when you are certain they will play?

3. (As a sports information director), exaggerate the physical characteristics of your players?

4. Allow tobacco companies to advertise in your game day magazines?

5. (As a sports television show producer), consider the physical beauty of both the men and women you select to host the show.

6. Direct your groundskeeper to not cover a soccer pitch or football field with a tarp before a rainstorm if scheduled to play a quicker team the next day.

7. (As a radio sports broadcaster), highlight the efficiency of your team and denigrate your opponents?

8. Report a sports story that will make you famous even when your sources are questionable?

9. (In states where betting on sporting events is illegal), list betting spreads in your publication?

10. (On your website) tell crude jokes and make lewd comments in order to increase visitors and, consequently, advertising revenue?

Do the Right Thing: Using Ethical Tools

Not everyone cares about ethical considerations. For some, ethics is an academic enterprise with no place in a practical world. In your class discussions, you may have already discovered this. For those who desire to be ethical, there are a number of tools that can be used to help one make ethical decisions.

THE CATEGORICAL IMPERATIVE

Often associated with Immanuel Kant, the categorical imperative assumes that there are universal absolutes regarding what is ethical and what is not. In assessing any particular act, what one needs to do is use the absolute as a guideline. The key to successfully implementing the categorical imperative is to be clear and accurate regarding the imperative. For example, a categorical imperative may be that it is wrong to lie. If one employs this imperative, then it would be unethical to do what is suggested in the "Ice Hockey Great" recruiting example.

UTILITARIANISM

John Stuart Mill wrote of an approach referred to as "The Greatest Happiness Principle." Essentially Mill's argument was that what made an act moral was whether the action benefited the greatest numbers of those affected by it. Obviously, the Categorical Imperative is at variance with Utilitarianism. The former argues that receivers' collective happiness is no yardstick. The yardstick is hard and fast. The latter argues that collective benefit is the primary yardstick. The key to employing Utilitarianism is identifying all stakeholders relevant to a particular issue. If you are assessing whether it is right to advertise tobacco products during a baseball game, then the stakeholders are indeed companies that will benefit from the sale of tobacco, schools that might reap valuable revenue from the advertisements, the networks that have as their lifeblood advertising money, but also impressionable youngsters who may begin to associate tobacco with successful sport achievement.

VEIL OF IGNORANCE

Philosopher John Rawls argues that justice should be blind, and this approach suggests that ethical arbiters go behind a veil to make decisions that do not take into consideration role, financial influence, or political power. The veil of ignorance, if people legitimately accept the challenge of standing behind it, guarantees dispassionate assessments and is likely to increase the chances of quality decision-making. If one stands behind a veil of ignorance in the "Website Decision" example, then financial issues are not a factor in the decision-making.

SITUATIONAL ETHICS

Situational Ethics was developed by Joseph Fletcher and argues that every ethical decision depends on the situation and not any absolute except for love. According to Situation Ethicists, determinations of what is right and wrong always depend on this lone criterion. "Whatever is the loving thing to do in any given situation is the right thing to do." This is a difficult tool to use because the word "love" can be interpreted variously. A key would be to not manipulate its meaning to satisfy a desired end. The reporter could justify not reporting the philandering behavior of the player because love compels him not to be a catalyst for destroying his marriage. Love could be used as the criterion for lying to the ice hockey recruit claiming that out of love, he is deceptive because he knows his school is the better fit for her.

ARISTOTLE'S GOLDEN MEAN

This refers to Aristotle's approach that between two poles in decision-making, there is a golden mean, which would make for an optimal decision. The mean, a statistical term referring to the arithmetic average of any sum, would be that decision that falls between the extremes. Such a mean, according to this approach, is a golden resolution to ethical dilemmas.

Test Yourself: Apply the Principles

Two tools that can be used to help one make ethical decisions are (a) the Categorical Imperative and (b) Utilitarianism. Consider the following questions. How would you assess each employing both tools? That is, what would your determination be if you used the Categorical Imperative, and what would be your determination if you used Utilitarianism.

- Should alcohol be advertised during the broadcasts of professional sporting events?
- Should physical attractiveness be a criterion when selecting sports television broadcasters?
- Should betting spreads be published in newspapers?
- Should lewd jokes be told on talk radio if producers think it will increase advertising revenue?
- Should college sports teams wear uniforms that endorse a particular brand? For example, should the uniforms show the Nike Swoosh?
- Should Sports Information Directors invite media representatives to dinners in the hope of obtaining more coverage for their teams?

Obviously, these approaches are only useful if sports communicators wish to employ them. Even so, the applications of any of the principles are a complex matter. It is relatively easy to contemplate morality. It's more difficult to be moral and ethical. The dollars and cents issues that surround sports are catalysts for instrumental rationality.

The problems with Kant's Categorical Imperative (or other ethical guidelines) are that few can agree on terms. What ethics means to me may have no meaning to you. Also, many of the absolutes that have been agreed upon have been codified into law. Therefore many of the issues not so codified become areas of disagreement without any real procedures for enforcement.

It's difficult to apply ethical yardsticks when people disagree on the number of inches to a yard or whether a situation needs to be measured at all. What's offensive to some is egalitarian to another. What's obscene to some is benign to another. Defining and controlling ethical behavior is like trying to add two numbers when the parties involved cannot agree on numeric values and give lip service to the rules of arithmetic.

Yet ethics is part of the fabric of sports communication. The question becomes to what extent is a sports organization, and those within it willing to work to ensure that communications are characterized by honesty and integrity.

Chapter Conclusion—Take-Aways

- Sports figures are often faced with difficult ethical choices. The results of these choices are often more discernible because of media and fan communication than choices made in other organizations.
- There are several obstacles that can preclude ethical decision-making.
  - Use of instrumental as opposed to value rationality.
  - Employing euphemisms to justify unethical behavior.
  - Rationalizing unethical behavior.
  - The normalization of unethical behavior such that the frequency and normalcy of it preclude dispassionate analysis.
- There are several tools that can be used to help athletes, coaches, and management make ethical decisions.
  - Categorical Imperative
  - Golden Mean
  - Utilitarianism
  - Veil of Ignorance
  - Situational Ethics
- The key to making ethical challenges in sports contexts is the willingness to behave—when confronted with ethical challenges—in accordance with articulated values.

QUESTIONS

1. What are the merits of Utilitarianism as opposed to the Categorical Imperative? Which tool do you think is more appropriate when facing ethical challenges in sports communication contexts?

2. In your experience, has the normalization of deviance been used to justify unethical practices in sports contexts?

3. In your experience, have you or sports organizations with which you're familiar used value rationality or instrumental rationality when faced with ethical choices?

4. Are codes of ethics significant methods for assuring that teams, coaches, and leagues adhere to organizational values? Why or why not?

Practitioner Perspective

Bob Donnan

Sports Photographer

© Bob Donnan/USA TODAY Sports/Newscom

Bob Donnan captures the moment when North Carolina Tar Heels forward Luke Maye (32) grabs a rebound over Virginia Cavaliers guard Kyle Guy (5) in the second half of the February 11, 2019, game.

AZ. What is SportShooter?

BD. SportShooter is a website started by Robert Hanashiro. It was an incredibly active site as the digital age of photography began and the business of photography was changing rapidly. It has very inexpensive dues and was both a great discussion board for ethics and the technical side of photography.

AZ. How do your photos find themselves into newspapers, magazines, and online?

BD. I work for USA Today Sports Images, a division of Gannett. All of the games that I cover are uploaded to their website.

Several pictures will be uploaded during the games I cover at halftime and then a larger selection after the game. I personally size and crop these images and put the captions on that describe what is happening in the game. They tell player, position, quarter, or half the picture was taken in.

It is especially important if it is the winning touchdown, basket, etc. at the end of the game. Once the pictures are on the site, they are distributed electronically to the Gannett papers and subscribing clients. They are also searchable by anyone wanting to purchase a picture.

If you look at a site like espn.com during a big game, you will see them change pictures every few minutes of the game. If you go to the USA Today Sports Images site http://www.usatsimg.com and type my name, you could see pages of pictures. What is more practical is to type in an athlete like LeBron James and also my name and see a smaller group of pictures.

AZ. What is the biggest challenge related to capturing sports images?

BD. Challenges are defined by the sport that you are trying to cover.

In the Olympics, it is the sheer logistics of so many events that all happen and how early you are able to get in position because of the other events that you cover.

In football, it is positioning on the field and the good fortune when the action comes your way. Part of this is anticipation of where the ball is going to go. In the NFL, there are well over fifty photographers on the sidelines, and you are trying to get the best version of a play.

In basketball, a challenge is setting up several cameras to catch different angles of a play.

AZ. Have you ever had an athlete or team be particularly appreciative of work you did capturing a moment?

BD. Relationships with teams are important. I have done a lot of work for my alma mater, UNC Chapel Hill, and have had several moments that were really appreciated.

Two examples are from UNC-Duke basketball games. The first is when Marvin Williams rebounded a missed foul shot and scored to beat Duke at the end of the game in 2005. I had put a camera up high from the side and it was a really clean look at the winning shot. The school has used that image a lot and it is also a large print that is displayed in the Smith Center.

The second was a punctuation mark at the end of this year's game where Theo Pinson screamed as he dunked the ball. It was a strong moment and everyone has a great picture but the camera that I put looking through the backboard glass is really strong and one of the best glass camera pictures I have ever taken. They wanted a copy of that picture for Coach Williams's office.

AZ. How important is it to establish networks between teams, leagues, and athletes so that you can have access to them? Any examples of situations where a relationship was key to such access?

BD. Relationships are always important. It is much easier when you have worked with people before and they know you. A level of trust is important and it helps you if you want to do anything out of the ordinary.

First Person   Hedons and Dolors

When I was a junior in college, I took a course called Ethics. It was, for the most part, a very dry class. The instructor was well-meaning, but his classes consisted mostly of him posing a question to the class that was uninspiring. Then the number (dwindling weekly) who attended a particular session would squirm, musing more about why we had decided to attend that day than about the specific inquiry.

However, despite this, there was something about the class for which I will forever be grateful.

To satisfy the requirements, we had to write three opinion papers. One asked us to compare the wisdom of two philosophers, John Stuart Mill and Immanuel Kant. If these thinkers had been discussed during a class session, I must have been dwelling about something else at the time. So, as the deadline approached for the paper, I hauled out the textbook and read about Mill's Utilitarianism and Kant's Categorical Imperative.

I was aghast. I could not believe that Utilitarianism was a philosophy of ethics that had earned any traction.

Utilitarianism is often called the Greatest Happiness Principle. It means essentially that things are ethical or right in proportion to the extent they tend to promote happiness and wrong if they tend to produce unhappiness or pain. The Categorical Imperative appears to be antithetical. It argues that behaviors are right because they inherently are right and wrong because they inherently are wrong, and it does not matter if something that is right does not cause pleasure.

I saw no merit to Utilitarianism. My twenty-year-old self was outraged by the idea. The only good news was that my revulsion made the writing of the paper relatively easy and made the course more interesting than it had been previously.

Since that time, I find myself attracted to lectures and debates and some articles that discuss Utilitarianism. Proponents (still around despite my undergraduate five-page rant) attempt to quantify pleasure and pain by counting hedons and dolors. A hedon is a unit of pleasure. A dolor a unit of pain. So to determine if something is right, count up the hedons, and count up the dolors. If the hedons outweigh the dolors, an action is right.

At one debate I attended, I was fascinated listening to two philosophers contentiously arguing that there were more dolors than hedons in a particular case, therefore rendering a decision unethical. One fellow in particular was really piling up the dolors because he couldn't seem to convince anyone that he was correct. What struck me as odd about this debate and any other attempt at quantifying was the subjectivity in determining what constitutes a hedon or a dolor.

Dolors and hedons. Can we really quantify these in a given situation and then count up the results? A coach has to determine whether to tweak the academic credentials of star players in order to make them eligible. A recruiter has to decide whether to embellish the qualities of the school in order to woo outstanding athletes to the school. Can you count up the collective hedons for playing the disqualified players or signing the deceived athletes and compare that to the dolors accrued by lying to authorities and young people and perhaps sullying the reputation of your program?

These are relatively easy examples. The actions are unethical. There are many more dolors, long term and short term, for lying to the players and authorities. Yet, there are other instances that are not as clear.

I am not as adamant as I was at twenty about the Greatest Happiness Principle versus the Categorical Imperative. I do think we need to respect hedons and dolors. We have to be careful not to manufacture dolors for others or accrue hedons at the expense of others. Maybe if we could carefully count hedons and dolors and genuinely respect how our actions and communications created dolors and hedons, we would find little that separates Utilitarianism from the Categorical Imperative.

Chapter 8

Fandom and Sports Communication

© Melinda Nagy/Shutterstock.com

Chapter in a Nutshell

Fans are the lifeblood of sports. This chapter discusses the nature of fandom, fan motivation, and approaches to communicating with these audiences.

Specifically, at the end of the chapter, students will be able to:

- Describe how fan communication can be seen through the lens of systems theory.
- Describe what is meant by Burke's concept of identification and how that applies to sports fandom.
- Discuss reasons that explain why people become fans.
- Identify best practices for communicating with fans.
- Identify how new media has affected fandom and participatory culture.

Sports Communication Prompts

- Below you will see statements pertaining to some aspect of communication and sports. For each item
  - Decide whether you agree or disagree with the statement.
  - Explain your rationale for the position.
  - Support your position with examples.
1. Radio sports talk and dedicated sports websites have created a society of crass people.
2. At halftimes, time outs, and other break times during sports broadcasts, it is important to entertain fans in the arena with music.
3. The appeal of the UFC reflects the large disparity among sports fans. Few who watch the Tennis Channel will watch UFC events. This is why dedicated sports networks make sense.
4. Fantasy football is bad for sport because it changes the nature of the game. That is, fans are playing a different game than the teams. Fantasy participants may cheer for a running back, for example, on an opponent's team, and that will dilute fans' allegiances to their own teams. Therefore, the professional leagues should discourage fantasy sports.
5. The effects of both conventional and new media become apparent when one looks at the surge in interest in soccer in America and basketball outside of America. Without the media, there would still be limited interest in soccer in the U.S. and basketball outside of the U.S.

You could replace all of the owners and the league would go on. You could replace all the players and the league would go on. But you can't replace the fans. If you don't have the fans, you're dead.

Houston Texans owner Bob McNair

For the most part the spectator's stake in the proceedings is the gratification that comes from identifying with success. The capacity of one person's actions to buttress the self-esteem of another is demonstrably a potent force—a force that has been exploited whenever possible by the entrepreneurs of sports events.

Michael Roberts
"The Vicarious Heroism of the Sports Spectator" *New Republic*

...the research that has been done, as well as the historical record, overwhelmingly shows that being a sports fan is good for us, good for humanity and good for the world."

Larry Olmstead
(*Fans.* 2021, p. 9).

Introduction

In Chapter 3, we introduced systems theory and discussed how that theory applies to communication in sports organizations. Systems theorists believe that an organization has to cultivate and nourish networks that link the organization to related entities in the relevant environment. Fans are essential audiences in any sports organization's relevant environment. This became very apparent during 2020, when sports were played without fans because of the pandemic. When fans returned to the stadiums and arenas in 2021, even a casual sports viewer heard and reheard broadcasters comment on the positive effects of fans on the sports experience. Whether one is looking at a team, a league, a university athletic department, a sports broadcasting network, a sports magazine, or a website—regardless of the sports organization—a key audience is the fans. Playwright Steven Sondheim commented, "The audience is the final collaborator on every show." Similarly, fans are essential collaborators in sports contexts.

A university athletic department needs to efficiently interact with alums, among other stakeholders. A dedicated sports network will want to expand its market share and consequently must cultivate and sustain potential consumers. A team must be responsive to its rabid supporters. In order to communicate effectively with these audiences, leagues, teams, and other sports entities have to understand the complex nature of fandom.

Fans can nourish a sports enterprise. A sports organization can nourish fandom. In the absence of that nourishment, a league, team, or network can become sickly. In the parlance of systems theory, there will be entropy.

Why are there Fans?

What makes adults who earn large salaries—who have paid well over fifty dollars for seats at a baseball game—thrust their arms into the air exuberantly when—after they have clawed over others—they secure baseballs that have landed in the stands? At Walmart, one can purchase an eight-pack of baseballs for $14.97.

What makes an otherwise tolerant individual berate officials at sports contests? What makes this individual, who might find discourteous language in most contexts inappropriate, bellow when an umpire makes an unfavorable decision?

What makes professionals who work calmly at high-pressure jobs become nervous watching a televised sports contest? What makes them pace or assume unnatural postures because they believe, somehow, that contorting a hand, or swinging a foot, will bring a player in another city good fortune?

Why are there fans?

The reasons that explain fandom may be related to Affect Theory, which will be discussed later in this chapter, or perhaps can be explained by Kenneth Burke's concept of identification—another topic soon to be discussed. Or perhaps the reasons for fandom are based on what is called *eustress*—another term defined later on.

People may become fans because of what biologist Edward Wilson contends is the natural human tendency "to form groups, drawing visceral comfort and pride from familiar fellowship, and to defend the group enthusiastically against rival groups" (Wilson, 2013, p. 57). Another explanation for fandom may be based on what researchers have called "BIRGing"—an acronym for "basking in reflected glory."

Fans may become fans because of any one of the reasons prolific fan researcher Dan Wann lists in his Sports Fan Motivation Scale: self-esteem benefits, escape, entertainment, aesthetics, group affiliation, eustress, acquisition of sports knowledge, and family bonding (Wann et al., 2019, p. 66).

Regardless of why fans become fans, there can be no debate that there are fans and that fans are passionate and, periodically, eccentric.

This is a passionate fan.

FANATICS

The word fan is an abbreviation for the word fanatic. Almost all those interested in sport, and even those who cannot comprehend fervid interest in sport, are likely aware of many for whom the label fan, short for fanatic, is apt.

In *Those Guys Have All the Fun*, a book about ESPN, Tim Kurkjian talks about the fanaticism of some of his colleagues at the network:

> There's a guy in our research department here named Mark Simon who could tell you who made the last out of every World Series back into the 1930s . . . We have another guy named Jeff Bennett who can tell you what every baseball card looks like from 1979 to 1985 . . . And we have Judson Burch who knows the number of every umpire in the Major Leagues. I didn't even know they had numbers. (Miller & Shales, 2011, 665)

Prolific and award-winning author Nick Hornby chronicles his fanaticism in the memoir *Fever Pitch*. Hornby is a manic supporter of Arsenal football. At one point in the memoir, he refers to a friend who is not as much of a zealot as he:

> My friend Simon managed only sixteen of the seventeen League games—he smashed his head on a bookshelf in London a few hours before the Grimsby game . . . his girlfriend had to take his car keys away from him because he kept making dazed attempts to drive from Fulham up to the Abbey. (Hornby, 1998, p. 141)

Among historian Doris Kearns Goodwin's many books is a memoir she authored about her childhood affection for the Brooklyn Dodgers. In it, *Wait Until Next Year*, she refers to people—including herself—who still, several decades later, wistfully speak about their fondness for the Brooklyn Dodgers. At one point, Goodwin recalls Bobby Thomson's ninth inning 1951 walk-off home run for the rival New York Giants that ended her beloved Dodgers' season. While only seven years old at the time,

Goodwin's recollections are vivid. She describes how she learned to keep score as a child and, as was typical, was keeping score in that fateful ninth inning. Her sister had, prior to Thomson's at-bat, predicted the homer. When the Giant actually did homer, Goodwin writes: "I threw down my scorebook, the last page never to be completed. For a moment I believed that my sister's prophecy had influenced the outcome and I hated her with all my heart" (Goodwin, 1997, p. 153).

Barry Levinson wrote and directed the movie, *Diner*. It is about a group of young men from Baltimore who are very dedicated Baltimore Colt fans. Levinson also directed the ESPN *30 for 30* documentary, *The Band That Wouldn't Die.* The documentary, as well as the movie, describes the emotional ties citizens of Baltimore had for its Colt football team. The events in *Diner* predate the decision by Colt owner Robert Irsay to move the team to Indianapolis. *The Band That Wouldn't Die* describes how much it hurt Colt fans when the team left Baltimore in the middle of the night in March 1984. In 2014, local television station WBAL acknowledged the sad anniversary of the departure with a report that began with the following words, "Nearly thirty years have passed since Baltimore sports fans woke up and found their beloved Baltimore Colts had picked up and moved to Indianapolis. It's a day that will live in infamy in Baltimore sports lore" (Roblin, 2014).

Legend has it that at 1 pm on the opening day of the 1984 season, the first season after the Colts had deserted Baltimore, a superfan, Hurst "Loudy" Loudenslager, took his seat in the vacant Baltimore Memorial Coliseum and stared at the empty field while the Colts started their game 600 miles away in Indianapolis.

Rebecca Watts's article, "The Florida Gator Nation Online," describes how fans of the University of Florida football team used social media to discuss the fortunes of the Gators and, virtually, embrace them. One fanatic upset about the hiring of a particular coach, Ron Zook, obtained the rights to the URL fireronzook.com before the soon to become beleaguered coach could assume the job (Watts, 2008, p. 253).

George Dohrmann, a Pulitzer Prize-winning author, wrote a 2018 book entitled, *Superfans*. In it, he describes obsessive sports fans who, even for readers who have strong allegiance to their teams, may seem maniacally preoccupied. One, a fellow who dressed up for Milwaukee Brewers' games as a banana and called himself "the rally banana," was distressed one day when he spotted another fan wearing similar garb. It had, after all, been his idea to dress up as a banana (Dohrmann, 2018, p. 76).

In *The Secret Lives of Sports Fans*, Eric Simons writes, "Sports fandom appears to be a species-level design flaw" (Simons, 2013, p. 10).

Flaw or not, the fanatics are out there. Many of them, and most, do not feel compelled to dress like a banana. Nevertheless, there are millions of fans, and they are the power source for the sports organizations they support.

Tomkins, Burke, and Wann

AFFECT THEORY

If you emphasize the first syllable of the word *affect*, you have a word that refers to the manifestations of emotion. Silvan Tomkins (not to be confused with Phillip Tompkins mentioned in other chapters) is credited as the originator of Affect Theory. Tomkins acknowledges that there is a distinction between affect and emotion, but as it relates to his theory, we can consider affect and emotion to be essentially synonymous.

Affect Theory provides a good floorboard for understanding the phenomenon of sports fandom. Tomkins argued that the various affects individuals experience can be placed in discrete categories. Most of these affect categories are negative, for example, anger, fear, and humiliation. A number of the affect categories are positive: enjoyment, interest, and excitement. The theory posits that mental health requires more positive affect than negative affect. Simply, if the balance of negative emotions overwhelms the positive emotions, you will feel sad. If the balance of positive emotions overwhelms the negative emotions, you will feel happy. The basic tenet of Affect Theory is that people typically attempt to maximize positive affect and minimize negative affect (Tomkins, 2008, p. xx). Therefore, in the parlance of Affect Theory, fans become fans because being a fan will "maximize positive affect." A review of George Dohrmann's *Superfans* supports the theory. In a number of cases, the fans he describes became fans when there was an emotional emptiness in their lives. Fandom filled the void with positive affect.

IDENTIFICATION

Another explanation for fandom relates to what rhetorician Kenneth Burke referred to as Identification. Burke contended that individuals identify to avoid isolation. He wrote: "Identification is affirmed with earnestness precisely because there is division" (Burke, 1969, p. 22). In other words, people identify with groups because the identification compensates for the division that can surface naturally because we are, after all, individuals. Consequently, people wear Detroit Red Wings jerseys and caps, particularly when they attend games, but also when they are out dressing casually. People buy and wear the gear of their teams to identify with others who share the same allegiances. When the Tampa Bay Buccaneers won the Super Bowl in 2021, all along beaches in Sarasota, fans were adorned with Buccaneer paraphernalia. Fans of the Bronx Bombers, wherever they may be, are reluctant to remove their Yankee caps. Visit Amazon, and you can purchase a blue hoodie sweatshirt for $13.99. If you would like a St. Louis Cardinals sweatshirt with probably the same fabric pedigree but with the words St. Louis Cardinals across your chest, it will cost between $41.24 (an on-sale item) and $74.99. People want to identify.

The aforementioned fan researcher Dan Wann created a tool called the Sports Spectator Identification Survey that measures the extent to which a fan identifies with a team. This SSIS instrument has been used and modified by many researchers (Kim et al., 2020, pp. 652-653).[1] Chapter 3 in *Superfans* is entitled, *What Exactly Are We Rooting For?* The chapter is subtitled with a quote from Wann: "It's Identification. Well, Duh!" (Dohrmann 2018, p. 32).

Simply, fans may become fans because of their desire to become part of a group of like-minded others. Fans identify with teams, and the teams to which fans have allegiance become part of the fan's identity. The aforementioned biologist Edward Wilson wrote, "People must have a tribe. It gives them a name in addition to their own and social meaning in a chaotic world" (Wilson, 2013, p. 57).

Lee Hammer is not a theorist. At one time, he was a program manager for the radio sports talk program, *The Ticket*. His comment about why people become fans of sport and identify with teams is simple: "Sports is our common denominator. You can be a blue-collar worker and you can talk sports on an equal level with the chairman of a Fortune 500 company" (Eisenstock, 2014, p. 215).

---

[1] As of January 2022 Wann's original 1993 work with Branscombe developing the SSIS has been cited over 1900 times.

Test Yourself: Apply the Principles

The Sport Spectator Identification Scale[2]
Instructions: Please list your favorite sports team.

Now answer each of the following questions with this team in mind by circling the most accurate number (i.e., response) to each item.

1. How important is it to you that the team listed above wins?

   Not Important 1 2 3 4 5 6 7 8 Very Important

2. How strongly do you see yourself as a fan of the team listed above?

   Not at All a Fan 1 2 3 4 5 6 7 8 Very Much a Fan

3. How strongly do your friends see you as a fan of the team listed above?

   Not at All a Fan 1 2 3 4 5 6 7 8 Very Much a Fan

4. During the season, how closely do you follow the team listed above via ANY of the following: in person or on television, on the radio, or televised news or a newspaper?

   Never 1 2 3 4 5 6 7 8 Almost Every Day

5. How important is being a fan of the team listed above to you?

   Not Important 1 2 3 4 5 6 7 8 Very Important

6. How much do you dislike the greatest rivals of the team listed above?

   Do Not Dislike 1 2 3 4 5 6 7 8 Dislike Very Much

7. How often do you display the above team's name or insignia at your place of work, where you live, or on your clothing?

   Never 1 2 3 4 5 6 7 8 Always

From International Journal of Sport Psychology, Vol. 24, issue 1 by D.L. Wann and N.R. Branscombe. Copyright © 1993 by Edizioni Luigi Pozzi. Reprinted by permission.

---

[2] In 2019 an article in *Sports Marketing Quarterly* presented a very slightly revised SSIS. In it, the options for each item had, as a lowest score, different labels. For example, for item 1, the lowest extreme was labeled A Little important. For item 2, Slightly a fan. There are some other minor changes. The article calls the revision of the SSIS, the SSIS-R (James et al, 2019, p. 34). As mentioned earlier in the chapter, researchers have employed other modifications of the original SSIS. See the 2020 article "How useful is each item in the Sport Spectator Identification Scale?: An item response theory analysis" (Kim, Lee, & Byon, 2020, p. 652).

Take a moment to complete the SSIS. What is your total score? According to Simons in *The Secret Life of Sports Fans*, if your score is less than 18, you are not much of a fan. If it comes in over 35, you are "seriously invested" (Simons 2013, p. 179). Wann categorized the nature of identification into four categories:

7–18 low identification;

19–35 moderate identification;

36–49 high identification;

50–56 extreme identification. (Dohrmann 2018, p. 42)

Participatory Culture

Henry Jenkins has written extensively about fandom and what is called Participatory Culture. His book *Fans, Bloggers, and Gamers: Exploring Participatory Culture* explains how fans not only identify with a collective but how their interactions with teams, i.e., their participation, can serve to alter the entities that are sports organizations. The phrase, participatory culture is used in contrast to consumer culture. In the latter, the receiver consumes the experience; in the former, the fan participates in the experience, and that participation in itself is an agent that can be transformative.

Communicating using social media has fueled participatory culture. It would be difficult to contend that audiences, even before social media, simply consumed what was witnessed. Later in this chapter, we will discuss the related Magic Bullet and Uses and Gratifications theories. However, at this point, and as it relates to participatory culture, consider how social media has accelerated the process of participation. Communicating using social media has allowed fans to participate immediately in sport discourse. The accelerated interaction has had effects. Teams inundated with tweets from fans may react in some way. In anticipation of posts on message boards, teams may be careful about what they say or do. Former sports talk hosts Mike Francesa and Christopher Russo, known informally as "Mike and the Mad Dog," take some if not most of the credit for bringing catcher Mike Piazza to the Mets because of the discourse they fueled on their popular afternoon sports talk show (Forer (director), 2017).

Talk radio is not social media, but the principle is the same. Interaction from participants, sports fans in this instance, can have effects. In an era where interactive media is increasingly common, these effects can be transformative.

Fever Pitch

Nick Hornby

Nick Hornby, a zealot fan, describes his sense that fandom is not observing but "Doing."

One thing I know for sure about being a fan is this: it is not a vicarious pleasure, despite all appearances to the contrary, and those who say that they would rather do than watch are missing the point. Football is a context where watching *becomes* doing—not in the aerobics sense, because watching a game, smoking your head off while doing so, drinking after it has finished and eating chips on the way home is unlikely to do you a whole lot of Jane Fonda good, in the way that chuffing up and down a pitch is supposed to. But when there is some kind of triumph the pleasure does not radiate from the players outwards until it reaches the likes of us at the back of the terraces in a pale and diminished form; our fun is not a watery version of the team's fun, even though they are the ones that get to score the goals and climb the steps at Wembley to meet Princess Diana. The joy we feel on occasions like this is not a celebration of others' good fortune, but a celebration of our own; and when there is a disastrous defeat the sorrow that engulfs us is, in effect, self-pity and anyone who wishes to understand how football is consumed must realize this above all things. I am a part of the club just as the club is part of me. (Hornby, 1998, p. 178–179)

EUSTRESS

Raney identifies several reasons for fandom in his article "Why We Watch And Enjoy Mediated Sports." One such reason is that people simply desire to be entertained. We watch sports because it is like going to a movie or watching a comedian—sports are entertaining. Another reason for watching sports is to pass the time and relax after a stressful day. We come home, have dinner, and look forward to the Bulls game because it helps us unwind. A third reason is that when our teams win, we actually feel better as if we ourselves were victorious. This sensation can bolster our sense of self. When our teams win, we Bask in the Reflected Glory. We BIRG. He refers to a fourth reason for watching sports as *eustress*.

The affix eu means good. Euthanasia denotatively means "good death." A euphemism is a good or tactful way to express something that, without the euphemism, might be expressed crudely. Euphony is a sweet or pleasing sound.

Eustress is a good type of stress. "Several studies report that fans tune into mediated sports because they like the positive emotions coming from the increased arousal and excitement experienced during viewing" (Raney 2006, p. 317). The feeling of tension a fan experiences before and during an important game is eustress.

Those who claim to be nervous before a big game, when they are not even remotely involved with the actual playing of the contest, are experiencing eustress. We miss the eustress when, for example, our team loses a seventh game in a preliminary playoff series. On August 6, 2021, fans of the Australian National basketball team likely sensed the absence of eustress. Their team had lost a semifinal game to the United States team in the Tokyo Olympics and would not advance to the gold medal round. U.S. fans, by contrast, enjoyed the eustress as they contemplated the challenges of playing France for a second time in the tournament. During the gold medal game in which the United States defeated France, fans of both teams experienced eustress. Reviewing the reaction of fans everywhere in anticipation of, and during, key games, one can see the joy of eustress.

Raney mentions other reasons for sports fandom. Some people watch sports to become experts. Like the ESPN staffer who knew all the players who made the last outs of the World Series, there are people who "take pride in being walking encyclopedias of sports knowledge and trivia" (Raney, 2006, p. 320). The television program *Sports Jeopardy*, a version of the popular quiz show, reveals that there are many who have a grasp on minute aspects of sports. Others become fans because they are taken by the aesthetic attractions of sports. There is a beauty to athleticism that can be engaging. Watching women's Olympic hockey star Kendall Coyne skate quickly while somehow keeping the puck on her stick; observing the graceful approach that Althea Gibson took to hitting a tennis ball; marveling at how LeBron James can hang in the air and maneuver—these are things of beauty that attract fans.

Raney, echoing positions taken by Wann, writes about how fandom satisfies group affiliation needs and companionship. It can be comforting to be a fan of America's team or to go to a Wrigleyville sports bar where everyone "knows your name" and cheers for the Cubs. Dohrmann contends that for many people, a fan group has usurped church membership or other community organizations as the primary binding agent in their lives (Dohrmann, 2018, p. xiii).

Finally, some fans watch sports because of economics. That is, they have bet on the games to "make it interesting." On June 5, 2018, the state of Delaware became the first state to take advantage of a Supreme Court ruling. The courts ruled that whereas prior to the ruling, the state of Nevada was the only state that allowed legal gambling, now, it could be legal in any state. Fans flocked to casinos. On Sunday, June 10, there were hour-long lines to place bets. One enthusiast who had driven to Delaware from Staten Island said, "This is the greatest thing on earth."

For some fans, the companionship and sense of belonging are what is important.

Those who rush to casinos to wager on sports are more sports fans than inveterate gamblers. In his book, *The Odds*, Chad Millman makes it clear that consistently winning a good deal of money betting on sports is unlikely. In my ethnography of sports bettors who bet on March Madness, I make the same point (Zaremba, 2009). There can be no doubt that gambling is becoming part of the fabric of sports and fandom in a manner that differs from what had been the case previously. Leagues and the networks that broadcast league games now embrace sports betting. That was hardly the case in the past. In 2021, prior to kickoff on NFL Sundays, former quarterbacks Boomer Esiason and Phil Simms offered their betting wisdom for the day. A 2021 issue of *Sports Illustrated* was entirely dedicated to gambling. The preface to the first article in the issue begins with these words: "What's changed in the three years since the Supreme Court granted all fifty states the rights to legalize sports betting? Everything" (Wertheim, 2021, p. 25). Gambling and sports are now legitimately intertwined.

Fair or Foul   Questions of Ethics

Which of the following do you consider fair, and which are foul:
- Shouting derisively using profanity when you disagree with a referee's call?
- Using social media to ridicule an athlete's performance?
- Creating a website dedicated to encouraging management to fire a coach?
- Cheering when an opponent is injured?

Communicating with Fans

HYPODERMIC NEEDLE THEORY; USES AND GRATIFICATION THEORY

Let's consider two contrasting theories that are foundational to understanding how teams should communicate with fans.

The Hypodermic Needle Theory, sometimes called the Magic Bullet Theory, assumes that audiences who consume media do just that—consume and are, consequently, influenced by the messages they consume. For example, according to this theory, a person who watched the 1960s Dick Van Dyke show consumed and internalized the messages on the show about marriage, friendships, male-female roles, work, parenting, and even what was or was not humorous. The Hypodermic Needle Theory assumes people are essentially sitting ducks who are persuaded, consciously or otherwise, by what they see or hear. Teenagers in the 50s and 60s who listened to a song about "one boy one special boy" would form or confirm their beliefs about the merits of monogamy. Teenagers in the 70s who listened to "Love the One You're With" would consider, if not subconsciously adopt, an alternative philosophy. The assumption with these theories is that the power of the media is overwhelming and consequently persuasive. According to the Magic Bullet Theory, sports fans who watch the NFL and various programming related to American football become more enthusiastic because the consumption of football begets greater appreciation for the game.

Uses and Gratification Theory is different. It assumes that consumers use the media for their needs and do not simply consume what is offered. Uses and Gratification Theory, therefore, assumes that sports fans seek out programs that they find valuable, enjoyable, and useful. Consequently, media managers provide programming that these fans find gratifying. For example, SportsCenter, postgame shows, and the NFL draft are all programs that were created to gratify voracious fans. Uses and Gratification Theory, as it relates to fandom, does not assume that fans become fans because they are overwhelmed and persuaded by what they consume. Rather, what is available to be consumed—is the result of fans' desires for such content.

TALK RADIO: THE TOY DEPARTMENT AND CANDY STORE

Life is a department store and sports is the toy department

Radio talk show host Ed (Superfan) Bieler
(Eisenstock, 2001, p. 5)

The emergence, existence, and proliferation of sports talk radio is a good illustration of how Uses and Gratification Theory applies.

On March 30, 1964, sportscaster Bill Mazer hosted the first talk radio program on WNBC radio in New York. The first caller was a teenager. The young man said he had only one question. Mazer said, "Ok. Go ahead." Then the caller asked the question that school kids throughout the city of New York debated for years in cafeterias, at little league games, and when they were supposed to be reading in study hall.

"Who's better," said the kid. "Willie Mays or Mickey Mantle?"

The great debate: Willie Mays or Mickey Mantle?

And so it began, interactive discussions on the air about sports. Discussions that satisfied a need—regardless of the hour—for fans to listen to, commiserate with, and argue with a community of like-minded others. These others, even in the middle of the night, could become riled up about an outfielder who could not hit the cut-off man, a point guard who did not make a high percentage of foul shots, or a coach who inexplicably used Goalie X instead of the clearly better Goalie Y. The legion of listeners to sports talk might hold on for an hour just to make an essential point about a fullback who, despite his running skills, regularly failed to pick up a blitz.

One of the more famous radio sports talk hosts is the aforementioned Christopher Russo, a Yale graduate who, during his on-air hours at least, is known as the Mad Dog. His former on-air partner, Mike Francesa, would sometimes just refer to Russo as Dog, an abbreviation. For example, "I think the Giants will beat the Cowboys on Sunday, but the Dog has a different opinion. Go ahead Dog, explain how the Cowboys can possibly win."

The fans who listened daily to Mike and the Mad Dog on WFAN sought out and reveled in this outlet that allowed for a public discussion about nuanced matters in the world of sports. At the height of his fame, Russo published a book entitled *The Mag Dog 100* that offered his opinion on 100 different sports questions such as: "What does it take to succeed as an NFL football coach? Which baseball players get all the glory but don't back it up? Which partners would you pick to play the ultimate round of golf? What sports moments are worth watching again and again? The introduction to the book begins with a revealing sentence: "Welcome to the candy store." (John & Russo, 2013, p. xv)

Eisenstock concludes his book *Talk Radio* with an explanation of its allure.

I have stumbled upon the core of sports talk radio. It lies in the connection between host and listener. Joe the waiter doesn't listen to sports talk because he gambles; getting winners was a bonus, a sign from God. He listens because of what sports meant so his soul. . . Sports exists to spirit us away from both the mundane and momentous decisions that clutter and conquer us. (Eisenstock, 2001, p. 242)

Practitioner Perspective

Paul Rogers

Former Head of Digital and Social Media AS Roma

Courtesy of Paul Rogers

Paul Rogers is the former Head of Digital Media at AS Roma, one of the world's most famous football clubs. In this role, Paul was responsible for the club's content activities across all digital and social platforms.

Prior to joining Roma in January 2015, Paul spent fourteen years working for Liverpool Football Club in the English Premier League. He was responsible for developing and leading the club's international media strategy—helping the club to communicate with over twenty-five million followers in eighteen different languages every day.

He joined Liverpool FC in 2001 after helping to launch the youth portal Liv4now.

Previously he worked at *Condé Nast* as a writer and sub-editor for *GQ magazine* as well as contributing weekly music columns and articles for the likes of *The Independent and Guardian newspapers, New Musical Express, iD magazine, The Face, Sky Magazine, Echoes, Blues & Soul, Hip-Hop Connection, Q, Smash Hits.*

In a very short time, Paul Rogers helped generate an international following for AS Roma. He earned a growing and glowing reputation for innovation and creativity while establishing the team's global brand.

Several writers commented on AS Roma's social media successes.

- "Roma's 3–0 rout of Barcelona was stunning, but I would like to make the argument that the performance from the club's English-language Twitter feed (@ASRomaEn) was even more impressive." (Yoesting)

- "Roma's Twitter output is frequently surreal. . . The posts are roaringly successful. (Henson)
- "AS Roma is to the player unveil [announcing the signing of a player to a team] what Picasso is to art" (A. Lewis)

AS Roma's website was honored with a "Best in Class" award in 2017 by the Interactive Media Awards. According to the club, Roma's official accounts generated more interactions on Twitter in June 2018 than any other Italian team and had the highest engagement rate among the Top 10 clubs in Europe.

While he was still working for AS Roma, I met with Paul and asked about his success communicating and engaging with fans.

AZ. What is your objective with AS Roma as it relates to communicating with fans?

PR. Our owner, Jim Pallotta, told me on day one that we were in the entertainment business and engaging with fans—and making content that brings our fans closer to the club—was the absolute goal. AS Roma started in 1927. However, Jim has said we are like a 91-year-old start-up, because until recently people beyond our supporters did not know enough about us. We had our fans, but our goal is to build a global brand out of what was before a corner store. We want to engage fans from around the world. We now communicate in thirteen different languages on social media—with official accounts in Italian, English, Arabic, Indonesian, Spanish, French, Portuguese, Greek, Bosnian, Turkish, Dutch, Persian, and Chinese.

Everything we do is for our fans; every decision we make starts with the fan in mind. Are we listening to fans? Are we engaging fans? Are we giving fans a voice? If we're not empowering our fans and making them feel closer to the club, we're doing it wrong.

In Rome, the fans are constantly bombarded by content about the club. There's the radio stations, the newspapers, the blogs, the social media feeds, the television shows, and the endless conversations everywhere you go about the club. Fans are free to consume the content they want to consume and it's our job to offer them something different that cuts through this noise and makes them feel not just closer to the club but actually part of it. We try and do that by giving fans a voice and a chance to engage.

A goal is to spread the fandom, not by poaching fans from their primary club. That is not likely to happen. A Liverpool fan is a fan from childhood. The affinity for Liverpool has been established, likely passed down from family members. Enthusiasm for Liverpool is not going to leave Liverpool just like enthusiasm for Roma will not leave Roma. However, we want to complement that fan base with an audience of those who see us as a second club to follow.

For example, in Spain there is Barcelona and Real Madrid. Between the two clubs there are some 209 million fans. Real Madrid fans are not going to support Barcelona, Barcelona fans are not going to follow Real Madrid, but there is a potential of 209 million fans who might desire to follow Roma as a second club. The second club is a massive market.

So our goal is to establish a global presence and engage the fans we have, as well as other fans who might see us as their second club.

AZ. What is essential for successful communication with fans?

PR. Remember we are in the attention industry. As communicators we have to realize your audience is not necessarily you, in that they don't necessarily think like you. You have to communicate to your audience. And you have to engage them. And you have to remember that good content is good content—and you have to have good content.

We did some crowdsourcing when I first started. We showed our website to audiences, and asked them to tell us what they did not like about it and tell us frankly. Fans respected us for that. They thought that was cool and gave us suggestions.

Then we suggested that if people had some artwork that would be good for our site to send their work to us. If people had articles they'd written but had not received a wide audience, we said that they should send these to us and we might publish them on our site. We were able to give people visibility. We became the first football club to implement this crowdsourcing approach to not just the design and functionality of the site, but also the content. We reached out and asked fans what content they wanted to consume and then empowered supporters to actually play an active role in creating that content, from photography, graphic design, and infographics to videos, opinion articles, and weekly columns.

In general what we do that works well is we are quick to react. We are frank. We are transparent and we use humor. Let's remember that sport is supposed to be fun. People work all week and they want to relax watching their favorite team. Football and following football ought to be fun. Football clubs can buy followers—particularly on Facebook and many do—but it's much harder to buy engagement. To ensure we organically generate great engagement metrics, we believe in entertainment—pure and simple—and being very down to earth.

Look, we take our work seriously, but we don't take ourselves seriously and that helps us make the experience for our fans fun.

It is also important to remember that everyone is their own personal brand. All receivers have their own brand. When you share something, you are contributing to your own brand. You see something from Roma that you want to share, you share it and it says something about you. It is as if people are creating their own online cv.

AZ. What success stories can you share?

PR. We've been fortunate to have had a number. Recently, we had success with a decision we made related to the 2018 World Cup. Since Italy did not have a team in the World Cup and therefore our fans would not have a team to root for, we decided to support Nigeria. There are 180 million fans in Nigeria. AS Roma adopted Nigeria in the World Cup competition and our social media was active supporting the team. We received a tremendous response from Nigerian fans, and also the Nigerian government. Some fans insisted that we must be from Nigeria to be as knowledgeable about Nigeria as we seemed to be. A radio program in England called "Talk Sports" aired a 15-minute segment on AS Roma with a professor commenting on the phenomenon of the Nigerian audiences.

We had a tremendous response from Iranian fans after a tweet. Our logo shows Romulus and Remus being suckled by the Capitoline Wolf taken from the myth surrounding the foundation of Rome. Iranian censors were concerned with the sexual nature of the image and when they broadcast our game, blurred the image of the suckling. This resulted in an outcry in a number of quarters. But we went with it. You may remember the advertisement that included two photos of a woman, one where she was wearing no make-up, and another where she had make-up. The ad copy read, if you don't love me like this—referring to the no make-up photo—then you can't love me like this—referring to the photo with cosmetics applied. So after the commotion regarding the censorship, we tweeted a photo of our logo, unblurred, juxtaposed with the blurred image. The text read, If you don't love me at my—referring to the unblurred photo. Then you can still love me at my—pointing to the blurred image. Very positive reaction, the extent of which even surprised us.

We've put out music playlists for rap, top 60s, various genres and this has endeared us to music aficionados who might adopt us as a second club and has certainly increased awareness of AS Roma.

Recurring Counsel: How Should Teams Communicate With Fans

A review of best practices related to communicating with fans provides the following recurring counsel.

SUBSTANTIVE CONTENT IS ESSENTIAL

As in any type of communication, it is important to have something meaningful to say when you communicate with fans. In the same way that regular team meetings have to be substantive in order to encourage players to attend and pay attention, messages from teams to fans have to be similarly valuable. Why visit a website or read an e-mail if the content repeats what you were able to get by watching a local news channel? Why read an inside story about the new goalie if the story has no inside information? The existence of sophisticated social media does not replace the need for quality content.

PLATFORMS

The platforms have changed. Teams need to make sure that fans can interact with the teams, and teams need to be prepared to respond to fan comments. Social media has revolutionized the way fans get their information. Fans expect opportunities to express their reactions and opinions. A team-produced newspaper, like the *Buffalo Bills Digest*, may still have an appreciable audience, but when you visit the team's website, you will see the following that indicates that the Bills recognize that interaction has to include more than a one-way vehicle. If you scroll to the bottom of the Buffalo Bills home page https://www.buffalobills.com/ you see six different ways that you can connect with the Bills:

CONNECT WITH US!

FACEBOOK Buffalo Bills	**TWITTER** buffalobills	**SNAPCHAT** BillsNFL
INSTAGRAM buffalobills	**YOUTUBE** Buffalo Bills	**EMAIL** News, promotions, ticket info & more

BEYOND THE GAME

Information that will engage fans does not only involve content about player statistics, game strategy, and upcoming contests. Content about player activities, hobbies, and favorite music groups can also be engaging. Almost no contemporary sports contest is without some complement beyond the game. Fans at Fenway Park sing Sweet Caroline at the bottom of the 8th, and it has become part of the experience of going to the game. Fans attending NFL preseason practices can bring along their youngsters, who may bounce around trampoline-like apparatus while the athletes take their repetitions.

Want to attend the Green Bay Packers training camp practices? If you went to the Packers website in search of information in the summer of 2018, you would learn that the "Packers Experience" was a "four day free festival for fans of all ages" offered by the team in honor of "100 Seasons," a celebration of the Packers' centennial season. There was "live music, a replica of a team locker room, USA football kids' clinics, Packers alumni question and answer sessions, photo stations, and prizes." And yes, one could attend the Packers' practices as well, which were held concurrently from July 26 through July 29. However, the "Packers Experience" extended beyond the hours of the practice.

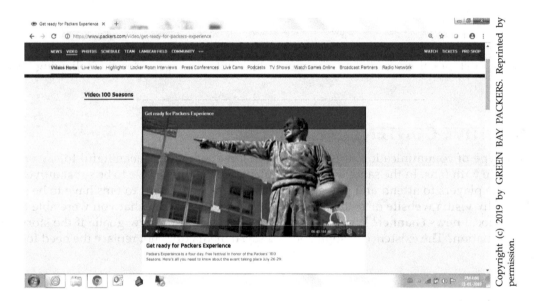

INCLUSIVENESS

Whereas thirty years ago, the predominant audience for sports messages were men, now—because of Title IX and other societal influences—the demographics of fandom are no longer monolithic. Nielsen reports that "Aside from the digital revolution, the rapid rise in the importance, influence, and value of female fans has been one of the most distinctive shifts in the sports marketing landscape in the last fifty years. We now see the impact of a second generation of young women growing up with a much higher chance of developing an interest in sport." (Nielsen Sports)

Frank Deford's memoir, *Over Time,* describes his life's work as a sports writer. At one point, he discusses his trip to Cameroon during the 1990 World Cup:

> . . . nothing touched me so much as when I went to Cameroon . . . I wanted to do a story from the point of view of the people down there, when little Cameroon was playing England in the quarterfinals . . . here was Cameroon's chance. It's one day in the sun. Cameroon scored the first

goal, too, and in the bar where I was watching, a short, fat lady next to me grabbed me and started dancing with me, and only if you could've seen the unbounded joy in her face. The photographer who was with me took a picture of that moment, and it's the only sports photograph I keep in my office. —It tells you better than anything else about the joy of sports—and the power, too, I suppose" (Deford, 2012, p. 275).

The joy and power of sports are at the roots of fandom. In a New York restaurant, a stranger having lunch two seats away from me explained, without any real encouragement, that he was a devout fan of the Pittsburgh Steelers yet always wagered against them. When I asked why he bets against the Steelers if he adores them, he said: "When I bet them to win, they lose. When I bet them to lose, they win. I don't want them to lose, so I bet them to lose because this way, either way, I win. I win if they win because I've bet them to lose. I win at least money if they lose because I've bet them to lose. Either way, if I bet them to lose, I win." There was no accompanying smile. Another person told me that he at one time ate two hot dogs before his beloved Syracuse Orangemen played an NCAA tournament basketball game. Since they were victorious in that game, he felt compelled to eat two hot dogs before every subsequent contest, even when he had contracted a stomach virus on the eve of the final. He wouldn't unequivocally acknowledge that there could be no correlation between eating the hot dogs and Syracuse's victory (Zaremba, 2009, 100–102). An oft-repeated but likely story alleges that a terminally ill Cleveland Brown fan requested in his last wishes that members of the Browns be his pallbearers. He made this request because he felt it would be fitting that the Browns let him down one last time.

An indication of the breadth, diversity, and, yes, fanaticism of fans can be found at a site called Mygameballs.com. This site is dedicated to those who attend ball games in an attempt to lead the league in foul balls they are able to obtain at the games. A person by the name of Dennis "the Beard" Mora, who attends Miami Marlins games, is featured in one article at the site. Mora had "hauled in a total of 846 balls . . . en route to being voted the 2017 Ballhawk of the Year." The Beard, however, has a long way to go to best all-time leader Zack Hample. Hample, a New Yorker and author of baseball books, is ahead in this year's competition.

Baseball collector Zack Hample shows off his astonishing collection of Major League baseballs he has gathered over the years.

Chapter Conclusion—Take-Aways

- Fans are essential to any sports organization.
- Creating networks to communicate with fans and for fans to communicate with teams is essential.
- Understanding the nature of fandom is important for any sports organization and sports communicator.
- Fans may become fans because of
  - Identification and group affiliation
  - Affect Theory principles
  - Eustress
  - *BIRGing*—Basking In Reflected Glory
  - Escape and entertainment
  - Aesthetic appreciation for a sport or athletes
- Social media has provided new methods for communicating with fans and for fans to communicate with sports organizations.
- Instances of fan reaction indicate the power of sports attraction.
  - Baltimore Colt and Cleveland Brown departures
  - Reaction to World Cup competition
  - Idiosyncratic fan behavior before, during, and after competitions

QUESTIONS

1. How can Affect Theory explain fandom? Eustress?

2. To which team do you have a strong affiliation? When did you begin cheering for that team? What do you do to follow the team? Do you consider your fandom healthy?

3. What is the best way for sports organizations to reach their fans with news of the team's activities?

4. How key is it for fans to be able to communicate their reactions to games during contests and after a game's conclusion?

First Person   2–1 in 508[3]

Larry Poppel, my dear childhood friend, is a very serious hockey fan. His team is the New York Rangers, and he follows them to the extent that he worries about them.

I do not share my friend's enthusiasm. Of the major team sports, hockey is actually my least favorite. But to support my life-long friend, I occasionally travel down to New York to sit with him in his season tickets in section 508[1] in Madison Square Garden.

Section 508 is populated by knowledgeable, loyal, and enthusiastic fans, just like Larry. They arrive at the games not like people out for an evening's entertainment but rather like blue-collar employees showing up for work. They lug—not their lunch pails—but their affection for the Rangers as they assemble, slide into their seats, and settle in as if they themselves are going to work. They collectively take a deep breath, hoist up their jeans, and prepare to watch their beloved Rangers.

Prior to 1994, the New York Rangers and its fans had endured the humiliation of not winning a championship in fifty-four years. Fans of opponents would often insult the Rangers by regularly jeering "1940, 1940" when opportunities presented themselves. Nevertheless, despite the taunts and past failures, every single night during a hockey season, the steadfastly devoted group in 508 would lumber up to the top tier of Madison Square Garden to join with the others in the arena to cheer for the New York Rangers.

It is not uncommon for people to refer to sports fanatics as "get a lifers." Even those who enjoy sports will comment disparagingly about fans who can not seem to get out of bed without worrying about the health of a goalie or whether a high school basketball star will be successfully recruited to play for a favorite university. Saying "get a life" to those fretting about such issues has become a way to suggest that there are other matters to consider in the world and that enthusiasm for sport can lead to a loss of perspective.

An incident reflecting such a loss of perspective took place one evening during a sports talk radio show. A listener called in ranting about an outfielder who had a tendency to play the field without enthusiasm. This laziness, according to the caller, turned singles into doubles and allowed runners on first to get to third easily. The caller was hoarse from shouting his complaint. In the course of his tirade, there was an audible crash and rumble in the background. The broadcaster interrupted the caller and asked:

"What was that?"

The fan responded evenly, "Ah, my wife tripped over a wire and fell down some stairs." Then without pausing for a second, the caller continued rasping, "It really burns my butt when Strawberry won't hustle after the single." Aghast, the talk show host shouted, "Sir, take care of your wife and get a life!"

---

[3] Madison Square Garden did not have a section 508 at the time this game was played. There was no fifth level. Larry Poppel (not his real name) sat in a different section. The number has been changed in case any season ticket holder in this section would prefer anonymity.

For far less egregious behaviors, the likes of the rabid folks in 508 have also heard the admonition and suggestion to "get a life."

In 1994, the Rangers seemed to have a legitimate chance to win the championship and take home the coveted Stanley Cup, the symbol of such victory. In each prior year, when Larry would talk optimistically about chances for the Cup, even he knew there was really no possibility of obtaining it. But in 1994, the Rangers had progressed easily through the first two playoff series, sweeping the hated New York Islanders and beating the Washington Capitols four games to one. The Rangers would play the New Jersey Devils in the penultimate round of the playoffs, and this was the key series. If the Rangers could defeat the Devils, they would likely play a weaker opponent in the finals. Therefore, the Devils seemed to present the only legitimate hurdle to winning the Cup. To the season ticket holders in section 508 and the rest of the get a lifers in Madison Square Garden, a Stanley Cup would be, literally, a dream come true.

Unfortunately, as the series with the Devils proceeded, the dream of securing the Stanley Cup seemed as if it would turn out to be yet another agonizing illusion for Ranger fans. After five games, the Devils led the best of seven series, three games to two, and were playing the sixth game on their home ice. After two periods of the sixth game, the Devils led the Rangers by a score of 3–1. My friend Larry was beyond depressed. He shut his television off at the end of the second period and urged his wife Angie to join him and go to sleep. Larry could not take watching a third period which resulted, once again, in a Cup-less Ranger season. He told Angie that if the Rangers were to miraculously overcome the 3–1 deficit and win, I would call and wake them up.

I called. The Rangers had stormed back in the third period to win the sixth game. The ringing of the phone roused Larry from his forced slumber. When he heard my voice, he reacted with stunned but joyous disbelief. He repeated my report in ecstatic short rasps to Angie. "The Rangers won. They came back. They won." Then, back to me, he said, "Al, you gotta come down for the seventh game."

On May 27, 1994—the Friday of Memorial Day weekend, I drove to New York and met Larry and Angie in a bar called Charlie O's. Charlie O's sat at the entrance to Madison Square Garden, and on this night—two hours before the opening face-off of the seventh game—Charlie O's was jammed, wall to wall, with keyed-up Ranger fans.

Larry told me that he and I would not be sitting next to each other for this game. In order to accommodate me as well as Angie, Larry had secured two seats from another season ticket holder. He and Angie would use the other tickets and be sitting in the tonier mezzanine section. I would be in hardscrabble 508 with a hockey pal of his named Richie. "Wait till you meet Richie," Larry said to me. "He's quite a character." To be "quite a character" among the distinctive population in section 508 would be no small achievement. Richie did not disappoint. About six feet tall and no more than 150 pounds, he arrived wearing a beat-up felt hat and reminded me of the Honeymooners character Ed Norton. With his lid not quite fitting securely on his head, Richie wiggled through the crowd at Charlie O's carrying a briefcase. He gave Angie a big hug and kiss, bear-hugged Larry, then looked at me. "You must be Poppel's friend."

"Yes."

"Ranger fan?'

"Tonight, I am."

"Better be, Poppel's friend. Better be."

Larry's season tickets were in the very front row of section 508, the fifth and sixth seats in from the aisle. I took the sixth seat, and Richie settled into the fifth. Directly in front of us was a three-foot brick wall with a metal guard rail. There is a walkway beyond the railing that is typically used by media personnel and photographers. For this deciding seventh game, the walkway had a dual purpose. Folding chairs were set up in the space to allow for additional spectators. The media folk and photographers would need to walk and stand behind these added customers. I noticed that among those in the folding chairs was a cluster of nuns. I wondered how they might react to the language that I knew would be cascading from our section during the course of this evening.

Seated to my right was a bull of a man. Not especially tall, maybe only 5'8", but he looked like he lived in a gym. This rock-hard fellow was all business. I tried to get him to converse, but he was too tense and focused. I managed to eke out that he lived in Albany, New York, drove the 120 miles down just for the game, and that he and his family were moving the next day to a new house.

"You're moving tomorrow? Your wife ok with that? I mean, is your wife ok about you coming down for the game since you're moving tomorrow?"

"No. She is not ok," he said.

He did not seem to want to elaborate on this issue or anything else. He was staring straight ahead at the ice.

Before the game, a photographer was walking behind the nuns in the aisle just below where Richie, I, and Albany were rooted. The photographer was tall and broad-shouldered. His hair, what was left of it, was closely cropped. His receding hairline and head shape had created an unusually expansive forehead. The photographer's brown eyes and everything about him seemed calm and relaxed, in stark contrast to the agitated others in my midst.

"You a fan, or just working?" I asked him.

"Just working. Hockey? Don't think so." He shook his head. "I do not know what you all see in this game."

"Just snapping pictures?"

"Just snapping pictures."

"Don't care if the Rangers win?"

"Just snapping pictures."

Right before the game began, I saw Richie fold his arms. Then he took his left hand and stretched it across his right arm. He proceeded to tap on the metal railing with his left hand. After this, he refolded his arms. Then he took his right hand and stretched it across his left arm to tap on a part of the railing closest to his left knee. He then refolded his arms and repeated these movements several times.

"What is that?" I asked.

"Just a little something I do," he answered.

I stared at him, confounded.

"Works best on metals," he said by way of explanation.

It was not until the second period that the first goal of this seventh game was scored. To the relieved joy of everyone around me, it was the Rangers who had made the score, and it stood up throughout the period. When I went to the men's room during the intermission, I stood at the back of a long line of fans, nearly all of whom were adorned in Ranger uniforms. In this queue of men waiting to use the toilet, an ear-splitting spontaneous chant of "Let's Go Rangers, Let's Go" was blasting against the tiles. At one point, the cheering lost some of its intensity. "Come on," screamed one of the faithful. "They need us now. Don't give up. They need us now." Again the chant picked up as if responding to a logical admonition. "Let's go, Rangers, Let's Go" between periods, in the bathroom, waiting to use the urinal.

The tension throughout the third period this night in Madison Square Garden was truly palpable. Richie was intense. It seemed as if every few minutes, he was doing his left hand over right hand, tapping hocus pocus on the railing. The Albany muscle man was staring straight ahead and had not said more than three words to me since our initial exchange before the first period.

The thin 1–0 lead continued to hold up as the minutes and seconds were draining off the clock. The fans in section 508 were wide-eyed and nearly delirious. This could be it. The Rangers might win this seventh game and then go on to play the lesser talented Vancouver Canucks, a team that could and would be defeated in the finals. The Rangers might win the Stanley Cup. The Rangers would finally win the Stanley Cup. Now there was only one minute left. Now thirty seconds. Now fifteen seconds. Ten, nine, eight. . .

And then, with 7.7 seconds left and the arena ready to burst with unrestrained glee, the Devils scored a goal sending the game into overtime.

Simon and Garfunkel. "Sounds of Silence." I have never heard such silence. Richie moaned as if he had been shot by an arrow. Albany's eyes flared. He looked like someone who had been waiting to see a sign on the New York State Thruway that read, "Albany 10 miles," but when he approached the marker, it read "Albany 1000 miles." During intermission, Ranger fans walked around the corridors in a communal daze. I saw a man using his left hand to prop up his right arm. Blood was oozing out from his knuckles. Someone asked, "Are you ok? What's wrong?"

"I punched the wall. That's what's wrong. Am I ok? The Devils scored with seven seconds left. Am I ok, this guy wants to know."

In the Stanley Cup, playoffs tied games are resolved by a procedure called sudden death. Additional twenty-minute periods are played until a goal is scored, resulting in an immediate victory for one team and a sudden death for the other. If no team scores in the first extra period, then the teams take a break, return to the ice and play a second sudden-death period. If necessary, there is another break, and then a third period is played. This process continues until there is a deciding goal.

For every zealot in Madison Square Garden on this night, the sudden death time in the arena was beyond tense. Any shot taken by the New Jersey Devils could mark the end of the game, series, and Stanley Cup hopes. Every time the Devils secured the puck and began skating toward the Ranger net, the air was sucked out of Madison Square Garden. And every time the Rangers skated back the other way, there was hope that maybe the result of this rush would be a victory. Back and forth. Hold your breath in. Let your breath out. Back and forth. Hold your breath in. Let your breath out.

There was no scoring during the first overtime period. I am not even a hockey fan, but I was limp with exhaustion. During intermission, the diehards were flopping around the concourses like noodles; spent fans who were dizzy from expenditure. After the first few rushes of the second overtime, I began to get pains in my chest. I tried to remind myself that I did not even like hockey, but this did not seem to help. The nuns were fiddling with something in front of me. At one point, the Devils raced up the ice and unleashed a screaming slap shot that the Ranger goalie managed heroically to kick away at the last second. The puck went careening into the stands, and play was temporarily halted. The whole arena gasped. I heard Joe Cool, the photographer, wheeze. He wheeled around. No longer a dispassionate observer, there were little droplets of perspiration on his very broad forehead. His brown eyes looked like two M&Ms, each swimming in its own bowl of milk.

"Wow. That was close. Wow," said Joe Cool, the photographer.

Prior to the ensuing face-off, I said something to myself that I had muttered throughout my life on occasion but had never previously meant literally. I said, "I don't know how much more of this I can take." I started thinking about what would happen if the Devils scored a goal. This place would crumble. I tried to imagine how the explosion of energy might manifest itself. There had to be a winner and a loser in this game. If the Rangers were to lose, Larry, Richie, and the 19,000 others in the arena would be crushed.

I thought that I had to calm myself and imagined some scenes in my life that were particularly comforting. I thought about my nephew's fifth birthday party when he decided to give a sweet if nonsensical speech to all those assembled. I remembered a day at the beach with a sweetheart many years prior. We had taken a bean bag to the ocean and were running pass patterns in the sand tossing the bag like a football back and forth. I tried to remember the sound of the ocean that day as we tossed the bag to each other and the serenity and. . . .

MATTEAU, MATTEAU, MATTEAU, MATTEAU, MATTEAU, MATTEAU.

A Ranger player by the name of Stephane Matteau had scored. Matteau had taken the puck at the side of the net and stuffed it past the Devil goaltender. The Garden erupted.

Immediately, with no thought to the contrary, I turned to Richie, and we embraced. An instant later, I did what came extraordinarily naturally. I wheeled around to my silent Albany neighbor—a person with whom I had exchanged less than twenty-five words in my life—and proceeded to share as ferocious a hug as any I have ever shared or will share. We all laughed and teared excessively as we walked up the aisle to exit. People were high-fiving everyone. It felt like everyone in the Garden was celebrating the birth of a baby. Richie and I met up with Angie and Larry when we got to the ground level, and our embrace was as meaningful as if we were congratulating them after their wedding. People were crying in the lobby as they hugged their friends.

We four decided we needed to stop for a bite. We found a tavern that was populated with other Ranger fans clad in their jerseys. We grabbed a table and observed the scene. Limp Ranger fanatics were shaking their heads, gazing at replays of the final goal on a television set propped above a bar. As I looked around the group, it seemed from the perspiration on their jerseys as if there was enough sweat on the apparel to convince a stranger that these guys themselves had skated some shifts. They were elated, wildly happy, drinking, toasting, tearing—this sudden death victory of a seventh game.

And as I looked at these spent Ranger fans in the restaurant, I started to think that to have this passion, to have this love for something, was special and was to be envied and emulated. These people had a passion. Sure, some could, can, and do become monomaniacal and irresponsible with that passion. But most of them had simply found something that thrilled them; something that they loved. It was something that brought them to Ranger games year after year, tapping on metal railings to bring the team luck.

I then thought about those who have no such passion in their lives, no zest for something; people who would never understand Richie, Larry, or the Albany guy. I thought that these folks who sit demurely through time never genuinely becoming excited about anything—whether it be hockey or stamps, basketball or coins—who never find or seek a place to invest their emotional energy—these people would be wise indeed to hurry up and get a life.

Reasons Why Fans Watch Televised Sporting Events	
• Aesthetic	• Family
• Companionship	• Group Affiliation
• Economics	• Learning
• Entertainment	• Release
• Escape	• Self-esteem
• Eustress	

From Raney, A. (2006). Why we watch and enjoy mediated sports. In Arthur and Bryant Jennings (Eds.), Handbook of Sports and Media Raney (pp. 313-327). Mahwah NJ: Lawrence Erlbaum.

Chapter 9

Communicating with the Public

© fitzcrittle/Shutterstock.com

Chapter in a Nutshell

Nearly always, the information we receive about sports has been mediated. We visit sports websites, review tweets, read newspapers, listen to radio, watch televised sporting events, watch sports documentaries, read books, watch sports movies, and listen to sports analysts. The public does not simply consume media; increasingly, the public participates in the generation of media. This chapter examines how sports figures, artists, and researchers communicate to and with the public.

Specifically, at the end of the chapter, students will be able to:

■ Identify incidents when athletes, coaches, and teams have shaped their images because of how they have communicated with the public.

■ Discuss the role of sports information directors.

■ Describe best practices of sports information directors.

■ Identify documentaries, films, and books that have shaped perceptions of sports and athletes.

■ Identify academic journals that publish scholarly research in sports communication.

Sports Communication Prompts

• Below you will see statements pertaining to some aspect of communication and sports. For each item

  ○ Decide whether you agree or disagree with the statement.

  ○ Explain your rationale for the position.

  ○ Support your position with examples.

1. A professional athlete should not use social media. It is too dangerous.

2. Most people do not get their sports news from newspapers or television. If you want to know about the Dolphins or the Heat, you go to the web, not the *Miami Herald* or Florida *Sun-Sentinel*.

3. A good sports information director is worth as much as a star athlete to a professional team. Likewise, establishing relationships with fans, the press, and members of the community is as essential for sports teams as wins or losses.

4. Movies, books, and tv shows about sports create the narrative about sports. For example, we say what we say about Michael Jordan because of the documentary, *The Last Dance*.

5. The majority of scholarly research in sports communication would be interesting and valuable to average fans if they invested the time reviewing the journals that publish this research.

The biggest change I've seen over four decades of covering sports is that everyone has become a citizen journalist.

Sports broadcaster Lesley Visser

Talk Radio. Philly Style. Flak Jacket Required

Sports author Michael Freeman

If a man watches three football games in a row he should be declared legally dead

Syndicated columnist Erma Bombeck

Introduction

How we think about sports is in large part a function of how sports figures and sports organizations communicate with us. Nearly always, the messages we receive about sports have been mediated. That is, in some way, we find out about sports and athletes via the media. On the same day, December 1, 2021, I learned why former Notre Dame football coach Brian Kelly decided to take the head football coaching job at LSU when I watched a replay of his press conference on YouTube; I read an Associated Press article and learned that the Women's Tennis Association had suspended tournament play because player Peng Shuai had received death threats; I visited Yahoo sports and discovered that Tampa Bay Buccaneer receiver Antonio Brown's ankle had still not healed and he would miss two more games. The very next day, I read on espn.com that Brown had been suspended for falsifying information about his vaccination status. I learned all this through the media. I did not bump into Brian Kelly, Peng Shuai, or Antonio Brown in Starbucks.

The media has a powerful effect on what we know, how we talk, and our attitudes about sports, teams, leagues, and athletes. In the parlance of communication studies, the media has an "agenda-setting" function as it relates to our understanding of sports and also "frames" content for us. More about agenda setting and framing later in this chapter.

Sports organizations are aware of the importance of communicating effectively with the public and the media's role in facilitating that communication. Consequently, teams, leagues, university athletic departments, and sometimes individual athletes themselves hire communication specialists. At the university level, these specialists are often called sports information directors or public relations officers. Sports organizations often hire administrators with titles like Directors of Communication and Marketing or Vice President for Public Relations. Pat Courtney, for example, is the Chief Communications Officer for Major League Baseball. Michael Bass is the Chief Communications Officer and Executive Vice President for the NBA and WNBA. Kate Hartman is the Chief Communications officer for the U.S. Olympic and Paralympic Committee.

These communication specialists are not the only people who communicate about sports to the public and, consequently, affect the narrative and discourse about sports. Authors, film producers, sports journalists, television producers, scholars, and fans themselves contribute to the narrative.

Sometimes communications with the public cast a positive light on sports. There are occasions when the opposite is true.

Throughout the text, we have discussed how analysts can look at communication through a transmission as well as a constitutive lens. These are discrete but complementary perspectives, and both are important. This is clearly apparent when we examine how sports organizations and athletes communicate with the public.

For example, at a most basic level, sports information directors need to communicate when games will be played, information about obtaining tickets, and facts about transportation to an arena. From a transmission perspective, communication analysts could examine how efficiently this type of information is received.

- Is there a mandatory vaccination policy for all who attend games?
  - Are season ticket owners aware of the policy?
- Is there a highway construction project that will affect transportation to a stadium?
  - Are fans given advance warning of the potential transportation challenges and provided alternatives?
- Is there a promotion for an upcoming game?
  - Are potential customers aware of the promotion?

The constitutive perspective is similarly important. When Jerry Jones, the owner of the Dallas Cowboys, declared in the summer of 2018 that all of his players would be compelled to stand for the national anthem, he was transmitting—or attempting to transmit—this policy to players, local and national/international media, fans, and political representatives. Concurrently, his message was shaping the image of the Cowboys, the league, and perhaps even the citizens of Dallas. When players are interviewed about their perspectives on this issue, they would attempt to transmit accurately their feelings about standing during the anthem. At the same time, the athletes would be shaping their relationships with various audiences.

Steps and Missteps

Sports information directors, certainly, are aware of the power of communication and the ramifications of what they say. Jean-Paul Sartre once said, "Words are loaded pistols," and this is a good metaphor to consider when we contemplate the importance of communication with the public. There have been times when sports figures have made regrettable comments during broadcasted or otherwise mass communicated interviews. Comments that sports information directors would never recommend. These remarks have had enduring effects on the sports figure's image and relationship with the public. What the athletes and coaches attempted to transmit might have been relatively benign. However, the constitutive effects of their communications left an enduring blemish, like a regrettable tattoo in a prominent place.

The public, for example, has associated Allen Iverson for years with comments he made about practice in 2002. Iverson was asked at a press conference why he was not practicing with the team. His response, if dispassionately digested, included a number of messages: When he is hurt, he can't practice. When he is tired, he should not practice. During games, he plays as hard as one can, so he should not be criticized for sitting out practice when tired or hurt. However, how Iverson said what he said—the emphasis on the word "practice" and the many times he said "practice"—made it seem as if he did not think that practice was necessary, at least for him.

(See his press conference here: https://www.youtube.com/watch?v=eGDBR2L5kzI)

"We're talking about practice. We're talking about practice. We ain't talking about the game. We're talking about practice, man."

From a constitutive perspective, this speech—and the repeated emphasis on the word "practice"—contributed to an image of Iverson as someone who did not respect the value of preparation and thought he was above the need for it. He might have simply desired to transmit that when hurt, he should not practice because compared to playing in a game, practice was relatively insignificant.

The late Dennis Green was a respected football coach for the Minnesota Vikings and subsequently the Arizona Cardinals. When Green coached Minnesota, he led the Vikings to the playoffs in eight out of the ten years he was head coach. His Viking teams twice went to the NFC championship game, one win shy twice of making the Super Bowl. Green did not fare as well in his three years with the Cardinals, but even with those losing seasons included, his career winning percentage was .546. Green has more head coaching victories than revered head coaches John Madden, Vince Lombardi, Bill Walsh, Jimmy Johnson, and Ted Marchibroda.

Nevertheless, despite his successes, what people remember most about Dennis Green were comments he made after a Monday Night Football game in 2006. That night, his 1-4 Cardinals had been defeating the previously undefeated Chicago Bears. The Cardinals were ahead by twenty points with seconds left in the third quarter. However, the Cardinals fumbled twice in the last fifteen-plus minutes, and both fumbles were returned for touchdowns. The Cardinals also gave up a punt return for a touchdown. This series of calamities resulted in the Bears taking the lead by one point in the last minutes of the game. Despite the stunning collapse, Green's Cardinals still had a chance to be victorious at the end, but a field goal attempt was unsuccessful.

In the postgame press conference, Green was understandably upset. In response to a question, he issued what was, out of context certainly, an irrational rant. The coach was asked about the Cardinals' excellent defense against the Bears. Green's team had intercepted Bears quarterback Rex Grossman four times during the contest. Instead of responding rationally to the inquiry, Green exploded with what would appear to many as an illogical rejoinder:

Unfortunately Dennis Green, despite his tremendous success as an NFL coach, is remembered often for comments he made to the media after a tough loss to the Chicago Bears.

The Bears were what we thought they were. What we thought they were. We played them in preseason. Who the hell takes the third game in the preseason like it's [expletive]? We played them the third game, everybody played three quarters. The Bears are who we thought they were. That's why we took the damn field. If you want to crown them, then crown their [expletive]. But they are who we thought they were. And we let them off the hook.

The fact is that throughout his career, Dennis Green was known as a mild-mannered coach. Yet what he became known for was not his won-loss record nor his typically controlled demeanor. What Dennis Green became known for was a strange rant that shaped the relationship he had with the public. As one columnist wrote after Green's death, ". . . that's a shame, as Green, who passed away at age sixty-seven in July, should be remembered for more than an unforgettable diatribe against his own team." (Gardner 2016)

Similarly, outstanding professional football coach Jim Mora is remembered less for his excellence and more for a twenty-two-word message he communicated to the public. Despite his record (Mora won even more games than Dennis Green but had a slightly lower win percentage), the coach is known for a reaction he had to a question at a postgame press conference. His team, the New Orleans Saints, had just lost ignominiously to the San Francisco 49ers in large part because the Saint offense had turned the ball over five times. After a long-winded and exasperated comment about how the defense was not at fault but rather the offense had played in a way that would preclude victory regardless of the level, Mora was asked about his team's chances of getting into the playoffs. His response was brief, "What's that? Ah — Playoffs? Don't talk about — playoffs? You kidding me? Playoffs? I just hope we can win a game! Another game".

Mora emphasized "playoffs" each time he said the word as if the prospect of making the playoffs was absurd. Each time he said "playoffs," he accompanied the utterance with a facial expression that suggested that it would be foolish to contemplate playoffs given his team's woeful performance. Despite the brevity of the message; Mora's 125 NFL career victories; the fact that twice the coach took over losing NFL teams and turned them into contenders; Mora's remarkable success in the USFL coaching for three seasons, each year taking his team to the championship game and winning two championships—despite his accomplishments, Mora is remembered for his "playoffs" twenty-two-word speech.

Jim Mora's long and illustrious career is often diminished by his "playoffs" speech.

There are other far more egregious examples. Lee Elia, a Chicago Cubs manager, went on a tirade after the Cubs lost a day game early one season. The fans had booed the team that day, and after the contest, Elia's remarks were remarkable. In a wild rant caught on a reporter's microphone, Elia excoriated the booing fans, using no fewer than forty expletives in the process. An expurgated excerpt from his remarks is below, and you can hear his rant at https://www.youtube.com/watch?v=uiVVbYK9HXw

"Blank those blankin' fans who come out here and say they're Cub fans that are supposed to be behind you rippin' every blankin' thing you do. I'll tell you one blankin' thing, I hope we get blankin' hotter than blank, just to stuff it up them three thousand blankin' people that show up every blankin' day, because if they're the real Chicago blankin' fans, they can kiss my blankin' blank right downtown and PRINT IT."

As is predictable, Elia's speech did not shape his relationship with fans positively. In August of that season, the manager was fired. The rant was in 1983. Decades later, Elia said that hardly a day would go by when he was not reminded of the tirade.

More recently, Cam Newton's comments at a press conference affected the relationship he has with the public. Newton, then the quarterback for the Carolina Panthers, was responding to questions at a press conference when reporter Jourdan Rodrigue asked what seemed like a conventional question, "I know you take a lot of pride in seeing your receivers play well. Devin Funchess has seemed to really embrace the physicality of his routes and getting those extra yards. Does that give you a little bit of enjoyment. . . "

During the question, Newton smiled when the reporter used the word "routes." When she finished the question, Newton commented, "It's funny to hear a female talk about routes."

Rodrigue was offended by the comment and afterward tweeted, "I don't think it is funny to be a female and talk about routes. I think it's my job." She subsequently issued a statement to the *Charlotte Observer*, "This afternoon I did my job as an NFL beat writer and asked Cam Newton a question about one of his receivers. I was dismayed by his response, which not only belittled me, but countless other women before me and beside me who work in similar jobs. I sought Mr. Newton out as he left the locker room a few minutes later. He did not apologize for his comments." Both the Association for Women in Sports Media and the Associated Press Sports Editors issued statements criticizing Newton and calling his comments "disrespectful" and "unacceptable."

Newton did eventually issue an apology. He said, "It was a lesson learned for me this whole week. My sarcasm trying to give someone kind of a compliment turned in ways I never would have even imagined." Nevertheless, the shape of Newton's relationship with the public was affected.

© Jeff Siner/TNS/Newscom

Cam Newton's response to a question changed the way he was viewed by the public.

There is an interesting sidebar to the incident. After the exchange between Newton and Rodrigue, a number of old tweets of Rodrigue's surfaced in which she seemed to be cavalier about racial prejudice. The reporter then turned to Twitter to apologize for these racist tweets. The apology may or may not have been transmitted effectively; that is, people may or may not have accepted it as a genuine statement of remorse. It is likely that there will be constitutive effects.

Not all mediated communications by athletes negatively shape their relationships. Olympic medalist Aly Raisman's public statements about sexual abuse have shaped her image positively as a champion for the rights of women. In an espnW feature, Raisman said, "I know that I'm one of the few that are being heard, so I just want to do right by people." Beyond the meaning of this specific message, Raisman is earning a reputation as a courageous athlete, and that will shape her persona positively. At the 2018 ESPY awards, Raisman and others who have spoken out about sexual abuse accepted the Arthur Ashe Courage Award and received a standing ovation from attendees.

Aly Raisman has become a spokesperson for the survivors of sexual abuse in the wake of the Larry Nassar case.

Using Social Media

Shortly after the Tampa Bay Buccaneers defeated the New England Patriots in October 2021, former Patriot player and current Buccaneer star Tom Brady used social media to express his appreciation for his former coach, owner, and fans. Reactions to his post were positive.

Brady's use of social media resulted in positive reactions, but it is not always the case that posts are well received. In late March 2009, the National Basketball Association fined Dallas Mavericks owner Mark Cuban $25,000 when Cuban criticized basketball officials on Twitter. At the time, Twitter may have been on the periphery of some radar screens, but not the National Basketball Association's. Quipped Cuban, you "can't say no one makes money from Twitter now. The NBA does."

When electronic typewriters replaced standard typewriters, there were administrative assistants who made the transition only very reluctantly. When word processing replaced the electronic typewriter, some people retired rather than learn how to use the new equipment. The advent of voice mail was greeted with disdain by technophobes, and it even took time for some workers to become comfortable with electronic mail. Teenagers now startle their grandparents with the speed at which they can "text" their friends. And teens serve as trainers for their elders as they explain the nuances and multiple applications of cell phones. The revolution in communication technology moves on and at such a rapid pace that whatever one can purchase now will be available in a more sophisticated version in months.

What has been collectively called social media has revolutionized communication in and beyond sports contexts. The title of Clay Shirky's book *Here Comes Everybody* is an accurate depiction of how social media has affected the communication landscape. We are no longer in a world where traditional gatekeepers determine what is disseminated to the public. We are in a world of what Jeff Howe has coined "crowdsourcing." All of us are involved with the dissemination of information and the concomitant construction of narratives about sport. And sport figures, as well as those who comment about sports, need to be cautious.

Social media has and will continue to evolve at a dizzying pace. However, the general concept behind social media will be the same. We are, or all of us can be, involved in the larger conversation as we have never been able to before. For public figures, including athletes, sports owners, sports journalists, coaches, and officials, the phenomenon of social media has brought both good and bad news. As Sheffer and Schultz write, ". . . social media use can create problems for athletes, many of whom are unaware of the repercussions of unfiltered communication." (Sheffer & Schultz, 2012, p. 212). Ann Pegoraro's article, "Look Who's Talking—Athletes on Twitter," makes the point more succinctly. "For every Twitter success, there are Twitter disasters" (Pegoraro, 2010, p. 501).

WHAT EXACTLY IS SOCIAL MEDIA?

Most people have a general idea of what social media is, but for many others, the meaning is nebulous. Also, there is the tendency to conceive of the various forms of social media as a monolithic entity. Add to this the fact that social media evolves rapidly, and there can be, and is understandable, confusion.

Social media is an umbrella phrase that describes a number of activities that integrate new technology with social interaction. Because of social media, all people have the capability of communicating to mass audiences. Social media allows individuals to "broadcast"—to the world if one so chooses—political perspectives, social activities, reviews of films and books, etc.

Social media has the effect of democratizing our society because more people now have a voice. Networks that previously could not as easily evolve form relatively effortlessly because of social media. You can be connected to high school alums who follow the fortunes of the swim team, like-minded Bronco fans, sports movie aficionados, and even people who wear sports-related attire.

Social media has created problems for athletes who have not considered the potential dangers.

Nearly all who read this, especially if you are a traditional eighteen- to twenty-three-year-old undergraduate, are aware of several categories of social media. Others with more laps around the track may not be as familiar with the various types. Social networking is enabled with applications like Facebook, MySpace, and Linked In. Blogs and podcasts facilitate ongoing conversations with parties who have common interests. The URL https://detailed.com/sports-blogs/ lists the top fifty sports blogs and regularly updates the list. No doubt, readers can argue that others deserve to be identified. Wikis and bulletin boards are repositories for information that people can share. Almost all readers of these pages will have used Wikipedia, an online encyclopedia that is different from its conventional predecessors because it is constantly updated, and individuals with information can add to the entries. Social media includes sites where you can share personal or organizational content, for example, Flickr for photographs and YouTube for video content.

A key feature of social media is interactivity. While the Tampa Bay Buccaneers are mounting a potentially game-altering drive, fans can opine about the wisdom of play selection and discuss reactions in real-time. A few decades ago, a fan upset at a referee's decision would have to wait until the game was over to squawk on talk radio or write a passionate letter to the editor. Social media allows for instant conversation.

Acknowledging that social media is a reality compels realists to understand it completely and measure its impact. Those who assess social media are concerned with "engagement," the number of unique likes, shares, or comments to a post; "traffic," the number of unique users who visit a website; "velocity," the relative change in daily attention to a site; "conversation ratio," how many comments are generated for each original posting and "participation ratio," percentage of account holders that actually participate with the social media as opposed to just read and "lurk" (Sinickas, 2004, pp. 76–87). Because many use search engines to research companies, organizations are concerned with SEO, an initialism for Search Engine Optimization. A team or league would like to create a site that will attract cyber explorers. Therefore a company will study the algorithms particular search engines employ. This way, a site can be created to optimize traffic, and users will be steered toward your site when exploring.

SOCIAL MEDIA COACHING

Because of the potential hazards associated with social media, communication specialists coach athletes about the proper use of social media. It's not uncommon for a first-week orientation session to include a lecture from an expert. A review of recommendations from these experts reveals a number of recurring points.

- Recognize the enduring nature of messages sent on social media. Unlike a spoken conversation, phone call, conventional letter, or even e-mail, messages posted on social media are "out there" and can be retrieved. "Screenshots of seemingly ephemeral posts or a simple copy-and-paste of a 'locked' tweet makes any message a potential time bomb" (J. Eisenberg, 2014, p. 8). Milwaukee Brewers pitcher and National League All-Star Josh Hader realized this during the 2018 All-Star game. When he was in high school, seven years prior, he had posted remarks that were homophobic and racist. These surfaced and created remarkable turbulence in his life. His claim was, "I was in high school. We're still learning who we are. I was in high school. You live and you learn. This mistake won't happen again." It may or may not happen again, but Hader is likely, regardless, to be remembered for his high school posts.

- Acknowledge the speed. Mark Twain is credited with saying, "A lie can be halfway around the world while the truth is putting on its shoes." Twain died in 1910. He had no idea how quickly messages, lies, or otherwise, can be halfway around the world in an era of social media.

- Remember that your messages are not just about you but your team, family, and league. When an incriminating post from Sonny Gray, a pitcher for the Yankees, surfaced after a particularly weak performance against the last-place Orioles, the damage transcended Gray himself and tainted the New York Yankees.

- Consider a post to be part of your brand, a representation of who you are. And therefore, post how you see yourself and want to be remembered.

- Avoid impulsive posting. Some recommend "a ten-minute rule." Waiting ten minutes when considering posting might allow one to consider the potential ramifications of the post. Sproull and Kiesler presciently—long before the rapid evolution of social media—wrote about "flaming" as a predictable second-level effect of new and emerging technology. Reputation consultant Michael Fertik has opined, "There is something in the Internet's secret sauce that brings out the snark in many of us" (Fertik, 2014). A recurring recommendation is to be vigilant about suppressing the snark when using social media.

- Be aware that several types of posts have created problems for individuals, teams, leagues, and various sports figures.
    - Complaints, e.g., "I am not getting enough playing time."
    - Disparaging teammates, opponents, the league.
    - Use of profanity.
    - Postings of improper photos that could be embarrassing to the persons in the image or those who've posted the pictures.
    - Revealing confidential information.
    - "Joking" when the punch line could offend individuals or groups.
    - Posting homophobic, sexist, racist comments regardless of whether the person to whom you are directing the comments is a "friend" or member of the offended group.

Despite this recurring counsel, a study by Sanderson, Browning, and Schmittel questioned whether student-athletes were receiving or absorbing this advice. In their study, while most student-athletes considered training on social media to be important, their perception of the messages they received was that they were either vague, admonishing, or related primarily to compliance (Sanderson, 2015, pp. 113–114). In other words, the subjects contended that recommendations were ambiguous, for example, "don't do anything foolish" or critical, "you really did something foolish," or concerned parochially with compliance issues, "If you do something foolish you could lose your eligibility."

Dallas Cowboy Jason Witten spent one year in the ESPN booth before coming out of retirement to rejoin the Cowboys in 2019 (retiring again in early 2021). In his year out of football, he wrote an essay for ESPN about social media. One comment therein was direct and to the point, "Negative social media can ruin a player." One has to be careful. Enduring damage to one's reputation can be self-inflicted.

Test Yourself: Apply the Principles

- We have discussed transmission and constitutive effects of communication throughout the text. Analyze the following from both a transmission and a constitutive perspective.
    - Cam Newton's comment about a female journalist being knowledgeable about pass routes.
    - Aly Raisman's interviews about sexual harassment.
    - Dennis Green's comments, "They are who we thought they were."
- Chapter 4 is about crisis communication. In what ways does social media create crises? In what ways can social media help crisis communicators?
- In Chapter 6, we talked about the social responsibility of sports figures. How can someone exercise their social responsibility using social media? Films and documentaries? Books?

Sports Information Directors

The College Sports Information Directors of America (CoSIDA) is an association of professionals who communicate to the public on behalf of their athletic departments. Generally, an SID's job is to "promote a university's sports teams to the media and community" (Whiteside, 2012, p. 143). Pedersen enumerates the traditional responsibilities to include

- Drafting media releases
- Coordinating media conferences
- Scheduling interviews with student-athletes, coaches, and athletic directors
- Developing and producing game notes and media guides
- Working with other institutions to share information when their teams compete
- Promote their teams through social media
- Provide social media training for coaches and athletes
- Monitor coaches' and athletes' use of social media. (Pedersen, 2017, p. 35)

It is a hectic job. On a single day, a SID could be doing several of the above activities for a number of different teams.

We discussed in Chapter 3 the importance of a systems theory approach to studying sports communication. This is an essential mindset for sports information directors. Much of their communications are directed externally, but effective internal communication is necessary for the externally sent messages to be accurate and timely.

In a comprehensive article about the evolution and state of college information directors, Stoldt writes that "organizations must both listen as well as be heard in order to ensure communication effectiveness" (Stoldt, 2012, p. 487). This point is made in the context of communicating with external publics. However, Stoldt continues to report that a challenge for sports information directors is a lack of respect from senior management, which may preclude access to necessary information or a seat at the table when decisions are made. The extent to which SIDs have access or are participants in decision-making will vary from institution to institution, but it is important for sports organizations to acknowledge that those who communicate with the public must be connected internally for the communication to be effective.

Practitioner Perspective

Matthew Houde

Sports Information Director

Courtesy of Matthew Houde

AZ. You work in sports information. What, generally speaking, do you do?

MH. We are responsible for managing the athletic communications operation, which disseminates information for all varsity sports to appropriate organizations, manage the department website and act as a liaison between the media and the university coaching staffs and student-athletes, in addition to participating in department initiatives and administrative responsibilities. We also serve as the department historians.

We wear a lot of hats in athletic communications. A lot of times, when a question pops up, the natural instinct of people is to ask the communications team and, more often than not, we have the answer.

AZ. Who are your most important external audiences? That is who, outside of the athletic department, do you need to interact with on a regular basis? Counterparts at other universities? Alums? Professional Teams? Local media? National media? Any other key external audiences?

MH. All of the above. As time has gone on, the field has shifted quite a bit. In the past, our focus was mainly on the media, but with social media taking over the way people consume content, our focus is now mainly on fans and recruits. We know that seventeen- to eighteen-year-olds are looking at the content teams produce on their social channels, so in a sense, we're now part of the recruiting process more than we ever were before.

We certainly interact with all of the constituents that you mentioned above to an extent, but the main focus is now on fans and recruits.

AZ. What is a typical workday like for you? Is there such a thing as a typical workday? Take me through a day in the middle of, for example, basketball and hockey season.

MH. The beauty of our job is that there is no typical workday. You can go into the office expecting one or two things, and then something can happen that completely turns your day on its head.

In the middle of basketball and hockey season, it's a grind. Both sports start in the fall, go through the winter and wrap up in the spring, so there isn't a lot of downtime.

On a game day, for example, we'll get to the arena around 9 a.m. and not leave until around midnight. During that time, we're prepping our game notes and game programs, setting up the press box for the night, setting up the scoring system to ensure that the official scoring and live stats are functioning, setting up the press conference for postgame.

During the game, we're in the press box cutting highlights, live-tweeting, creating graphics for social media, writing our game story, and tending to the needs of any media members in attendance. After the game, we coordinate the postgame press conference with the head coach and select student-athletes (a press conference after a win is a lot more enjoyable than the alternative!).

We also post our game recap on our website and distribute it to the media, post the box score to our website and send it to the conference office and the NCAA, post the end of game graphic on social media and answer any questions the media may have. We're always the first to arrive and the last to leave the press box on game day.

Then, if the game is on a Friday, we're back in the office once all of that is done, getting ready for the game the next night. Rinse and repeat.

AZ. How important is it for you to be in touch with internal audiences in order to do your job? Do you work with coaches on teams? Game day statisticians? Players themselves? Any other internal audiences?

MH. It's crucial. It isn't a stretch to say that we spend more time with our teams during the season than we do with our families. I speak with my coach and players every day at the arena, even if we don't have anything work related to talk about—having a strong culture throughout the team; from players to coaches to the support staff, is critical to team success, and we've been fortunate over the last several seasons to have that.

On a game day, everyone on the support staff needs to be in sync. We interact with the operations and facilities team constantly, and game day statisticians are also vital to the game day operation.

AZ. Can you provide some examples of successful communication that have come as a result of meaningful access to important sources?

MH. My daily interactions with our men's hockey team are a perfect example. We're fortunate to have all of our offices in the same building, which allows us to communicate face-to-face daily.

With our team, there aren't any surprises, and I'm in constant communication with our head coach on the daily comings and goings of the team. As I mentioned above, a culture has been created within that team where we truly are a family. There's an incredibly high level of trust across the board and an understanding that everything we do is for the benefit of the team and our student-athletes. That attitude from everyone involved with the program has led to a sustained level of success over the last five seasons or so.

AZ. How has social media affected your job?

MH. Social media has completely changed the job. When you think of a "sports information director," you may think of the old press release that gets sent out and then shows up in the newspaper the next day.

Today, the press release is dying, if not already dead. The way that people consume content has totally changed. Instead of picking up a newspaper to find out about what happened in the game last night, you log on to Twitter or Instagram and check the score.

People's attention spans are also so narrow now that you only have seconds to make an impression on somebody, which is why you see more graphic design and video elements implemented into what we do.

We're also aware of who we're catering our content toward now. millennials. They'd much rather look at a photo or a video than read a long press release, so we've changed our approach in an effort to make a positive impression of the most people in the shortest time frame possible.

AZ. Does CoSIDA help?

MH. Certainly. It's a great asset for any sports information director, and we've been able to send a member of the staff to their annual convention to network and interact with other communications professionals to bounce ideas off one another to positively impact our organization.

AZ. What would you recommend for students who are interested in pursuing a career in sports information?

MH. Get involved early. Every school with varsity athletics has an athletic communications office. Some are obviously smaller than others, but we all need additional hands. You may not be paid at first, but if you're truly interested in the field, it's a great way to network and build a skill set that can lead to jobs down the road.

Movies, Documentaries, Books, and Sites

Are you knowledgeable about sports?

What do you know about Michael Jordan's Chicago Bulls, Texas high school football? The life of minor league baseball players? The All-American Girls Professional Baseball League? What is your understanding of basketball fandom in small-town Indiana?

Who was Jake LaMotta?

What do you know about the world of sports agents?

What do you know about minor league hockey?

Why was the miracle in *Miracle* a miracle?

Who are the Ninety-Niners?

What do you know about Brian Piccolo?

Who is the Italian Stallion?

What was Peyton Manning's childhood like?

What do you know about the Celtics-Lakers rivalries of the 80s?

How did Nelson Mandela affect the success of the Springboks?

A good deal of what we know about sports is a function of the movies and documentaries we've seen, books and periodicals we've read, dedicated sports television programs we've watched, and sports-related websites we visit. Most undergraduates taking this course were not born until the early twenty-first century. Nevertheless, if you are interested in sports and a consumer of sports films or a reader of sports books, you may be able to answer at least half of the questions above.

You probably know what you know about Texas high school football because you read the book *Friday Night Lights* or saw the film of the same name, or watched the television series also called *Friday Night Lights*. You know about the U.S. 1980 Olympic hockey victory over the Soviet Union, not because you were alive then, but because of the film *Miracle*. What you know about The All-American Girls Professional Baseball League is likely derived from the Penny Marshall film *A League of Their Own*. You may know about avid Hoosier fans because of the oft-replayed film *Hoosiers*.

Your perceptions of minor league ice hockey may have been affected by watching the Paul Newman film *Slap Shot*. What you know about the great women's soccer team that won the World Cup in 1999, you may have learned from seeing the ESPN *Nine For IX* documentary, the *99ers,* or reading the book, *The Girls of Summer*. You never saw Jake LaMotta fight, but you may know about him because of the Oscar-nominated movie *Raging Bull*.

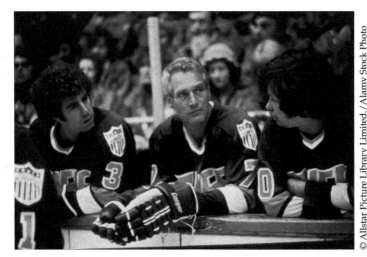

Slap Shot, 1977

Brian's Song was a made for TV film that was first broadcast in 1971. It was based on Gayle Sayers's autobiography *I Am Third*. Piccolo, a running back for the Chicago Bears, was, apparently, a fine person. However, his football credentials were not sufficiently outstanding to make him anything other than a trivia question had it not been for the film and the book.

We know about the tribulations of Rocky Balboa's life as if he were an actual person. What we know about the challenges of being a boxing contender comes from movies like *Million Dollar Baby* and the multiple *Rocky* iterations.

Peyton Manning's childhood, the Lakers and Celtics rivalry, and the political turbulence surrounding the 1995 Rugby World Cup are all likely familiar to sports fans to whatever extent they are because of documentaries in the ESPN *30 for 30* series.

AGENDA SETTING AND FRAMING

Billings et al. write that the media is an entity that "constructs, delivers, and digests sporting events" (Billings, 2018, p. 11). One might debate whether the media actually constructs sporting events, though a strong argument can be made that leagues like the NFL, for example, would never have flourished as they have without media coverage, specifically television. The 1958 NFL championship game between the New York Giants and Baltimore Colts has been called the greatest game ever played. This claim, of course, could be contested. But what cannot be contested is that because the game was televised, and because it was exciting, and because it became obvious that football could be captured by television, the 1958 media event catapulted football to the front line of fan and network executive consciousness.

Networks will also dictate some requirements for sports broadcasts that can affect, in the eyes of purists at least, the fabric of the game—in effect, becoming a player in the construction of the event. Extensive halftime shows, for example, in the Super Bowl, alter the normal protocol for a game. The need to sell advertising for hockey broadcasts has affected the flow of play in a period. There may be other good reasons, but the initiation of the tiebreaker in tennis allowed networks to cover an event with some sense of when it would end. There are still time variations between a three-set and a five-set match, but without tie breakers, any one set could last hours.

Whether one agrees or disagrees that the media actually constructs sporting events, one cannot dispute that the media, wittingly or otherwise, sets our agenda and frames what we know about sports.

In the last chapter, we discussed the Hypodermic Needle Theory. Two related theories are Agenda Setting and Framing. These two may seem similar to the Hypodermic Needle Theory and even similar to each other, but there are meaningful if subtle distinctions.

The Hypodermic Needle Theory suggests that viewers or readers of media simply consume what is communicated to them. Much like a patient is affected by an injection, consumers of sports films, books, and periodicals read a story about, for example, soccer star Alex Morgan, and consume what is written in the article about her. Agenda Setting theorists do not necessarily agree that audiences simply consume what they read or see. However, the theory suggests that what audiences read or see depends on what they have the opportunity to read or see. Essentially the theory argues that the media sets the table for the consumer. Zeng et al. write that "Media agenda-setting refers to the deliberate coverage of topics or events with the goal of influencing public opinion" (Zeng et al., 2011, p. 40).

We know about Alex Morgan because there has been an article, documentary, or sports program segment about her. If there were no stories about athletes like Alex Morgan or women's soccer, there would be relatively limited concomitant discourse about women's soccer.

Gatekeeping is a term that refers to how media representatives select what does and what does not get through the metaphoric gate and through to media audiences. Consequently, gatekeepers serve as a filter. This makes sense. All sports news, for example, cannot be on tonight's *SportsCenter* program. Someone has to determine what is presented. All sports stories will not be made into documentaries. The *Athletes in Limbo* faculty basketball team I played on never had a film, book, or documentary produced about it. Nobody on our team pursued such an opportunity but had we done so, some gatekeeper would have determined that this probably was not the best subject for a film. If gatekeepers do their job dispassionately, then they will select the most important sports stories to be on *SportsCenter*, most relevant subjects to examine in a documentary, the most significant sports figures to write books about. And then our agenda will be set. We may learn about and subsequently discuss Texas high school culture and football, Nelson Mandela and the Springboks, and the Ninety-Niners.

It should be obvious, however, that it is possible, if not likely, that the agenda can be set because of a person or group's hidden agenda. A radio sports talk station that broadcasts all Chicago White Sox games may not entertain callers who want to praise the Chicago Cubs. There have been a number of studies, for example, that examine whether women's sports are less popular than men's in part because consumers are exposed to men's events more than women's. Scheadler and Wagstaff write, ". . . female athletes still experience significantly less and different media coverage than their male counterparts" (Scheadler & Wagstaff, 2018, p. 1). Eagleman's study of newspaper portrayals of gymnasts in the 2012 Olympics illustrated the media's "power to impact society's views on gender and reinforce long-held stereotypes about gender" (Eagleman, 2015, p. 245). Interested readers can look at the work of Scheadler, Cranmer, and Eagleman to examine their studies in this area that analyze whether viewers' agendas and frames are set to privilege male sports. The short answer is that they seem to be. Consequently, what we speak about, develop an interest in, and spend resources to follow, may be affected. As Olympian Kendall Coyne commented in her Practitioner Perspective interview found in Chapter 1, "If our games received more exposure, there would be greater interest in our sport."

In short, as opposed to Hypodermic Needle Theory, Agenda Setting Theory does not contend that media audiences are force-fed and simply consume what is offered. Agenda Setting Theory does suggest that we are provided limited menu items, sometimes deliberately.

Framing Theory is very closely related to Agenda Setting. When media frame, they select "some aspects of a perceived reality [that] make them more salient in a communicating text, in such a way as to promote a particular problem definition, causal interpretation, moral evaluation, and/or treatment recommendation" (Entman, 1993, p. 52).

In other words, how we perceive what we are exposed to depends on how the exposed content is presented. Cranmer et al. explored *ESPN the Body Issue* in terms of how women, as opposed to men, were being portrayed. The authors write that traditionally images of female athletes de-emphasized their athleticism and emphasized their sexual allure. While there had been some suggestion that this tendency was declining, the research suggests that there is still evidence that the framing of female athletes is different from the framing of male athletes (Cranmer et al., 2014, p. 146).

In essence, Framing Theory contends that even when items are placed on the agenda, how that content is framed for the consumer affects the conclusions that can be drawn and subsequent discourse. H.G. "Buzz" Bissinger's decision to write a book about Texas high school football (and Addison-Wesley's decision to publish it) put Texas high school football on the agenda. But the orientation Bissinger takes on the subject is what frames the event for the reader. What he chose to place within the frame was not a story about Xs and Os but a story reflecting the interdependent relationship between culture, community, and sports.

Think of a camera metaphor. If you were at a stadium and were taking a picture to show a friend about your experience at the game, what would be within the frame of the picture? Would you do a close-up of the goalie? Would you try to capture how well the pitch was manicured? Would you capture the thousands of cheering fans? How you framed the picture would affect the viewers' takeaways. Similarly, in the media coverage of sports, how a producer or author frames an event will affect what the receiver could potentially perceive and retain.

While they often have been depicted negatively, agenda-setting and framing need not, consciously at least, be such. Consider the early research conducted in sports communication. One could contend, accurately, that most of the research done in the first years focused on sports communication and media.

Consequently, this set the agenda for students and researchers. There was, however, nothing nefarious about this, and the field is now morphing, as is evident in this text to include the multifaceted way sport and communication are linked. Researchers may have framed their analysis of, for example, dedicated sports networks so that readers would learn about numbers of viewers and revenue generated—or—researchers could have framed such analysis in terms of how dedicated sports networks have affected culture and leisure time. Neither approach to the framing choices would necessarily have been designed to promote a hidden agenda. There can be "bias in the booth," as is the title of Dylan Gwinn's recent book, but there isn't always.

In general, one has to be careful when discussing what we know about sports or any other subject not to blame the media for distorting reality. The media is not some lurking nemesis plotting to affect our consciousness and souls. Certainly, there are people whose motives when communicating about phenomena are based on self-interest or political agendas. Yet that is not always the case. As discussed in earlier chapters—and as specifically referenced in Uses and Gratification Theory—what is presented to us by the media is in part a reflection of consumer interest. The media is not the enemy. To some extent, the media is us.

Academic Research

Students in this class who enrolled, at least in part, because of interest in sport are probably aware of bleacherreport.com, or espn.com and mainstream publications like *Sports Illustrated* or *ESPN The Magazine*. As discussed in the last section, many of you became knowledgeable about some issues because of books you've read or films you've seen. If you read *The Boys in the Boat,* you are far more familiar with the world of crew than you'd been previously. If you viewed the documentary *Let Them Wear Towels,* you've become knowledgeable about the tribulations women journalists have faced when attempting to do their jobs. Regardless of how many sports books, films, documentaries, blogs, or sites you've read, watched, or regularly visit, it is likely that you are not as acquainted with another way information about sports communication is available to the public.

Scholarly journals are typically not taken to the beach, yet for those with an interest in a particular field, they can be an extraordinarily valuable source of information. A *Sports Illustrated* article may discuss issues of race and sport, but a study in an academic publication will provide far more depth and can be, for those excited about sports communication, a springboard for future exploration.

There are many scholarly journals that publish articles about sports communication. As you have read through the text, you've seen references to a number of these and may have reviewed the bibliography at the conclusion of the text. As sports communication continues to grow, research in the field will keep pace, and what is available to the public about the linkage between communication studies and sports will mushroom.

Below is a list of some of the dozens of journals that publish in the area. For each, you will find a sample article, an edited abstract, and the article citation for those who would like to read the piece in its entirety. As you will see, the research reflects a noteworthy breadth. In this sample alone, there are articles about media framing; women's televised sports; athletes speaking out in protest; rowdy fan communication; nonverbal messages of athletes' tattoos; player perceptions of coaches' communication competencies; effects of team social responsibility on the communication grapevine; effects of "cancer" teammates on team cohesion; crisis communication approaches; sports team websites, and other—to an enthusiast's eye—engaging topics.

INTERNATIONAL JOURNAL OF SPORT COMMUNICATION

Sample: SportsCenter: A Case Study of Media Framing U.S. Sport as the COVID-19 Epicenter

Summary: This case study examined how the cancellation or postponement of sports as a result of COVID-19 was framed across twenty-two episodes of SportsCenter in the early weeks of the pandemic.

Citation Bell, Travis R. 2021. "SportsCenter: A Case Study of Media Framing U.S. Sport as the COVID-19 Epicenter." *International Journal of Sport Communication* 14 (2): 298–317.

COMMUNICATION AND SPORT

Sample Article: One and Done: The Long Eclipse of Women's Televised Sports, 1989–2019.

Summary: This study compares men's vs. women's televised sports over a thirty-year period. The results suggest that there has been little change in the disproportionate coverage of women's and men's sports.

Citation: Cooky, Cheryl, LaToya D. Council, Maria A. Mears, and Michael A. Messner. "One and Done: The Long Eclipse of Women's Televised Sports, 1989–2019." *Communication & Sport* 9, no. 3 (June 2021): 347–71.

CRITICAL STUDIES IN MEDIA COMMUNICATION

Sample Article: Rewriting activism: the NFL Takes a Knee

Summary: This article examines the broadcasts of NFL games after September 22, 2017. On that date, President Trump spoke disparagingly of players who protested during the national anthem. Athletes subsequently continued to demonstrate. The article discusses the methods used by the NFL to describe and, according to the author, obscure the intentions of the protestors to protect the NFL brand.

Citation: Lopez, J. K. (2021). Rewriting activism: the NFL takes a knee. *Critical Studies in Media Communication, 38*(2), 183–196.

INTERNATIONAL JOURNAL OF SPORTS MARKETING AND SPONSORSHIP

Sample Article: Sport League Website: An Effective Marketing Communication Tool for Corporate Sponsors.

Summary: The authors examine the effects of website interactivity, website fit, and website credibility on viewers' attitude toward corporate sponsor advertisements and willingness to click on a banner advertisement to search for more information.

Citation: Kim D, Walker M, Heo J, and Koo G.-Y. Sport League Website: An Effective Marketing Communication Tool for Corporate Sponsors. *International Journal of Sports Marketing and Sponsorship 18, no.* 3 (2017): 314–27.

JOURNAL OF SPORTS MEDIA

Sample Article: "'I Got Beat, and He Deserves to Win': Image Repair Strategies Used by Athletes Who Lost Big Games"

Summary: This study examines image repair strategies used by athletes who have been defeated in key contests. The findings suggest that bolstering, defeasibility, and corrective action are used extensively. Athletes often praise their opponents and indicate what they have learned from their defeats.

Citation: Ostrowsky, Michael, and Kevin Stein. ""I Got Beat, and He Deserves to Win": Image Repair Strategies used by Athletes Who Lost Big Games." *Journal of Sports Media* 15.1 (2020): 75–97.

JOURNAL FOR THE STUDY OF SPORTS AND ATHLETES IN EDUCATION

Sample Article: Media Perceptions And Constructions Of Race And Sports: Reflections On The Duke Lacrosse Scandal.

Summary: The authors argue that media coverage of the alleged Duke rape incident followed racial narratives that shaped public perceptions. In addition, the authors contend that the media coverage reflects how sports in the United States can galvanize public attention.

Citation: Hughes, R., Giles, M., Haywood, J., & Snipes, J.. Media perceptions and constructions of race and sports: Reflections on the Duke lacrosse scandal. *Journal for the Study of Sports and Athletes in Education, 11*(3), (2017)161–174.

JOURNAL OF APPLIED SPORT PSYCHOLOGY

Sample Article: Coaches' Perspectives of a Negative Informal Role: The 'Cancer' within Sport Teams.

Summary: The authors examine the negative, informal role of a team "cancer"—defined as an athlete who expresses negative emotions that spread destructively throughout a team. The research explores the influence of the "cancer" as that influence relates to group functioning.

Citation: Cope, C., Eys, M., Schinke, R., & Bosselut, G. Coaches' Perspectives of a Negative Informal Role: The 'Cancer' within Sport Teams. *Journal of Applied Sport Psychology, 22*(4), (2010). 420–436.

JOURNAL OF SPORT AND SOCIAL ISSUES

Sample Article: "Real Men Stand for Our Nation": Constructions of an American Nation and Anti-Kaepernick Memes

Summary: The authors describe the context of Colin Kaepernick's protests and the 2020 United States presidential election. The article analyzes internet memes related to Kaepernick and what they reveal in terms of race, gender, and politics.

Citation: Dickerson, N., & Hodler, M. (2021). "Real Men Stand for Our Nation": Constructions of an American Nation and Anti-Kaepernick Memes. *Journal of Sport and Social Issues*, 45(4), 329–357.

JOURNAL OF SPORT BEHAVIOR

Sample Article: Female Athletes' Perceptions Of Head Coaches' Communication Competence.

Summary: As the title suggests, the article explores the relationship between female athletes and their perceptions of head coaches' communication skills. Results indicated that coaches perceived themselves as communicatively competent, while athletes' perceptions were positive but not as strong.

Citation: Haselwood Denise M., Joyner, A. Barry, Burke, Kevin L., Geyerman, Chris B., Czech, Daniel R., Munkasy Barry A., & Zwald, A. Drew. Female athletes' perceptions of head coaches' communication competence. *Journal of Sport Behavior, 28*(3) (2005).

COMMUNICATION QUARTERLY

Sample Article: Memorable Messages From Fathers to Children Through Sports: Perspectives From Sons and Daughters

Summary: Memorable messages are those that people (a) retain for a long time and (b) consider to be a major influence during their lifetime. The author examines memorable messages that children report receiving from their fathers while actively or passively participating in sports.

Citation: Starcher, Shawn C. Memorable Messages From Fathers to Children Through Sports: Perspectives From Sons and Daughters. *Communication Quarterly* 63, no. 2 (2015): 204–20.

SOCIOLOGY OF SPORT JOURNAL

Sample Article: Off-Colour Landscape: Framing Race Equality in Sport Coaching

Summary: The authors examine whether coaching sustains institutional racial processes that normalize and privilege whiteness.

Citation: Rankin-Wright, A., Hylton, K., & Norman, L.. Off-Colour Landscape: Framing Race Equality in Sport Coaching. *Sociology of Sport Journal, 33*(4), (2016)1–30.

SPORTS MARKETING QUARTERLY

Sample Article: The Effects Of Perceived Team Performance And Social Responsibility On Pride And Word-Of-Mouth Recommendation.

Summary: As the title suggests, the researchers investigated the relationships among pride, team performance/corporate social responsibility, and word of mouth recommendations. The results suggest that both fans' perception of team performance and social responsibility significantly influence pride and word-of-mouth recommendations.

Citation: Chang, M., Kang, J., Ko, Y., & Connaughton, D. The effects of perceived team performance and social responsibility on pride and word-of-mouth recommendation. *Sport Marketing Quarterly, 26*(1), (2017). 31.

SPORT IN HISTORY

Sample Article: The 'Reel' Jesse Owens: Visual Rhetoric And The Berlin Olympics

Summary: This article considers how the Owens' footage from the 1936 Olympics was used to support American exceptionality and mitigate the stigma of Nazi ideology.

Citation: Milford, M. The 'reel' Jesse Owens: Visual rhetoric and the Berlin Olympics. *Sport in History, 38*(1), (2018). 96–117.

SPORT JOURNAL

Sample Article: "Talking Bodies: Athletes & Tattoos as Nonverbal Communication."

Summary: The authors discuss how professional and collegiate basketball players perceive tattoos and how tattoos act as a channel for nonverbal communication in this population.

Citation: Belkin, Sam, and R. Dale Sheptak Jr.. "Talking Bodies: Athletes & Tattoos as Nonverbal Communication." *Sport Journal* 1. 2018.

THE SPORTS LAWYERS JOURNALS

Sample Article: "A Rope, A Tree, Hang the Referee": Exploring the First Amendment Boundaries of Offensive Fan Speech Regulation in College Sports

Summary: The author contends that public universities and colleges in the United States have a limited ability to regulate offensive fan speech. However, the author suggests that there are permissible speech restrictions and strategies that public institutions can implement to attempt to reduce the impact of offensive fan speech.

Citation: David M. Ullian. "A Rope, a Tree, Hang the Referee!": Exploring the First Amendment Boundaries of Offensive Fan Speech Regulation in College Sports. *Sports Lawyers Journal* 23 (2016).

Fair or Foul — Questions of Ethics

- When Joe Theisman played for Notre Dame, the sports information director suggested that they change the pronunciation of his name from THEESMAN to THIGHSMAN so that he would have a better chance of winning the Heisman trophy. Was this fair or foul?
- Some social media sites use foul language. This can be alluring to some visitors. Is it fair or foul to use foul language on a sports social media site?
- Some films about real-life sporting events do not accurately depict what took place. For example, in the movie *The Express*, about the life of college football great Ernie Davis, the film changes the score of one game and the sequence of scores in another to create more drama than was actually the case. Is this fair or foul?
- When excerpting a press conference response from a player or coach, a broadcaster or web writer may exclude the context of an incident and highlight the incendiary portions of a response to make it seem like more of a rant. Is this Fair or Foul?

Chapter Conclusion—Take-Aways

- The persona of sports figures is a function of how they communicate with the public. Sometimes a few ill-advised words can change the discourse about teams, players, and sports organizations.
- More often than not, communication with the public is mediated. New interactive media has had a powerful effect on the image of athletes and teams.
- Sports information directors for teams have diverse and challenging responsibilities.
- Films, books, and movies have affected the narrative of sports.
- Several academic publications explore sports communication issues from a scholarly perspective.

QUESTIONS

- Which sports movies, television programs, or books have had the greatest influence on you?
- In what ways are documentaries like *30 for 30* or *Nine for IX* valuable for sports fans in ways that books and magazines are not?
- In your opinion, what are the greatest challenges for sports information directors?
- In what ways has social media helped athletes give back to the community?
- Which of the articles identified in the section on scholarly journals seems as if it would be most valuable to you in your career or graduate studies? Explain.

Top 10 Sports Movies
According to the American Film Institute identified in Screenrant August 19, 2021

1. *Rocky*	7. *Slap Shot*
2. *Raging Bull*	8. *The Hustler*
3. *Rocky*	9. *Caddyshack*
4. *Pride of the Yankees*	10. *Breaking Away*
5. *Hoosiers*	11. *National Velvet*
6. *Bull Durham*	12. *Jerry Maguire*

Top 10 Sports Books
As identified by MansionBet blog January 2021

1. **The Sweet Science—A.J. Liebling**	6. **Paper Lion—George Plimpton A Season on the Brink—John Feinstein**
2. **Fever Pitch—Nick Hornby**	7. **A Rough Ride—Paul Kimmage**
3. **Friday Night Lights. H.G. Bissinger**	8. **Only a Game-Eamon Dunphy**
4. **Scabiscuit-Laura Hillenbrand**	9. **Ball Four—Jim Bouton**
5. **Open-Andre Agassi**	10. **Moneyball-Michael Lewis**

Top 10 Sports Documentaries
According to Stacker.com February 2021

1. *Hoop Dreams*	6. *The King of Kong*
2. *Man on Wire*	7. *Senna*
3. *Over the Limit*	8. *When We Were Kings*
4. *Free Solo*	9. *Athlete*
5. *Murderball*	10. *Touching the Void*

Top 10 Most Popular Sports Websites
(According to Detailed.com December 13, 2021

1. **Yahoo sports**	6. **Sky Sports**
2. **Bleacher Report**	7. **FanSided**
3. **The Athletic**	8. **TSN**
4. **Essentially Sports**	9. **Clutchpoints**
5. **theScore.com**	10. **Sportsnet.ca**

First Person   Swimsuit Edition

Not much in the way of articles in the swimsuit edition of Sports *Illustrated*. Not much in the way of sports either. And not much in the way of swimsuits.

What you have in the "swimsuit" issue is skin. Nobody is playing tennis or volleyball or basketball. Models decked out in next to nothing adorn the pages. And you don't need to be a sleuth to discern that many of the women are exposed in a way that could get them arrested in a public place.

One year the women were photographed in their "swimwear" on each of the continents. For example, the magazine's cover featured a woman in Antarctica. She was wearing a bathing suit bottom and a parka over her naked top. She hadn't zipped up the parka. She's working on getting her hood on and, in so doing, has her elbows pushing in on her chest. You couldn't mistake her for a Hank or Charlie.

As I flipped through the magazine, I saw that some of the models weren't wearing bathing suits at all, just threads over portions of their bottom and something sort of covering on the top. One model had nothing covering her top and, judging by her pose and facial expression, was not contemplating NFL rule changes.

The ads are also revealing. Taylor Made Golf Clubs peddled a driver with two photos taken from reverse angles. The text, "Nice top. Even Nicer Bottom." The ad is adjacent to the photo of a model who has pulled a transparent tube around her naked top.

The photos in and of themselves do not bother me. The intimations of intimacy do not bother me either. What bothers me is that photographs like these, in a publication ostensibly about sports, do nothing to alleviate the problem of women in sports being assessed on the basis of criteria other than their athleticism. What bothers me is the hypocrisy.

During the broadcast of a championship football game, Brent Musburger, the announcer, commented on the pulchritude of the girlfriend of the Alabama quarterback. The woman was in the stands, and a cameraperson got her in the lens. Musburger remarked that she was a looker.

He was excoriated in the next day's media.

Musburger's comments were sophomoric for sure. However, how can agents of the press cite his comments as an abomination when *Sports Illustrated* is publishing the swimsuit issue and getting a pass?

Last Sunday night, I turned on the set at eight, ready to watch the NBA All-Star game. When I did this, I did not see the athletes. I saw instead the pre-game show. A singer was doing something akin to singing while a group of women dressed provocatively was dancing provocatively.

This bothers me not because I am a prude or concerned with the innocents who were watching. I'd much prefer that kids watch gyrations than movies where people get shot or blown up. What bothers me is that the same people who screamed foul when there was a "wardrobe malfunction" in the Super Bowl, who yelp for abstinence, who squawk when a school district wants to have a substantive sex education curriculum, and who want to ban novels from school curricula because there are references to intimacy in them, a percentage of these same people must be watching the NBA dancers and buying the swimsuit issue of *Sports Illustrated*. This has to be the case, or else the *S.I.* issue wouldn't be so filled with ads, and the NBA would not have a pre-game show that appeals to prurient interests.

So, it is fine if you want to criticize an announcer for making a frat boy comment. However, make sure you are similarly critical when other mediated communications reflect insensitivity to women in more insidious ways.

References Zaremba

Abeza, G., O'Reilly, N., & Nadeau, J. (2014). Sport communication: A multidimensional assessment of the field's development. *International Journal of Sport Communication*, 7(3), 289–316.

Alder, J. (nd). *Culture and Coaching: The shadow of team values.* https://playerdevelopmentproject.com/the-shadow-of-team-values/

Alford, S., & Garrity, J. (1990). *Playing for Knight: My six seasons with Coach Knight.* New York: Simon and Schuster.

Allen, M., & Caillouet, R. (1994). Legitimation endeavors: Impression management strategies used by an organization in crisis. *Communication Monographs*, 61(1), 44–62.

Anderson, R. J. (2014). *Tarnished Heels: How unethical actions and deliberate deceit at the University of North Carolina ended "the Carolina Way".* Rock Hill, S.C.: Strategic Media Books.

Angelou, M. (February 17, 2009). An interview with Maya Angelou. *Psychology Today*. Retrieved from https://www.psychologytoday.com/us/blog/the-guest-room/200902/interview-maya-angelou

Auerbach, R., & Fitzgerald, J. (1985). *On and off the court.* New York: London: Macmillan; Collier Macmillan.

Axon, R. (2018). *Women in sports. Title levels the playing field.* Minneapolis, Minnesota: SportsZone.

Bascon-Seda, & Ramirez-Macias, G. (2020). Are E-Sports a sport? The term "sport" in checkmate. *Movimento.* Porto Alegre, Brazil, 26. https://doi.org/10.22456/1982-8918.97363

Bass, A. (2019). *One goal: A coach, a team, and the game that brought a divided town together.* New York: Hachette Books.

Belanger, K. (2016). *Sports and entertainment. Invisible seasons: Title IX and the fight for equity in college sports.* Syracuse, New York: Syracuse University Press.

Bell, J. B. (1987). *To play the game: An analysis of sports.* New Brunswick: Transaction Books.

Bell, T. R. (2021). SportsCenter: A case study of media framing U.S. Sport as the COVID-19 epicenter." *International Journal of Sport Communication* 14 (2): 298–317.

Belth, A. (2006). *Stepping up: The story of Curt Flood and his fight for baseball players' rights.* Persea Books: New York.

Belkin, Sam, and R. Dale Sheptak Jr.. "Talking Bodies: Athletes & Tattoos as Nonverbal Communication." *Sport Journal* 1. 2018.

Bennett, A. (October 17, 2017). *How the hell did North Carolina get away with this? Media react to NCAA ruling on UNC.* Retrieved from https://www.newsobserver.com/sports/college/acc/unc/article179133761.html

Benoit, W.L. (1995). Sears' repair of its auto service image: Image restoration discourse in the corporate sector. *Communication Studies*, 46(1–2), 89.

Berlow, L. H. (1994). *Contemporary world issues. Sports ethics: A reference handbook.* Santa Barbara, California: ABC-CLIO.

Bestall, C., Freeman, M., McCreary, L., Fox, T., Smith, M., & ESPN (Television Network). (2015). *The 16ᵗʰ man*. Distributed by Beyond Home Entertainment, DVD

Bien, L. (November 28, 2014). *A complete timeline of the Ray Rice assault case*. Retrieved from https://www.sbnation.com/nfl/2014/5/23/5744964/ray-rice-arrest-assault-statement-apology-ravens

Billings, A. C., Butterworth, M. L., & Turman P. D. (2018). *Communication and sport: Surveying the field*. Los Angeles: Sage.

Billings, A. C., & Hardin, M. (2014). *Routledge handbook of sport and new media*. London: Routledge.

Bissinger, B. (1990). *Friday night lights: A town, a team, and a dream*. Reading, Massachusetts: Addison-Wesley Publisher.

Bissinger, B. (2005). *Three nights in August: Strategy, heartbreak, and joy, inside the mind of a manager*. Boston: Houghton Mifflin.

Blaney, J., Lippert, L. R., Smith, J. S., & ProQuest. (2013*). Repairing the athlete's image: Studies in sports image restoration*. Lanham, MD: Lexington Books.

Bok, S. (1999). *Lying: Moral choice in public and private life*. New York: Vintage Books.

Bondy, S. (May 9, 2018). David Fizdale stresses culture and accountability as Knicks introduce him as head coach. *New York Daily*. Retrieved from http://www.nydailynews.com/sports/basketball/knicks/knicks-introduce-david-fizdale-new-head-coach-article-1.3977779

Bowden, M. (2008). *The best game ever: Giants vs. Colts, 1958, and the birth of the modern NFL*. Washington DC: Atlantic Monthly Press.

Branca, R. (2014). *A moment in time: An American story of baseball, heartbreak, and grace*. New York: Scribner.

Brazeal, L. (2012). Belated remorse: Serena Williams's image repair rhetoric at the 2009 U.S. Open. In Blaney et al., *Repairing the athlete's image: Studies in sports image restoration*. Lanham, MD: Lexington Books.

Broadcast Media Group (Directors). (2013). *One night in March: The story of Mississippi State in the 1963 NCAA tournament*. Broadcast Media Group, DVD.

Brummett, B. (2014). *New agendas in communication. Sports and identity: New agendas in communication*. New York: Routledge.

Bryant, H. (2018). *The heritage: Black athletes, a divided America, and the politics of patriotism*. Boston: Beacon Press.

Bullis, C. A., & Tompkins. P. K. (1989). The forest ranger revisited: A study of control practices and identification. *Communication Monographs* 56(4), 287–306.

Burke, K. (1969). *A rhetoric of motives*. Berkeley: University of California Press.

Callahan, T. (2020). *Gods at play: An eyewitness account of great moments in American sports*. New York: W.W. Norton & Company

Caplan, A. L., & Parent B. (Eds.), (2017). *The ethics of sport: Essential readings*. New York: Oxford University Press.

Carey, J. W., & Adam G. S. (2008). *Communication as culture: Essays on media and society, revised edition* (2nd ed.). Hoboken: Taylor & Francis.

Carlyle, T. (2017). *On heroes, hero-worship, and the heroic in history: Six lectures, reported, with emendations and . . . additions* (classic reprint). London: Forgotten Books.

Carter, I. (July 21, 2007). *NBA referee may have bet on games*. Retrieved from http://www.washingtonpost.com/wp-dyn/content/article/2007/07/20/AR2007072000764.html

Chang, M., Kang, J., Ko, Y., & Connaughton, D. The effects of perceived team performance and social responsibility on pride and word-of-mouth recommendation. *Sport Marketing Quarterly, 26*(1), (2017). 31.

Clarey, C. (February 22, 2007). Wimbledon to pay women and men equal prize money. (Sports Desk). *The New York Times.* https://www.nytimes.com/2007/02/22/sports/tennis/23cnd-tennis.html

Clavane, A. (2014). *Does your rabbi know you're here?: The story of English football's forgotten tribe.* New York: Quercus.

Clavio, G. (2012). Emerging social media and applications in sport. In Pederson (Ed.), *Routledge Handbook of Sport Communication* (pp. 259–268). Oxfordshire: Routledge.

Clemmons, A. K. (2018). The whole package: Without a dominant veteran superstar; the men's basketball team has succeeded by exceeding the sum of its parts. *Virginia.*

Cohan, W. D. (2014). *The price of silence: The Duke Lacrosse scandal, the power of the elite, and the corruption of our great universities.* New York: Scribner.

Cohen, J. R. (1999). Advising clients to apologize. (legal advice). *Southern California Law Review, 72*(4), 1009–1069.

Cohn, L. (2008). *Cohn-head: A no-holds-barred account of breaking into the boys' club.* Guilford, Conn.: Lyons Press.

Colletti, N., & Reaves J. A. (2017). *The big chair: The smooth hops and bad bounces from the inside world of the acclaimed Los Angeles Dodgers general manager.* New York: G.P. Putnam's Sons.

Cooky, C., Council, L. D., Mears, M. A., & Messner, M. A. (2021). One and done: The long eclipse of women's televised sports, 1989–2019. *Communication & Sport* 9, no. 3 (June 2021): 347–71.

Coombs, T. (1999). Information and compassion in crisis responses: A test of their effects. *Journal of Public Relations Research, 11*(2), 125–142.

Coombs, T. W., & Holladay, S. (2001). An extended examination of the crisis situations: A fusion of the relational management and symbolic approaches. *Journal of Public Relations Research, 13*(4).

Coombs, W. T. (2015). *Ongoing crisis communication* (4th ed.). Thousand Oaks: Sage Publications.

Cooper, C. (2009). *Extraordinary circumstances: The journey of a corporate whistleblower.* Hoboken: Wiley.

Cope, C., Eys, M., Schinke, R., & Bosselut, G. Coaches' Perspectives of a Negative Informal Role: The 'Cancer' within Sport Teams. *Journal of Applied Sport Psychology, 22*(4), (2010). 420–436.

Corben, B., Gordon, D., Mandt, M., Swade, J., Coodie, C., Mitchell, F., et al., (Directors). (2013). *Ghosts of Ole Miss.* 30 For 30. ESPN Home Entertainment.

Craig, R. (2001). Communication in Sloane, T. O. (ed). *Encyclopedia of rhetoric.* Oxford: Oxford University Press, 125–136.

Cranmer, G. (2019). *Athletic coaching: A communicative perspective.* New York: Peter Lang.

Cranmer, G. A., Brann, M., & Bowman, N. D. (2014). Male athletes, female aesthetics: The continued ambivalence toward female athletes in ESPN's The Body Issue. *International Journal of Sport Communication, 7*(2), 145–165.

Crawford, G. (2004). *Consuming sport: Fans, sport and culture.* London: Routledge.

Cumming, S., Smith, R., & Smoll, F. (2006). Athlete-perceived coaching behaviors: Relating two measurement traditions. *Journal of Sport & Exercise Psychology, 28*(2), 205–231.

Curry, J., & Wilson, D. (December 19, 2007). Clemens strongly denies allegations by his ex-trainer. *The New York Times.* D 1.

Curtis, Charles (2018) "Fox News host tells LeBron James to 'shut up and dribble' after Trump criticism." https://ftw.usatoday.com/2018/02/cleveland-cavaliers-lebron-james-fox-news-laura-ingraham-shut-up-and-dribble-donald-trump-response-uninterrupted-video

Dainton, M., & Zelley, E. D. (2019). *Applying communication theory for professional life: A practical introduction* (4th ed.). Thousand Oaks, California: SAGE Publications.

Dance, F. (1970). The concept of communication. *Journal of Communication*, 20(2).

David M. Ullian. "A Rope, a Tree, Hang the Referee!": Exploring the First Amendment Boundaries of Offensive Fan Speech Regulation in College Sports. *Sports Lawyers Journal* 23 (2016).

Deford, F (1984) "The Toughest Coach That Ever Was" Sports Illustrated, April 30, 1984 pages 44-61.

Deford, F. (2012). *OverTime: My life as a sportswriter*. New York: Atlantic Monthly Press.

Denison, D. R. (1996). What is the difference between organizational culture and organizational climate? A native's point of view on a decade of paradigm wars. *The Academy of Management Review* 21(3); 619–19.

DeVito, C. (2001). *The ultimate dictionary of sports quotations*. New York: Facts on File.

DeVito, J. (2006). *Human communication: The basic course* (10th ed.). Boston: Allyn and Bacon.

Dezenhall, E., & Weber, J. (2007). *Damage control: Why everything you know about crisis management is wrong*. New York: Portfolio.

DiCaro, J. (2021). *Sidelined: Sports, culture, and being a woman in America*. New York: Dutton.

Dickerson, N., & Hodler, M. (2021). Real men stand for our nation: Constructions of an American nation and anti-Kaepernick memes. *Journal of Sport and Social Issues*, 45(4), 329–357.

Didinger, R., & Macnow, G. (2009). *The ultimate book of sports movies: Featuring the 100 greatest sports films of all time*. Philadelphia, PA: Running Press Book.

Dinich, H., Rittenberg, A., & VanHaaren, T. (August 10, 2018). *The inside story of a toxic culture at Maryland football*. Retrieved from http://www.espn.com/college-football/story/_/id/24342005/maryland-terrapins-football-culture-toxic-coach-dj-durkin

Dohrmann, G. (2018). *Superfans: Into the heart of obsessive sports fandom*. New York: Ballantine Books.

Donaghy, T., & Scala, P. (2010). *Personal foul: A first-person account of the scandal that rocked the NBA*. Cincinnati, Ohio: Clerisy Press.

DuPree, D. (November 22, 1983). *Jones: Doubly sweet second time around*. Retrieved from https://www.washingtonpost.com/archive/sports/1983/11/22/jones-doubly-sweet-second-time-around/6b486b35-21ea-4e67-81f5-013163ee7762/?utm_term=.813c9d398e95

DuVernay, A, Williams, V., King, B.J., McEnroe, J., Sharapova, M., Allaster, S., Scott, L., Walker, A., Anderson, J., Jowell, T. J., Gulsar Corat, S., Flink, S. Roberts, S., Bryant, H., Clarey, C. Jelani Cobb, W., Fontaine Smokey D., Murray, C., Averick, S., Jafa, A., Reid, K., Charles, H., Bostic, K., Riddlore, (Rapper), Aybee, Walizadeh, O. ESPN Films (Firm), Forward Movement (Firm), Kandoo Films, and Team Marketing (Firm). *Venus Vs*. ESPN Films, DVD.

Eagleman, A. N. (2015). Constructing gender differences: Newspaper portrayals of male and female gymnasts at the 2012 Olympic games. *Sport in Society*, 18(2), 234–247.

Eisenberg, E. (1984). Ambiguity as strategy in organizational communication. *Communication Monographs*, 51, 227–242.

Eisenberg E., & Witten, M. (1987). Reconsidering openness in organizational communication. In Hutchinson, K. (Ed.), *Readings in organizational communication*. Wm C. Brown. Originally published in *Academy of Management Review* 12(3), 418–426.

Eisenberg, E., Goodall, M. H. L., & Trethewey, A. (2014). *Organizational communication: Balancing creativity and constraint* (7th ed.). Boston: Bedford/St. Martin's.

Eisenberg, J. (2014). How to teach your student-athletes about responsible online social networking. *Neumann University Institute for Sport, Spirituality, and Character Development*. (Presentation).

Eisenberg, J. B. (2014). Circumventing hazards of social media and the student athlete. *Journal of NCAA Compliance*, 5. Excerpts from *How to teach your student-athletes about responsible online social networking*. https://sportslitigationalert.com/circumventing-the-hazards-of-social-media-and-the-student-athlete/

Eisenstock, A. (2014). *Sports talk: A journey inside the world of sports talk radio*. New York: Atria Books.

Entman, R. M. (1993). Framing: Toward clarification of a fractured paradigm. *Journal of Communication*, 43(4), 51–58.

Entine, J. (2000). *Taboo: Why Black athletes dominate sports and why we are afraid to talk about it*. New York: Public Affairs.

Etnier, J. L. (2020). *Coaching for the love of the game: A practical guide for working with young athletes*. Chapel Hill: University of North Carolina Press.

Fagan, K. (2021). *All the colors came out: A father, a daughter, and a lifetime of lessons*. New York: Little, Brown and Company.

Fainaru-Wada, M., & Fainaru, S. (2013). *League of denial: The NFL, concussions, and the battle for truth*. New York: Crown Archetype.

Feeley, T. H., & Melissa J. Y. (1998). Humans as lie detectors: Some more second thoughts. *Communication Quarterly*, 46(2), 109–126.

Feinstein, J. (1986). *A Season on the brink: A year with Bob Knight and the Indiana Hoosiers*. New York: Macmillan.

Feinstein, J. (2021). *Raise a fist, take a knee: Race and the illusion of progress in modern sports*. New York: Little, Brown and Company.

Fertik, M. (April 20, 2014). Ten commandments of smart social media use. *Inc.* https://www.inc.com/michael-fertik/10-commandments-smart-social-media.html

Feynman, R. (1988). An outsider's inside view of the challenger inquiry. *Physics Today*, 41(2), 26–37.

Feynman, R. P., & Leighton, R. (1992). *What do you care what other people think*?: Further adventures of a curious character as told to Ralph Leighton. London: Grafton.

Feynman, R. P. (1985). *Surely you're joking Mr. Feynman!* New York: W.W Norton.

Fink, S. (2013). *Crisis communications: The definitive guide to managing the message*. New York: McGraw-Hill Education.

Fink, S. (1986, 2002). *Crisis management: Planning for the inevitable*. New York: American Management Association.

Fisher, M. (2009). *A terrible splendor: Three extraordinary men, a world poised for war, and the greatest tennis match ever played*. New York: Crown.

Fleder, R. (2017). *The sports bucket list: 101 sights every fan has to see before the clock runs out*. New York: Harper Design.

Ford, C. V. (1996). *Lies!, Lies!!, Lies!!!: The psychology of deceit*. Washington, DC: American Psychiatric Press.

Forer, H.H., Diaz, M., Francesca, M., & Russo, C. (2017). *Mike and the Mad Dog*. ESPN Films (Firm), ESPN Home Entertainment, and Team Marketing (Firm). ESPN Home Entertainment, DVD.

Foster, G., Greyer, A., & Walsh, B. (2006). *The business of sports: Text and cases on strategy and management*. Mason, OH: Thomson/South-Western.

Frank, M., & Feeley, T. (2003). To catch a liar: Challenges for research in lie detection training. *Journal of Applied Communication Research*, Volume 31, No 1, February 2003: pp 58-75.

Freeman, R. Edward. (2018). *Strategic management: A stakeholder approach*. Cambridge: Cambridge University Press

Freeman, M. (2000). *ESPN: The uncensored history*. Dallas, Texas: Taylor Publishers.

Freedman, S. G. (2013). *Breaking the line: The season in Black college football that transformed the sport and changed the course of civil rights*. New York: Simon & Schuster.

French, P. A. (2004). *Ethics and college sports: ethics, sports, and the university. Issues in academic ethics.* Lanham, MD: Rowman & Littlefield.

Frey, D. (1994). *The last shot: City streets, basketball dreams*. Boston: Houghton Mifflin.

Frommer, F. (June 12, 2012). Clemens lawyer again attacks key witness. *San Diego Union*. Retrieved from http://www.sandiegouniontribune.com/sdut-clemens-lawyer-again-attacks-key-witness-2012jun12-story.html

Gardner, Sam (2016) "10 Years Ago Today, Dennis Green Unleashed One Of The Nfl's Most Famous Rants." November 15, 2016 https://www.foxsports.com/stories/nfl/10-years-ago-today-dennis-green-unleashed-one-of-the-nfls-most-famous-rants

Dan Gartland (2017) Gregg Popovich Issues Blistering Takedown of 'Soulless Coward' Donald Trump https://www.si.com/nba/2017/10/16/gregg-popovich-donald-trump-soulless-coward

Gibb, J. R. (2008). Defensive Communication. In Mortensen, C. D. (Ed.)., *Communication theory* (NEEDS PAGES). Piscataway, NJ: Transaction Publishers.

Glickman, M. (1996). *The fastest kid on the block*. Syracuse: Syracuse University Press

Goldman, T. (July 25, 2017). *Study: CTE found in nearly all donated NFL player brains.* https://www.npr.org/2017/07/25/539198429/study-cte-found-in-nearly-all-donated-nfl-player-brains

Goleman, D. (2005). *Emotional intelligence*. New York: Bantam Books.

Goleman, D. (2006). *Social intelligence: The new science of human relationships*. New York: Bantam Books.

Goodman, B. (Producer). (2013). *The Fight*. RMIT University. DVD.

Goodwin, D. K. (1997). *Wait till next year: a memoir*. New York: Simon & Schuster.

Gordon, J., & Smith, M. (2015). *You win in the locker room first: The 7 C s to build a winning team in sports, business and life*. Hoboken: John Wiley & Sons..

Gossett, L. (2006). Falling between the cracks control and communication challenges of a temporary workforce. *Management Communication Quarterly* Fall 2006, 376–415.

Grant, J., Sabellico, T., & O'Brien, P. (2007). *The Black Aces : Baseball's only African-American twenty-game winners*. San Diego: Aventine Press.

Gray, J. (2021). *Talking to GOATS*. New York: William Morrow.

Gubar, J. (2015). *Fanaticus: Mischief and madness in the modern sports fan*. Lanham: Rowman & Littlefield.

Gwinn, D. (2015). *Bias in the booth: An insider exposes how sports media distort the news*. Washington, DC: Regnery Publishing.

Hamilton, M. (2013). Coaching, gamesmanship, and intimidation. In Simon, R. L. (Ed.), *The ethics of coaching sports: Moral social and legal issues* (pp. 137-149). Boulder: Westview Press.

Hample, Z. (2007). *Watching baseball smarter: A professional fan's guide for beginners, semi-experts, and deeply serious geeks*. New York: Vintage Books.

Hauch, V., Sporer, S. L., Michael, S. W., & Meissner, C. A. (2016). Does training improve the detection of deception? A meta-analysis. *Communication Research*, 43(3), 283–343. https://doi.org/10.1177/0093650214534974

Harkness, J.B., Husain, M., Phipps, W. Teel, D., National Collegiate Athletic Association, Pathway Productions, & Cinema Guild. (2008). *The Game of Change: Documenting the 1963 Mississippi State Vs. Loyola (Ill.) basketball game*. NCAA, DVD.

Haselwood Denise M., Joyner, A. Barry, Burke, Kevin L., Geyerman, Chris B., Czech, Daniel R., Munkasy Barry A., & Zwald, A. Drew. Female athletes' perceptions of head coaches' communication competence. *Journal of Sport Behavior, 28*(3) (2005).

Hearit, K.M. "'We Didn't Do It' To 'It's Not Our Fault' The Use Of Apologia In Public Relations Crises." In W. N. Elwood (Ed). *Public Relations Inquiry As Rhetorical Criticism: Case Studies of Corporate Discourse and Social Influence* Westport, CT:Praeger. 1995 117–134.

Helgeland, B. Produced by Tull, T., Directed by Ford, H., Linklater, H., Boseman, C., Beharie, N., Merriman, R., Black, L., Meloni, C., Holland, A., Isham, M., Warner Bros. Pictures (1969), Legendary Pictures, Warner Bros. Entertainment, and Warner Home Video (Firm). Performed by Ford, H., Linklater, H., Boseman, C., Beharie, N., Merriman, R., Black, R., Meloni, C., & Holland, A. (Screenplay).*42.* (2013). Warner Bros. Entertainment, Inc.

Henderson, D. (2009). *The Media savvy leader: Visibility, influence, and results in a competitive world*. Bandon, OR: Robert D. Reed.

Henry, R. A. (2000). *You'd better have a hose if you want to put out the fire: The complete guide to crisis and risk communications: professional tips, tactics, dos, don'ts and case* histories. Windsor, CA: Gollywobbler Productions.

Henson, M. *Celebration GIFS and elaborate transfer announcements: roma, bristol city and clubs' increasingly use of social media.* https://thesetpieces.com/latest-posts/celebration-gifs-elaborate-transfer-announcements-roma-bristol-city-and-clubs-increasingly-innovative-use-of-social-media/

Herbeck, D. (2004). Sports metaphors and public policy: The football theme in Desert Storm discourse. In Beer, F. A., & De Landtsheer, C. (Ed.), *Metaphorical world politics* (pp. 121-139). East Lansing: Michigan State University Press.

Herrold, R. M. (2010). *The 20 worst teammates in sports history.* https://bleacherreport.com/articles/443185-the-20-worst-teammates-in-sports-history

Hoffer, R. (2018). *Something in the air: American passion and defiance in the 1968 Mexico City Olympics.* Lincoln, Nebraska: University Of Nebraska Press.

Holley, M. (2011). *War room: Bill Belichick and the Patriot legacy.* New York: !t Books

Hopper, R. (1976). *Human message systems.* New York: Harper & Row.

Hornby, N. (1998). *Fever pitch.* New York: Riverhead Books.

Hughes, R., Giles, M., Haywood, J., & Snipes, J.. Media perceptions and constructions of race and sports: Reflections on the Duke lacrosse scandal. *Journal for the Study of Sports and Athletes in Education, 11*(3), (2017)161–174.

Hugenberg, L. W., Haridakis, P.M., & Earnheardt. A.C. (2008). *Sports mania: Essays on fandom and the media in the 21st century.* Jefferson, N.C.: McFarland.

Infante, D., Rancer, A., & Womack, D. (2003). *Building communication theory* (4th ed.). Waveland Press.

Jackson, R. (2020). *The Game is not a game: The power, protest, and politics of American sports.* Chicago: Haymarket Books.

Jacobson, S. (2009). *Carrying Jackie's torch: The players who integrated baseball-and America.* Chicago: Chicago Review.

Jeffrey D. James, Elizabeth B. Delia, and Daniel L. Wann. (2019). "No" is not "Low": Improving the assessment of sport team identification. *Sport Marketing Quarterly*, 28(1), 34–45.

Jay, K. (2004). *Columbia histories of modern American Life. More than just a game: Sports in American life since 1945.* New York: Columbia University Press.

Jenkins, H. (2006). *Fans, bloggers, and gamers: Exploring participatory culture.* New York: New York University Press.

Jennings, A. (2007). *Foul!: The secret world of FIFA: Bribes, vote rigging and ticket scandals*. London: HarperSport.

Jones, D. G., & Daly, E. L. (1992). Sports ethics in America: A bibliography, 1970–1990. *Bibliographies and indexes in American history, No. 21*. New York: Greenwood Press.

Kahn, R. (1972). *The boys of summer*. New York: Harper & Row.

Kassing, J., Billings, A., Brown, R., Halone, K., Harrison, K., Krizek, B., & Turman, P. (2004). Communication in the community of sport: The process of enacting, (re)producing, consuming, and organizing sport. *Annals of the International Communication Association*, 28(1), 373–409.

Kay, M. (2021). *CenterStage: My most fascinating interviews--From A-Rod to Jay-Z*. New York: Scribner.

Kelly, R. (2018). *The worst teammates in sports history*. https://www.stadiumtalk.com/s/worst-teammates-sports-history-5b06341772304cac

"Kicking Down Barriers: Sarah Fuller makes history as kicker for Vanderbilt football team." *Vanderbilt Magazine*. February 18, 2021

Kim D, Walker M, Heo J, and Koo G.-Y. Sport League Website: An Effective Marketing Communication Tool for Corporate Sponsors. *International Journal of Sports Marketing and Sponsorship 18, n*o. 3 (2017): 314–27.

Kim, K., Lee, S., & Byon, K. (2020). How useful is each item in the Sport Spectator Identification Scale?: An item response theory analysis. *International Journal of Sports Marketing & Sponsorship*, 21(4), 651-667

King, Billie Jean, Johnette Howard, and Maryanne Vollers. 2022. *All in : An Autobiography*. Toronto: Vintage Canada.

King III, G. A. (November 6, 2017). *Brian Cashman speaks: "Why Yankees moved on from Joe Girardi*. https://nypost.com/2017/11/06/brian-cashman-speaks-why-yankees-moved-on-from-joe-girardi/

Koreivo, S. (2011). *Tales from the tailgate*. Bloomington, Indiana: Author House.

Kraut, R. (1980). Humans as lie detectors. *Journal of Communication*, 30(4), 209–218.

Kreps, G. L. (1986). *Organizational communication: Theory and practice*. New York: Longman.

Krone, K., Jablin, F., & Putnam, L. (1987). Communication theory and organizational communication: multiple perspectives. In Jablin, F., Putnum, L., Roberts, K., & Porter, L. (Eds.), *Handbook of organizational communication*. Sage pp 18-40.

Kuhn, G. (2015). *Playing as if the world mattered: An illustrated history of activism in sports*. Oakland: PM Press.

Lardner, R. (1991). *You know me Al: A busher's letters*. New York: Collier Books.

Lasswell, H. D. (1948). The structure and function of communication in society. In Lyman Bryson, L. (Ed.), (pp. 37–51). New York: Harper and Brothers.

L'Etang, J. (2013). *Sports public relations*. London: Sage.

Leavy, J. (2003). *Sandy Koufax: A lefty's legacy*. New York: Harper Perennial.

Leavy, J. (2010). *The last boy: Mickey Mantle and the and of America's childhood*. New York: Harper Perennial.

Leven, E., Feist, F., Brooke, P.R., Peck, C. K., & Alpha Video Distributors (Directors). (2004). *The basketball fix*. Alpha Video.

Levinson, H. (1973). Asinine attitudes toward motivation. *Harvard Business Review*, 51(1), 73.

Lewis, A. (August 18, 2018). *What next for football's weird social media craze*. https://www.cnn.com/2018/08/16/football/roma-social-media-video-unveil-patrik-schick-manchester-united-spt-itl/index.html

Lewis, L. Jr. (May 3, 2018). *Redskins issue statement regarding cheerleader accusations*. https://redskinswire. usatoday.com/2018/05/03/redskins-issue- statement-regarding-cheerleader-accusations/

Lewis, M., & Hugg, C. (2015). Review implications, best practices for student–athletes' social–media use. *College Athletics and the Law*, 12(9), 1–3.

Levinson, B. (Director), ESPN Films (Firm), Baltimore Pictures (Firm), Severn River Productions, ESPN Home Entertainment, and Team Marketing (Firm). Produced by Bonner, L., Flint, S., & Sosnoff, J. (2010). *The band that wouldn't die*. ESPN Home Entertainment, DVD.

Leyden, E., Loth, T., & Foudy, J. (Producers). Directed by ESPN Films (Firm), ESPN Home Entertainment, and Team Marketing (Firm). (2013). *The 99ers*. ESPN Home Entertainment, DVD.

Littlefield, B. (June 6, 2005). *Hollywood scores a 'miracle' with locker room speech*. http://www.wbur.org/onlyagame/2015/06/06/us-miracle-olympics-herb-brooks

Longman, J. (2000). *The girls of summer: The U.S. women's soccer team and how it changed the world*. New York, New York: HarperCollins.

Lopez, J. K. (2021). Rewriting activism: the NFL takes a knee. *Critical Studies in Media Communication*, 38(2), 183–196.

Lopiano, D. A. (2014). *Athletic director's desk reference*. Champaign, IL: Human Kinetics.

Lucas, J., Luke, D., Voight, J., Bruckheimer, J., Gartner, J., Walt Disney Pictures, & Jerry Bruckheimer Films. Screenplay by Cleveland, C., & Gilois, B. Performed by Lucas, J., Luke, D., & Voight, J. *Glory Road*. (2006). Walt Disney Home Entertainment, DVD.

Lumpkin, A. (2017). *Modern sport ethics: A reference handbook* (2nd ed.). Contemporary World Issues Series. Santa Barbara, California: ABC-CLIO An Imprint of ABC-CLIO, LLC.

Macht, N. L. (2019). *They played the game: Memories from 47 major leaguers*. Lincoln: University of Nebraska Press

Maller, B. (February 16, 2012). *Jeremy Lin TV graphic raises concerns*. http://www.thepostgame.com/blog/dish/201202/knicks-jeremy-lin-tv-graphic- controversy

Mandell, Nina, (2018) Charles Barkley on 'SNL' to athletes: Keep speaking up https://www.pnj.com/story/sports/ftw/2018/03/04/charles-barkley-opens-saturday-night-live-with-strong-monologue-on-athletes-speaking-up/111080908/

Manusov, V., & Billingsley, J. (1997). Nonverbal Communication in Organizations. In Yuhas Byers, P. (Ed.), Organizational communication: Theory and behavior (p. 66). Boston: Allyn and Bacon.

Maraniss, A. (2014). *Strong inside: Perry Wallace and the collision of race and sports in the south*. Nashville: Vanderbilt University Press.

Maraniss, D. (2008). *Rome 1960: The Olympics that changed the world*. New York: Simon & Schuster.

Maraniss, D. (1999). *When pride still mattered: A life of Vince Lombardi*. New York: Simon & Schuster.

Markovits, A. S, and Rensmann, L. (2010). *Gaming the world : How sports are reshaping global politics and culture*. Book Collections on Project Muse. Princeton: Princeton University Press.

Markula Center for Applied Ethics. *What role does ethics play in sports?* https://www.scu.edu/ethics/focus-areas/more/resources/what-role-does-ethics-play-in-sports/

Mays, W., Shea, J., & Costas, B. (2020). *24: Life stories and lessons from the Say Hey Kid*. New York: St. Martin's Press.

McBride, J. (January 10, 2018). Kyle Van Noy feeling a spring in his step. *Boston Globe*. Retrieved from https://c.o0bg.com/sports/patriots/2018/01/09/kyle-van-noy-feeling-spring-his-step/2d0dE0kS0ZBOD80SaJTEjO/story.html?p1=AMP_Recirculation_Pos5

McClure, A.K, & Frank and Virginia Williams Collection of Lincolniana (Mississippi State University. Libraries). (1990). *Lincoln's yarns and stories: A complete collection of the funny and witty anecdotes that made Abraham Lincoln famous as America's greatest story telle*r. Chicago: J.C. Winston.

McCombs, M. E., & Shaw, D. L. (1972). The agenda-setting function of mass media. *Public Opinion Quarterly*, 36(2), 176–187.

McEnroe, J., & Kaplan, J. (2003). *You cannot be serious*. New York: Berkley Books.

McGuire J., & Melton McKinnon, L. (2012). "Big Mac" with a side of steroids: The image repair strategies of Mark McGwire. In Blaney, J. R, Lippert, L. R., & Smith, J. S. (Eds.), *Repairing the athlete's image: Studies in sports image restoration* (pp. 27-40). Lanham, MD: Lexington Books, 2012. 27–40.

McKenna, Henry, (2017) Bill Belichick shares his take on sitting around and singing kumbaya all day" Henry McKenna December 15, 2017 https://patriotswire.usatoday.com/2017/12/15/ bill-belichick-shares-his-take-on-sitting-around-and-singing-kumbaya-all-day/

McMurray, J. (June 5, 2018). *Even today, Willie Mays remains a giant in baseball history*. https://www. smithsonianmag.com/smithsonian-institution/event- today-willie-mays-remains-giant-baseball-history-180969229/#sy1h4chIwSzuBGS7.99

McNamee, M. J, & S. J Parry. (1998). *Ethics and sport*. London: E & FN Spon.

Meggyesy, D. (2005). *Out of their league*. Lincoln: University of Nebraska Press.

Messner, M. A. (2002). *Taking the field: Women, men, and sports. sport and culture series, v. 4*. Minneapolis: University of Minnesota Press.

Meyers Drysdale, A., & Ravenna, J. (2012). *You let some girl beat you?: The story of Ann Meyers Drysdale*. New York: Behler Publications, LLC.

Mez J, Daneshvar DH, Kiernan PT, et al. Clinicopathological Evaluation of Chronic Traumatic Encephalopathy in Players of American Football. *JAMA*. 2017;318(4):360–370.

Milford, M. The 'reel' Jesse Owens: Visual rhetoric and the Berlin Olympics. *Sport in History, 38*(1), (2018). 96–117.

Miller, J. A., & Shales, T. (2011). *Those guys have all the fun: Inside the world of ESPN*. New York: Back Bay Books.

Millman, C. (2002). *The Odds: One season, three gamblers, and the death of their Las Vegas*. Cambridge, Mass.: Da Capo.

Mitchell, F., Gates, G.P., Durand, M., Yamano, W. (Directors), ESPN Films, ESPN (Television Network), and Team Marketing (Firm). (2010). *The legend of Jimmy the Greek*. ESPN Films, DVD.

Modaff, D. P., Butler, J. A., & DeWine, S. (2017). *Organizational communication: Foundations, challenges, and misunderstandings* (4th ed.). New York: Pearson.

Montville, L. (2021). *Tall men, short shorts: The 1969 NBA Finals: Wilt, Russ, Lakers, Celtics, and a very young sports reporter*. New York: Doubleday.

Morgan, W. J., Meier, K.V., & Schneider, A. J-A. (2001). *Ethics in sport*. Champaign, IL: Human Kinetics.

Mosbacher, D., & Yacker, F. (Producers). Screenplay by Mallimson, G. Directed by Nyad, D., Leibrecht, G., Parks, T., Woman Vision Productions, & Wolfe Video (Firm). (2010). *Training rules: No drinking, no drugs, no lesbians*. Wolfe Video LLC, DVD.

Murray, Jim (1990) Before Writing Him Off, Remember What He Did. https://www.latimes.com/ archives/la-xpm-1990-01-11-sp-418-story.html

NBA Voices Home Page. https://voices.nba.com/about/

Newcomb, T. M. (1966). An approach to the study of communicative acts. In Smith, A.G. (Ed.), *Communication and Culture* (pp. 66-79). New York: Holt, Rinehart and Winston

Nielsen Sports. *Women and sport: insights into the growing rise and importance of female fans and female athletes*. https://issuu.com/repucom.net/docs/women-and-sport-repucom/1

No author. (February 18, 2021). Kicking Down Barriers: Sarah Fuller makes history as kicker for Vanderbilt football team, Vanderbilt Magazine. https://news.vanderbilt.edu/2021/02/18/kicking-

No author. (May 6, 1981). The troubles, and triumph of Billie Jean. (Billie Jean King) (editorial). *The New York Times*, A 30.

No author. (February 2017). *Hbr guide to emotional intelligence*. Harvard Business Review Guides. Boston, Massachusetts: Harvard Business Review Press.

O'Connor, I. (2018). *Belichick: The making of the greatest football coach of all time*. Boston, New York: Houghton Mifflin Harcourt.

O'Hair, D., Stewart, R. A., & Rubenstein, H. (2007). *A speaker's guidebook: Text and reference* (3rd ed.). Boston: Bedford/St. Martins.

Olmsted, L. (2021). *Fans: How watching sports makes us happier, healthier, and more understanding* Chapel Hill, North Carolina: Algonquin Books of Chapel Hill

Ostrowsky, M., & Stein, K. (2020). "I got beat, and he deserves to win": Image repair strategies used by athletes who lost big games. *Journal of Sports Media* 15.1 (2020): 75-97.

Palmatier, R. A., & Ray, H. L. (1993). *Dictionary of sports idioms*. Lincolnwood, Ill.: National Textbook.

Parry, J. (2019). E-sports are not sports. *Sport, Ethics and Philosophy*, 13(1), 3–18. https://doi.org/10.1080/17511321.2018.1489419

Parsons, P., & Institute of Public Relations (Great Britain). (2004). *Ethics in public relations: A guide to best practice*. London: Kogan Page.

Paul, J., & Strbiak, C.A. (1997). The ethics of strategic ambiguity. *Journal of Business Communication*, 34(2): 149–159.

Pedersen, P. M., Laucella, P.C., Miloch, K. S., & Fielding, W. L. (2007). The juxtaposition of sport and communication: Defining the field of sport communication. *International Journal of Sport Management and Marketing* 2(3), 193.

Pedersen, P. M. (2017). *Strategic sport communication* (2nd ed.). Champaign, IL: Human Kinetics.

Pegoraro, A. (2010). Look who's talking—athletes on Twitter: A case study. *International Journal of Sport Communication*, 3(4), 501–514.

Penny, L. (2005). *Your call is important to us: The truth about bullsh*t*. New York: Crown.

Peterson, R. (1999). *Only the ball was white: a history of legendary Black players and all-Black professional teams*. New York: Gramercy Books.

Pluto, T. (2007). *Loose balls: The short, wild life of the American Basketball Association*. New York: Simon & Schuster Paperbacks.

Roberts, R., Rosenthal, J., & Foudy, J. (Producers). Directed by DuVernay, A., Lax, L., Stern Winters, N., Sundberg, A., Stern, R., Ellwood, A., Storm, H., Arnold, J., Kheshgi, S., Lynch, S., Leyden, E., Ewing, H., & Grady, R. (Directors). (2013). *Nine for IX*. ESPN Films (Firm), ESPNW, ESPN, Inc, Team Marketing (Firm), and ESPN Home Entertainment. ESPN Inc, DVD.

Potter, S. (2015). *The theory and practice of gamesmanship, or, the Art of winning games without actually cheating*. (e-book). Auckland, New Zealand: Pickle Partners Publishing.

Powell, S. (2008). *Souled out?: How Blacks are winning and losing in sports*. Champaign, IL: Human Kinetics.

Raney, A. (2006). Why we watch and enjoy mediated sports. In Arthur and Bryant Jennings. A., & Jennings, B. (Eds.), *Handbook of sports and media* (pp. 313-327). Mahwah, NJ: Lawrence Erlbaum.

Rankin-Wright, A., Hylton, K., & Norman, L.. Off-Colour Landscape: Framing Race Equality in Sport Coaching. *Sociology of Sport Journal, 33*(4), (2016)1–30.

Rapinoe, M. (2020). *One life.* New York: Penguin Press.

Reilly, R., & Armstrong, L. (2008). *Hate mail from cheerleaders and other adventures from the life of Reilly.* New York: Sports Illustrated Books.

Rhoden, W. C. (2006). *40 million dollar slaves: The rise, fall, and redemption of the Black athlete.* New York: Crown.

Roberts, M. (November 23, 1974). The vicarious heroism of the sports spectator. *New Republic.*

Roblin, R. (March 20, 2014). *Baltimore to mark 30 years since Colts left.* https://www.wbaltv.com/article/baltimore-to-mark-30-years-since-colts-left/ 7085966

Rock, L. (July 29, 2017). As women's sport grows, athletes find they can't stay silent in the era of Trump. *The Guardian.* https://www.theguardian.com/sport/2017/jul/29/womens-sport-activism-and-political-protest-planned-parenthood

Rodriguez, D. (2016). *Sport communication: An interpersonal approach.* Dubuque, IO: Kendall Hunt.

Roethlisberger, F. J., W. J Dickson, Harold A. Wright, Carl H. Pforzheimer, & Western Electric Company. (1939). *Management and the worker: An account of a research program conducted by the Western Electric Company,* Hawthorne Works, Chicago. Cambridge, Mass.: Harvard University Press.

Rosen, C. (2003). *The wizard of odds: How Jack Molinas almost destroyed the game of basketball.* New York: Seven Stories Press.

Rule, H. (2018). *Women in sports media. Women in sports.* Minneapolis, Minnesota: SportsZone, Abdo Publishing.

Ryan, J. (2020). *Intangibles: Unlocking the science and soul of team chemistry.* New York: Little Brown & Company.

Salovey, P., & Mayer, J. (1990). Emotional intelligence. *Imagination Cognition and Personality*, Volume 9 (3).

Sanderson, J.; Browning, B., & Schmittel, A. (2015). Education on the digital terrain: A case study exploring college athletes' perceptions of social-media training. *International Journal of Sport Communication*, 8(1), 103–124.

Saunders, J., & Bacon, J. U. (2017). *Playing hurt: My journey from despair to hope.* New York: Da Capo Press.

Scarborough, A. (March 21, 2018). *Kentucky's Calipari warns team to not 'drink the poison'.* https://abcnews.go.com/Sports/kentuckys-calipari-warns-team-drink-poison/story?id=53913739

Scheadler, T., & Wagstaff, A. (June 5, 2018). States sports academy exposure to women's sports: Changing attitudes toward female athletes. *Sport Journal. 1.*

Schein, E. H. (1999). *The corporate culture survival guide: Sense and nonsense about culture change.* Warren Bennis Signature Series. San Francisco, Calif.: Jossey-Bass.

Schein, E., & Schein, P. (2019). *The corporate culture survival guide* (3rd edition). Hoboken: John Wiley and Sons.

Schnall, Marianne (2009) An Interview with Maya Angelou https://www.psychologytoday.com/us/blog/the-guest-room/200902/interview-maya-angelou

Schworm, P. (February 16, 2009). A sorry state of affairs public apologies becoming a 'tenor of the times'. *Boston Globe.*

Seeger, M. W., Sellnow, Timothy L., & Ulmer, Robert R. (1998). Communication, organization, and crisis. *Communication Yearbook*, 21, (pp. 231–275).

Sen, F. & Egelhoff, W. (1991). Six years and counting: Learning from crisis management at Bhopal. *Public Relations Review*, 17(1), 69–83.

Serazio, M. (2019). *The power of sports: Media and spectacle in American culture. Postmillenial pop.* New York: New York University Press

Shamsky, A., & Sherman, E. (2020). *After the miracle: The lasting brotherhood of the '69 Mets.* New York: Simon & Schuster Paperbacks.

Sheffer, M. L., & Schultz, B. (2012). The new world of social media and broadcast sports reporting. In Pedersen, P. (Ed.), *Routledge handbook of sport communication* (pp. 210–218). Routledge.

Shirky, C. (2008). *Here comes everybody: the power of organizing without organizations.* New York: Penguin Press.

Shirley, P. (2008). *Can I keep my jersey?: 11 teams, 5 countries, and 4 years in my life as a basketball vagabond.* New York: Villard.

Silver, M. (September 19, 2008). Davis wants to win. . . just not on the field. *Yahoo Sports Exclusive.*

Simon, R. L. (Ed.). (2013). *The ethics of coaching sports: Moral social and legal issues.* Boulder: Westview Press.

Simon, R. L. (2004). *Fair play: The ethics of sport* (2nd ed.). Boulder, Colo.: Westview Press.

Simons, E. (2013). *The secret lives of sports fans: The science of sports obsession.* New York: Overlook Duckworth.

Sinickas, A. D. (2004). *How to measure your communication programs: a practical manual for maximizing the effectiveness of your messages and media* (3rd ed.). Laguna Woods, CA: Sinickas Communications Pub.

Sinickas, A. (June 24, 2008). *Measuring your social tools.* Presentation at 2008 International Association of Business Communicators Meetings. New York, New York.

Smith, A. L. (1973). (Molefi Kete Asante). Transracial communication. *Prentice-Hall speech communication series.* Englewood Cliffs, N.J.: Prentice-Hall.

Smith, C. (2022). *E-sports are not sports.* https://www.contendercary.com/blog/csports are not sports

Smith, G. (March 2, 1998). *Eyes of the storm.* https://www.si.com/ vault/1998/03/02/239460/ eyes-of-the-storm-when-tennessees-whirlwind-of-a-coach-pat-summitt-hits-you-with-her-steely-gaze-you-get-a-dose-of-the-intensity-that-has-carried-the-lady-vols-to-five-ncaa-titles

Smith, J. M., & Willingham, M. (2015). *Cheated. The UNC scandal, the education of athletes, and the future of big-time college sports.* Lincoln: Potomac Books, an Imprint of the University of Nebraska Press.

Smith, J. S. (2012). Bad Newz Kennels: Michael Vick and Dogfighting. In Blaney, J. R., Lance R. Lippert, L. R., & Smith, J. S. (Eds.), *Repairing the athlete's image: Studies in sports image restoration* (pp. 151–168). Lanham, MD: Lexington Books.

Smoll, F. L., & Smith, R. E. (2006). Enhancing coach-athlete relationships: Cognitive-behavioral principles and procedures. In Dosil, J. (Ed.), *The sport psychologist's handbook* (pp. 19–37). Chichester, UK: John Wiley & Sons Ltd.

Spears, M. J., & Washburn, G. (2020). *The Spencer Haywood rule: Battles, basketball, and the making of an American iconoclast.* Chicago: Triumph Books.

SPJ Code of Ethics. https://www.spj.org/ethicscode.asp

Sperber, M. A. (2000). *Beer and circus: How big-time college sports is crippling undergraduate education.* New York: H. Holt.

Springer, S. (June 24, 2918). It's time for change. *Boston Globe* p. C16.

Sproull, L., & Kiesler, S. (1991). *Connections: New ways of working in the networked organization.* Cambridge, Mass.: MIT Press.

St. John, A., & Russo, C. (2013). *The Mad Dog 100: The greatest sports arguments of all time.* New York: Three Rivers Press.

Starcher, Shawn C. Memorable Messages From Fathers to Children Through Sports: Perspectives From Sons and Daughters. *Communication Quarterly* 63, no. 2 (2015): 204–20.

Stern, N., Lax, L. (Directors), & ESPN Films. (2013). *Pat X0: A life spent at the Summitt*. Directed by ESPN Films, DVD.

Stern, R., Sundberg, A., Ludtke, M., Smith, C., Visser, L, Brennan, C., (Directors), Break Thru Films, ESPN Films (Firm), ESPN Home Entertainment, and Team Marketing (Firm). Lupton, S. (Producer). (2013). *Let them wear towels: behind closed doors were closed minds*. ESPN Home Entertainment, DVD.

Stevens, S. S. (1950). Introduction: A definition of communication. *Journal of the Acoustical Society of America*, 22.

Stoldt, C., Dittmore, S. W., & Branvold. S.E. (2012). *Sport public relations: Managing stakeholder communication* (2nd ed.). Champaign, IL: Human Kinetics.

Stoldt, C. (2012). College athletics communications. In Pedersen, P.M. (Ed.)., *Routledge handbook of sport communication* (pp. 482–491). Abingdon, England: Routledge.

Sullivan, T. (June 5, 2018). *Everybody's yelling, nobody's hearing about the national anthem*. https://www.bostonglobe.com/sports/patriots/2018/06/05/there- are-winners-nfl-anthem-standoff/BNB6x4bpN0HCcomD2mhMXM/story.html

Sullivan, T. (September 26, 2021). Athletes often targets on social media. *Boston Globe* p. c1

Summitt, Head, P., & Jenkins., S. (2013). *Sum it up: 1,098 victories, a couple of irrelevant losses, and a life in perspective*. New York: Crown Archetype.

Sweet, D. (2019). *Three seconds in Munich: The controversial 1972 Olympic basketball final*. Lincoln: University of Nebraska Press.

Swift, E. M. (March 3, 1980). The golden goal. *Sports Illustrated*.

Taylor, F. (2014). *The principles of scientific management*. Mansfield Centre, Connecticut: Martino Publishing

Taguiri, R. (1968). The concepts of organizational climate. In Taguiri, R. and Litwin, G.H. (Eds.), *Organizational climate: Exploration of a concept* (pp. 16–20). Boston. Harvard University Press.

Thomas, E. (2005). *More than an athlete*. Atlanta: Moore Black Press.

Thomas, E. (2018). *We matter: Athletes and activism*. Brooklyn: Akashic Books.

Thompson, J. (2022). *I came as a shadow: An autobiography*. New York: Henry Holt Paperbacks.

Thornton, P. K., Champion, W.T., & Ruddell, L. (2012). *Sports ethics for sports management professionals*. Sudbury, MA: Jones & Bartlett.

Tignor, S. (April 9, 2015). 1973: Arthur Ashe breaks sporting color barrier in South Africa. *Tennis*.

Timm, P. R., & De Tienne K. B. (1995). *Managerial communication: A finger on the pulse* (3rd ed.). Englewood Cliffs, NJ: Prentice Hall.

Titus, M. (October 13, 2017). *North Carolina was always going to get off in the NCAA's 'paper class' investigation*. https://www.theringer.com/2017/10/ 13/16471704/north-carolina-academic-fraud-ncaa-investigation-findings

Tomkins, S. S., & Silvan S. Tomkins Institute. (2008). *Affect imagery consciousness: the complete edition: the positive effects, the negative affects*. Vol. Book 1, Vol. 1-2. New York: Springer Publishing.

Tompkins, P. K. (1993). *Organizational communication imperatives: Lessons of the space program*. Los Angeles: Roxbury Pub.

Tompkins, P. K. (2005). *Apollo, Challenger, Columbia: The decline of the space program: a study in organizational communication*. Los Angeles: Roxbury Pub.

Tompkins. P.K. (1984). The functions of human communication in organization. In C.C. Arnold, C.C., & J. W. Bowers, J.W. (Eds.), *Handbook of rhetorical and communication theory* (pp. 659–719). Boston: Allyn and Bacon.

Totino, S., Laskas, J. M., Smith, W., Baldwin, A., Mbatha-Raw, G., Howard, A., Reiser, P., Wilson, L., Akinnuoye-Agbaje, A., Morse, D., & Brooks, A. (Directors). Landesman, P. Performed by Smith, W., Baldwin, A., Mbatha-Raw, G., Howard, A., Reiser, P., Wilson, L., Akinnuoye-Agbaje, A., Morse, D., & Brooks, A. (Screenplay). (2017). *Concussion.* Universal Sony Pictures Home Entertainment Nordic.

Tucker, D. L., & Wrench, J.S. (Eds.), (2016). *Casing sport communication.* Dubuque, Iowa: Kendall Hunt Publishing.

UCSUSA, Union of Concerned Scientists. (2017). The NFL tried to intimidate scientists studying the link between pro football and traumatic brain injury. https://www.ucsusa.org/intimidating-scientists-documenting-link-between-pro-football-and-traumatic-brain-injury#

Vaughan, D. (1996). *The Challenger launch decision: Risky technology, culture, and deviance at NASA.* Chicago: University of Chicago Press.

Veazey, K. (2012). *Champions for change: How the Mississippi State Bulldogs and their bold coach defied segregation.* Charleston, SC: History Press.

Veal, A. J. and Simon Darcy (2014). *Research methods in sport studies and sport management: A practical guide.* London: Pearson.

Visser, L. (2017). *Sometimes you have to cross when it says don't walk: A memoir of breaking barriers.* Dallas: BenBella Books.

Vyorst, D., Riegert P. (Directors), & Laemmle/Zeller Films. (2009). *The first basket.* Laemmle/Zeller Films, DVD.

Wainstein, K. L., Jay III, A. J., Depman Kukowski, C., Cadwalader, Wickersham & Taft, and University of North Carolina at Chapel Hill. (2014). *Investigation of irregular classes in the Department of African and Afro-American Studies at the University of North Carolina at Chapel Hill.* United States: Cadwalader.

Walker, S. (2017). *The captain class: The hidden force that creates the world's greatest teams.* New York: Random House.

Wann, D. L., & James, J. D. (2019). Sport *fans: The psychology and social impact of fandom* (2nd ed.). New York: Routledge.

Wann, D. L., & Branscombe, N. R. (1993). Sports fans: Measuring degree of identification with their team. *International Journal of Sport Psychology*, 24(1), 1–17.

*Ward, R. (2012). Reggie Jackson in no-man's land. In Ward, R, *Renegades* (pp. 207-234). Blue Ash, Ohio: Tyrus Books. Originally from Ward, R. (1977). Reggie Jackson in no-man's land. *Sport*, 64.

Ware, S. (2011). *Game, set, match: Billie Jean King and the revolution in women's sports.* Chapel Hill: University of North Carolina Press.

Ware, S. (2007). *Title IX: A brief history with documents. The Bedford series in history and culture.* Boston: Bedford/St. Martins.

Washburn, G. (September 27, 2017). Chemistry is the first lesson for Celtics. *Boston Globe.* https://www.bostonglobe.com/sports/celtics/2017/ 09/26/chemistry-first-mission-for-celtics/Gcx4SVgGIomNLchNEIy58H/story.html

Watts, R. (2008). The Florida gator nation on line. In Hugenberg, L. W., Haridakis, P.M., & Earnheardt, A.C. (Eds.), *Sports mania: Essays on fandom and the media in the 21st century* (pp. 243-256). Jefferson, N.C.: McFarland.

Weinzimmer, L., Franczak, J., & Michel, E. (April 2008). Culture-performance research: Challenges and future directions. *Journal of Academy of Business and Economics.*

Welter, J. (2017). *Play big: Lessons in being limitless from the first woman to coach in the NFL.* New York: Seal Press.

Wertheim, L. J. (2021). *Glory days: the summer of 1984 and the 90 days that changed sports and culture forever.* Boston: Houghton Mifflin Harcourt

Wertheim, L J. (2021). Follow the money. *Sports Illustrated* 132, no. 9 (2021): 26.

West, J., & Coleman, J. (2011). *West by west: My charmed, tormented life.* New York: Little, Brown.

Whiteside, E. A. (2014). New media and the changing role of sports information. In Billings, A.C., and Hardin, M. (Eds.) *Routledge Handbook of Sport and New Media.* Abingond, England: Routledge. Chapter 13.

Wickersham, S. (2021). *It's better to be feared: The New England Patriots dynasty and the pursuit of greatness.* New York: Liveright Publishing Corporation.

Wilkens, L., & Pluto, T. (2014). *Unguarded: My forty years surviving in the NBA.* New York: Simon & Schuster.

Williams, V. (June 26, 2006). Wimbledon has sent me a message: I'm only a second-class champion. *London Times,* p. 21.

Wilson, E. O. (2013). *The social conquest of earth.* New York: Liveright Publishing Corp.

Wolff, A. (2003). College basketball: Ghosts of Mississippi: Forty years ago a courageous college president defied a court order and sent his team to face Black players in the NCAA. *Sports Illustrated* 98(10), p. 160.

Wood, E., Hunnam, C., Forlani, C., Alexander, L. and Odd Lot Entertainment (Firm), (Directors). (2005). *Green Street hooligans.* Reel DVD distributor.

Wright, J., McCartney, B., Podhoretz, J. (Directors). (2016). *The Gospel According to Mac.* ESPN and Team.

Yoesting, T. (April 10, 2018). *WTF did Roma's Twitter feed just do?* https://the18.com/soccer-entertainment/roma-twitter-reacts-barcelona-champions-league

Zaremba, A. J. (2009). *The madness of March: Bonding and betting with the boys in Las Vegas.* Lincoln: University of Nebraska Press.

Zaremba, A. J. (2021). *Organizational communication* (4th ed.). Dubuque, Iowa: Kendall Hunt publishing.

Zaremba, A., & Wiseman, F. (2015). Communication challenges in university athletic department: Preempting crises. *Journal of Sports Management and Commercialization,* 6(3).

Zeng, G., Go, F., & Kolmer, C. (2011). The impact of international TV media coverage of the Beijing Olympics 2008 on China's media image formation: A media content analysis perspective. *International Journal of Sports Marketing and Sponsorship,* 12(4), 39–56.

Zenovich, M (Director)., Cooney, J. (Attorney), Darby, S., Chafe, W. H., Starn, O., Meadows, S., Yaeger, D., Bannon, B., Johnson, R. D., Seligmann, K., Cheshire, J. B., Neff, V. J., Sheehan, R., Coleman, J. E., Burnette, D., Cardoni, J., ESPN Films (Firm), Lightbox (Firm), ESPN Home Entertainment, and Team Marketing (Firm). *Fantastic lies.* (2016). Produced by P. G Morgan. ESPN Home Entertainment, 2016. DVD.

Zirin, D. (2013). *Game over: How politics has turned the sports world upside down.* New York: New Press.

Index